THE
MIRACLES
OF
EXODUS

THE
MIRACLES
OF
EXODUS

A Scientist's Discovery of

the Extraordinary Natural Causes of

the Biblical Stories

COLIN J. HUMPHREYS

HarperOne
An Imprint of HarperCollinsPublishers

HarperOne

Grateful acknowledgment is given to the following for permission to use the figures in this book. Every effort has been made to obtain permissions. 1.2: From a 1680 English Bible, Bible Society Library, Cambridge University. By permission of the Syndics of Cambridge Univeristy Library. 1.3: based a a map in *The NIV Study Bible,* 1992, Hodder & Stoughton. 2.2: From *The Lower Jordan Valley* by Isaac Schattner (Series title: *Scripta Hierosolymitana,* vol. 11). Jerusalem, the Hebrew University, 1962. 2.3: From *From Sinai to Jerusalem* by Leen and Kathleen Ritmeyer, Carta, Jerusalem, 2000. 4.3: From *The Northern Hegaz* by Alois Musil, published in 1926 by the American Geographical Society. 5.1: From the 1469 Cologne Bible, Bible Society Library, Cambridge University. By permission of the Syndics of Cambridge University Library. 6.3: © Corbis/Bettman. 9.1: From a 1680 English Bible, Bible Society Library, Cambridge University. By permission of the Syndics of Cambridge University Library. 9.2: From the 1469 Cologne Bible, Bible Society Library, Cambridge University. By permission of the Syndics of Cambridge University Library. 10.1: From the 1469 Cologne Bible, Bible Society Library, Cambridge University. By permission of the Syndics of Cambridge University Library. 11.2: © Corbis/Bettman. 11.3: © Corbis/ Bettman. 11.4: © Corbis/Bettman.

Unless otherwise noted Bible quotations are from the NIV.

FIRST HARPERCOLLINS PAPERBACK EDITION
PUBLISHED IN 2004
Designed by Joseph Rutt

Library of Congress Cataloging-in-Publication Data is available upon request.
ISBN 978–0–06–058273–9

23 24 25 26 27 LBC 15 14 13 12 11

CONTENTS

PART 4. THE ROAD TO THE RED SEA 151

PART 5. DISCOVERING MOUNT SINAI 261

PART ONE

SETTING THE SCENE

*1.1. View from the top of the traditional Mount Sinai,
Jebel Musa, in the Sinai Peninsula.*

ONE

UNLOCKING THE SECRETS
OF THE EXODUS

*Mount Sinai was covered with smoke, because the Lord descended on
it in fire. The smoke billowed up from it like smoke from a furnace,
the whole mountain trembled violently, and the sound of the trumpet
grew louder and louder. Then Moses spoke and the voice of God answered him.*

Exodus 19:18, 19

As I stood in the red light of the rising sun shining on the summit of Mount Sinai in the Sinai Peninsula, I sensed something
was wrong. Why was this particular mountain special? Why
had Moses led the Israelites about three thousand years ago to this
mountain and not to one of the other mountains in the Sinai Peninsula, or even farther afield? To be sure, this mountain was majestic, but
so were the other mountains visible from the top of Mount Sinai (see
figure 1.1). There appeared to be nothing special about this particular
mountain.

And then I looked down to the dry and truly barren land below.
How could two million Israelites, or even twenty thousand with their
flocks and herds of animals, have survived for about a year at the desolate foot of Mount Sinai? There was little water and virtually no vegetation, apart from stunted acacia bushes dotted sparsely about. How
could they have survived forty years of wandering in this barren
wilderness? I knew that the Old Testament described the Israelites as
living on quail, but these are migratory birds that pass over the Sinai
Peninsula only in spring and autumn. In any case, the Bible texts refer
to the Israelites eating quail on only two occasions, each for a few

days. How were the Israelites, and their flocks and herds that lived on grass and plants, to survive at other times in the desolate wilderness of the Sinai Peninsula?

There, in the spring of 1995, standing on the top of the traditional Mount Sinai, also called Jebel Musa, the Mountain of Moses, I resolved to tackle the problem of finding the real Mount Sinai. I knew that many historians and biblical scholars had worked on this problem, but I had an idea for a completely different approach: a more comprehensive study using the understanding of nature provided by modern science. I am a scientist, and as we will see later, looking at the events of the Exodus through the lenses of science does indeed enable us to solve the puzzle of what really happened three thousand years ago. However, the science has to be applied in the context of our knowledge of the ancient Israelites and ancient Egyptians. We will need to understand the history and the geography of the countries involved in the route of the Exodus. We will need to study the main source of information on the Exodus: the Old Testament.

Science and Miracles

Why might a scientific approach be useful in helping to solve the problems of the Exodus? Science involves the study of the universe, including our planet Earth, using detailed observation, logical thinking, and experiment. Scientists try to understand nature and answer questions like how a lunar eclipse occurs or how metals conduct electricity or how our brain works. The account of the Exodus abounds in extraordinary events reported to have occurred in nature, including a burning bush that wasn't consumed, the ten plagues of Egypt, a pillar of fire and a pillar of cloud in the sky, the Red Sea being forced back so that the Israelites could cross then returning so rapidly that the Egyptian army was drowned, water from a rock, special food called manna, a mountain blazing with fire at its summit, and the River Jordan ceasing to flow, which enabled the Israelites to cross. These events are reported as occurring in our natural world, and some are explicitly stated in the Bible to have had a natural cause. We should therefore expect that present-day science may have an important contribution to make in our understanding of the events of the Exodus. Indeed, as we will see later in this book, I believe there is a natural explanation for all of the events listed above. In many cases this enables us to pinpoint geographically where these events must have occurred, and thus we can reconstruct the extraordinary Exodus journey. As far as I am aware, this is the first time that science (geology, biology, physics, chemistry, and mathematics), in combination with history, geography, archaeology, ancient languages, and the Old Testament text, has been used to reconstruct the route of the Exodus.

A natural explanation of the events of the Exodus doesn't to my mind make them any less miraculous. As we will see, the ancient Israelites believed that their God worked in, with, and through natural events. What made certain natural events miraculous was their timing: for example, the River Jordan stopped flowing precisely when the Israelites were assembled on its banks and desperate to cross. I will give a detailed natural explanation of this miracle in the next chapter. I believe this natural explanation makes this miracle more, not less, believable.

About This Book

Like most books, this one is meant to be read from the front to the back. However, if you want to know what happened at the crossing of the Red Sea, for example, then you can go straight to the relevant chapter. I've tried to write this book so that each chapter is reasonably self-contained. I do hope, however, that you won't read only the "highlight" chapters on miracles like the Red Sea crossing. To do so would be to miss fascinating chapters like "The Lost Site of Etham," which doesn't involve miracles at all and is about finding a lost biblical site. It is only if you read the book straight through, from cover to cover, that you can see how the epic events of the Exodus unfold. Only then can you appreciate just how remarkable and amazing the Exodus was.

As I've said above, this book brings together knowledge from science, history, geography, archaeology, ancient languages, and the Bible to try to understand what really happened at the Exodus. I'm well aware that as a scientist I don't have expertise in all these areas, so I've done a large amount of reading and I've consulted with experts in these areas. In particular, Robert Gordon, the Regius Professor of

Hebrew in the University of Cambridge, has kindly read and commented upon every chapter in this book. Robert is an international expert in Hebrew and the Old Testament. Others I've consulted with include Alan Millard, professor of Hebrew and Ancient Semitic Languages in the University of Liverpool, John Ray, professor of Egyptology in the University of Cambridge, and William Facey, director of the London Centre of Arab Studies. Alan is an international authority on the Bible, ancient Israel, and Middle Eastern languages. John is a world expert on ancient Egypt. William has substantial knowledge about ancient Arabia. So, in writing this book I've interacted with some of the leading experts in the world, who have put me right and given me help in a number of places. However, the new interpretations of the Exodus story in this book are mine. Many of these interpretations are totally new and not to be found in any other book.

Summary of the Exodus Story

As you know, the Exodus story starts with the Israelites in Egypt. They were slaves, helping to build cities for a cruel and oppressive pharaoh. One day Moses was born. His mother hid him in a basket among the reeds along the bank of the river Nile, because the Egyptians were killing the Hebrew male babies. Miraculously he survived. Pharaoh's daughter heard him crying, rescued him, and brought him up in an Egyptian palace. When Moses had grown up he saw an Egyptian slavemaster beating a Hebrew slave, and Moses, in his anger, killed the Egyptian. Moses then feared for his own life and fled to the land of Midian, outside of Egyptian control.

While in Midian, Moses visited Mount Sinai and saw an amazing sight: a burning bush with flames of fire leaping out, but the bush didn't burn up as expected; it just kept on burning. At this fiery bush Moses heard the voice of God telling him to lead the Israelites out of Egypt, bring them to Mount Sinai, and then take them to the promised land of Canaan.

So Moses returned to Egypt and asked Pharaoh to let the Hebrew slaves go, but Pharaoh refused. God then sent ten plagues of increasing severity upon the Egyptians until Pharaoh finally yielded and allowed the Israelites to leave. A pillar of cloud by day and a pillar of fire by night were in front of the Israelites, guiding them to Mount Sinai.

However, after they had left Egypt, Pharaoh changed his mind and had his army pursue them, trapping them at the Red Sea. Remarkably, a strong wind drove back the sea so that the Israelites could cross. When Pharaoh's army followed them, the sea rapidly returned and his army was swept into it and drowned.

The Israelites, free at last, continued their journey toward Mount Sinai. Along the way a number of extraordinary events occurred: Moses turned bitter water sweet using a piece of wood; the Israelites ate a mysterious substance called manna and caught and ate large numbers of quail; Moses obtained water from a rock when the Israelites were thirsty. Finally the Israelites reached Mount Sinai and found it to be an awesome sight: emitting fire and smoke, and a sound like a trumpet blast. Here on Mount Sinai Moses received the Ten Commandments, and here also the Israelites rebelled and built an idol to worship: a golden calf (see figure 1.2, pg. 8).

After building the Ark of the Covenant and a portable Tabernacle at Mount Sinai, the Israelites left this holy mountain, traveled through various deserts, and finally entered the promised land by crossing the river Jordan. The river was in full flood when they arrived but it miraculously stopped flowing while they stood at the water's edge so that they could walk across the dry riverbed to the other side. The Israelites had reached the promised land of Israel after an extraordinary journey, and a nation was born.

Is the Exodus Story True?

Before we go further, we should ask whether the account of Moses, the Exodus, and Mount Sinai recorded in the Bible really happened. Biblical scholars hold a range of views on this. The traditional view is that Moses was a real person and one of the great figures of world history, who was responsible for leading the Israelites out of Egypt, giving them the Ten Commandments on Mount Sinai, and establishing the Nation of Israel. This traditional view regards the biblical account of the Exodus in the Old Testament as a factual account of what really happened. At the other end of the spectrum is the view that Moses never existed and the whole account of the Exodus is fiction invented

Moſes breaketh the Tables.   Exod: 32.

And it came to paſs as ſoon as he came nigh unto the camp that he ſaw the calf, and the dancing: and Moſes anger waxed hot, and he cast the tables out of his hands and brake them beneath the mount. Verſe 19/22

1.2. *Moses with the Ten Commandments, from a rare 1680 English Bible.*

to fulfill a theological purpose. Many scholars occupy positions in between these two viewpoints, accepting the existence of Moses and a "desert period" but differing in the amount of detail in the biblical accounts they would regard as describing what really happened and how much actually goes back to Moses.

My approach to the description of Moses and the Exodus in the Bible is going to be as a scientist who tests and weighs the evidence. If ancient writings, whether Egyptian, Babylonian, or Hebrew, claim to describe real historical events, my belief is that, tentatively, we should take them seriously and see if they make sense and fit the evidence available to us today. If they do not make sense, then we may be justified in treating them as historical fiction (that is, a fictional story cleverly written so that it appears to be historical fact). But first, surely we should take seriously the claims of the authors that they are describing factual events. Therefore, tentatively, I am going to take the Old Testament writings about the Exodus seriously. In my research I found that these writings are remarkably accurate and coherent. But I also found that much of the traditional interpretation of these writings is wrong, particularly regarding the geography of the Exodus. (The map on pg. 10 (1.3) shows the Sinai Peninsula with the conventional route of the Exodus.)

The true story of the Exodus is even more amazing than the traditional interpretation. It was an extraordinary journey. It was so extraordinary that I believe that, as you read this book, you will never forget it.

A key conclusion of this book is that the real Mount Sinai is not in the Sinai Peninsula. For many readers this may be hard to accept because the name of Sinai has been attached for so many centuries to a particular mountain in the Sinai Peninsula that it has become a time-honored identification. People now assume that Mount Sinai must be in the Sinai Peninsula because of the spell cast by the name. However, the tradition that Mount Sinai is in the Sinai Peninsula goes back no further than the third century A.D., when groups of Christian monks began to spring up in the Sinai Peninsula. One of these groups claimed that a particular mountain was Mount Sinai, and later a famous monastery, St. Catherine's Monastery, was built halfway up the mountain, but there was no evidence that this was the real Mount Sinai. So this is a very late tradition, arising about fifteen hundred

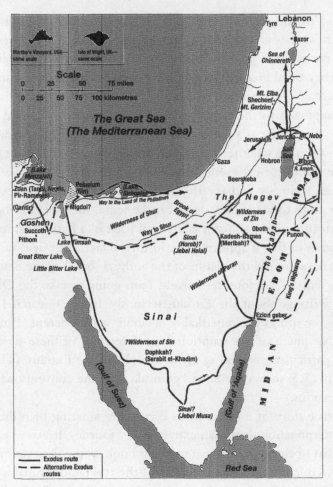

1.3. Map of the Sinai Peninsula showing the conventional route of the Exodus, plus alternative routes proposed by others. Based on map in The NIV Study Bible, *1992, Hodder & Stoughton. Note a probable error in this map: ancient Rameses is almost certainly at modern Qantir and not at modern Tanis (see chapter 3).*

years after the events of the Exodus. However, can we now find the true Mount Sinai, over three thousand years later?

I want you to read this book as though you are a detective, analyzing the clues given about the Exodus in the Old Testament writings in the light of the modern scientific knowledge I will provide. I would also like you to try to time-travel—to go back three thousand years in time into the mind of Moses. This is what I frequently tried to do. If we can understand how and why Moses would have reacted in different situations, and how the biblical writers described these situations in the language of the time, then we are well on our way to solving the problems of the Exodus.

I write *problems* in the plural because in order to locate the true Mount Sinai, it turns out that there are a number of separate but interlocking problems to be solved. Unless all these problems are solved, then we cannot convincingly locate Mount Sinai. It is like having a case with many different combination locks on it, each of which must be unlocked before we can open the case to reveal what is inside. In this book we will try to solve the problems of the Exodus one by one. It is essential that we do not underestimate the difficulty of the challenges involved. Nearly all recent books state that reconstructing the route of the Exodus and finding the true Mount Sinai are now impossible. For example, the *Oxford History of the Biblical World* states:

> Thus, despite decades of research, we cannot reconstruct a reliable Exodus route based on information in the biblical account. Nor, despite intensive survey and exploration by archaeologists, are there remains on the Sinai Peninsula or in Egypt that can be linked specifically to the Israelite Exodus. Barring some future momentous discovery, we shall never be able to establish exactly the route of the Exodus.

Never say never! Using a combination of the biblical account, historical records, and present-day science, I believe it is possible to reconstruct the Exodus route and hence to locate the real Mount Sinai, but in order to do this, we are going to need very clear thinking about the Bible, history, and science. It is synthesizing viewpoints from these various angles—biblical, historical, and scientific—that makes this book different from all others written about the Exodus and that enables us to determine what happened three thousand years ago.

Five Key Questions

My aim in writing this book is to answer five key questions about the Exodus:

1. Is the story coherent and consistent?

2. Is the story factually accurate?

3. Can we understand the miracles?

4. Has the Exodus text been misinterpreted?

5. Can we reconstruct the Exodus route and find the true Mount Sinai?

I believe these are really important questions. I plan to have answered them by the end of this book.

As I wrote this book, another question emerged in my thinking. Three thousand years ago, the Israelites regarded the events of the Exodus as clear evidence for a "guiding hand." Is this interpretation of the Exodus credible today in our modern scientific world? Does the Exodus provide evidence for a guiding hand? Readers may be surprised by the pointers that emerge in this book.

A Road Map of This Book

Let me explain the sequence of the chapters in this book, and why I've ordered them in this way. Readers may well think it curious that in the next chapter I consider a remarkable event that happened at the very end of the Exodus journey: the crossing of the river Jordan. Why do I start here, at the end, rather than at the beginning? Because the mystery of how the Israelites were able to cross the river Jordan, which was normally far too wide at that point for people to cross, offers a clear test case of how the miracles of the Exodus story can be explained naturally, while not being explained away religiously at all. In addition, this story illustrates just how accurate the Old Testament is, both in terms of the detailed geography of where the crossing occurred, and in terms of the description of the event itself. Chapter 2 therefore establishes the main theme of this book, that science has a key role to play in understanding the events of the Exodus, and I use the crossing of the river Jordan as a clear demonstration of this.

If we are to understand any event in detail then we have to know roughly when it happened. It turns out that the date of the Exodus is a long-running controversy, and I try to solve that controversy in chapter 3. Knowing the date of the Exodus then enables us to say who the pharaoh probably was at the time of the Exodus. In addition, some scholars explain the crossing of the Red Sea and many of the plagues of Egypt as being due to a massive eruption of a volcano called Santorini. Knowing the date of the Exodus enables us to say that in fact the eruption of Santorini had nothing to do with it!

The first three chapters form Part 1 of this book, called "Setting the Scene." The book then mainly follows the chronological order of the Exodus, as given in the Old Testament, starting with the birth of Moses in Egypt and ending with the Israelites at Mount Sinai (the real one, that is!). Chapter 4 starts with the birth of Moses and then describes how he fled to the land of Midian to escape the fury of Pharaoh. We use the findings of archaeologists and explorers to discover what the mysterious land of Midian was like three thousand years ago. When Moses was in Midian he traveled to Mount Sinai and there he encountered the burning bush. Chapter 5 looks in detail at what could have kept the bush burning and provides a natural explanation for this.

Chapter 6 examines why the Bible calls Mount Sinai the Mountain of God and shows that the Old Testament description of Mount Sinai matches closely the description of an erupting volcano, down to points of minute detail. I argue that the biblical description of Mount Sinai is the world's oldest known description of an active volcano.

While at the burning bush, near Mount Sinai, Moses received his momentous mission to lead the Israelites out of Egypt, as described in chapter 7. How many people were involved in the Exodus? Was it really as many as two million? I look at this much-debated question in chapter 8, and arrive at a clear answer. As we've seen earlier, Pharaoh refused to let the Israelites leave Egypt and so God sent ten plagues of increasing severity. These are discussed in chapters 9 and 10, where it will be shown that the plagues form an intimately connected sequence of natural events.

After the terrible tenth plague, the death of the firstborn, Pharaoh finally agreed to let the Israelites go. In chapter 11 I use archaeology to identify the starting point of the Exodus, Rameses, and the next stopping place, Succoth, and I also explain scientifically the pillar of cloud and the pillar of fire that guided the Israelites to Mount Sinai. Chapters 12 and 13 ask, and answer, the long-debated question of where was the biblical Red Sea that the Israelites crossed. Was it an inland Sea of Reeds, or the Red Sea?

The lost biblical site of Etham, close to the Red Sea crossing point, is identified for the first time in chapter 14 using a variety of biblical clues. Chapter 15 then describes how Pharaoh brilliantly trapped the Israelites so that they really had no escape route—except to cross the Red Sea. The science underlying the Red Sea crossing is described in chapter 16, as is the drowning of Pharaoh's army by the rapidly returning water.

Chapter 17 tentatively identifies several biblical sites on the route to Mount Sinai and gives natural mechanisms for Moses' sweetening bitter water with wood. Chapter 18 describes quail, manna, and obtaining water from a rock in terms of our modern scientific knowledge. I also consider here the biblical clue of the dew that acts like a fingerprint to enable us to identify the Desert of Sin.

In chapter 19 the site of the real Mount Sinai is discovered using a combination of biblical clues and modern science. It is shown that there is only one mountain in the world that satisfies in detail the biblical description of Mount Sinai. A fascinating connection with the ancient Moon-god is also revealed. We have finally arrived at the true site of what is probably the most significant mountain in the world: Mount Sinai.

In the Epilogue I answer the five key questions about the Exodus raised earlier in this chapter and also comment on whether the Exodus story gives evidence for a "guiding hand."

Our introduction and scene setting are now finished. Come with me on an amazing detective adventure to reconstruct the extraordinary journey taken by Moses three thousand years ago. As you will see, it really is one of the greatest true stories ever told.

TWO

CROSSING THE RIVER JORDAN

Now the Jordan is in flood all during harvest. Yet as soon as the priests who carried the ark reached the Jordan and their feet touched the water's edge, the water from upstream stopped flowing. It piled up in a heap a great distance away, at a town called Adam in the vicinity of Zarethan, while the water flowing down to the sea of the Arabah [the Dead Sea] was completely cut off. So the people crossed over opposite Jericho.

Joshua 3:15, 16

So what really happened at the crossing of the Jordan? Picture the scene. The Israelites are standing on one side of the river Jordan in flood. They gaze longingly across to the land on the other side—their promised land of Canaan. They have waited forty long years to possess this land, and now, tantalizingly, it is within their sight, yet it seems as far away as ever as the floodwaters rush by in torrents. The situation looks hopeless. But suddenly the raging river stills and the water flow reduces to a tiny trickle, as if a giant tap has been turned off. The Israelites cannot believe it. They shout and sing as they dance across the riverbed and triumphantly claim the promised land on the other side.

Many people say, "What a wonderful children's story! What a fabulous fairy tale!" But can it possibly be true? How can we know what really happened three thousand years ago? Most people, even most biblical scholars, believe the story of the crossing of the river Jordan to be a legend. But I believe that looking at this story through the lenses of science can prove, beyond reasonable doubt, that the Jordan stopped flowing exactly as described in the Old Testament. But first we need to put the story into context and analyze exactly what the Bible says about crossing the river Jordan.

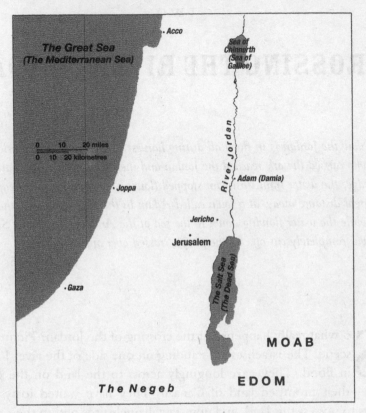

2.1. The Dead Sea and the River Jordan.

Crossing the Jordan was the final stage of the Exodus journey: the climax. About forty years earlier Moses had led the Israelites out of Egypt. They had then crossed the Red Sea, received the Ten Commandments at Mount Sinai, and traveled through various deserts. Toward the end of these travels Moses had died and Joshua had taken over as the new leader of the Israelites. They had tried to enter directly the promised land of Canaan but had been driven back, so Joshua had led them north up the eastern side of the Dead Sea and then up the east side of the river Jordan (see map 2.1).

However, there was a major problem: as we've seen, the land the Israelites wanted to enter, the promised land of Canaan (part of which is now called Israel), was on the west side of the river Jordan, and they were on the east side. What happened next is vividly described in the passage from the Old Testament book of Joshua quoted at the start of this chapter. This passage contains a curious detail that I think is a key clue to understanding what really happened. Try reading it again and see if you can spot this clue.

In a really good detective story the minor clues usually hold the key. If a mystery could be solved using only the major clues, then the solution would be simple. So it is with the events of the Exodus: if the various problems could be solved using only the major clues, then they would have been solved long ago. Hence, in solving any long-standing problem, whether in history or in science, the details are key.

The detail that caught my attention in the account of the crossing of the river Jordan is that the water stopped flowing, not where the Israelites were gathered, which one might expect if the story had been invented, but a great distance away at a town called Adam in the vicinity of Zarethan. Something had stopped the water flowing at this place called Adam. What could it have been, and is it possible to find out about this over three thousand years later?

The Geography of the Jordan Crossing

A feature of the story that really stands out is the careful attention paid to geography. The writer is effectively saying, "This is where these amazing events really happened: I will point you to the precise spot." So he doesn't just tell us that the people crossed the river Jordan, he tells us that they crossed the Jordan opposite Jericho. He doesn't just write that the water stopped flowing a great distance away, he pinpoints where: at a town called Adam in the vicinity of Zarethan. For good measure he tells us these places are all upstream of the Dead Sea. The writer(s) did not intend the route of the Exodus to be a mystery, and it would not have been for the original audience. The problem we face today in reconstructing the route of the Exodus is in locating ancient place-names that have long been forgotten. For example, where did the Jordan stop flowing? Not at a town called Alice, but at a town called Adam. However, if you look on a modern map of the state of Jordan, you will find no town called Adam. Is it possible to locate the ancient town of Adam after three thousand years?

One point that puzzled me was that ancient Hebrew texts contained only consonants and no vowels, so how was the word *Adam* written in ancient Hebrew? I needed to ask my Hebrew experts, Robert Gordon and Alan Millard, a few questions. "I've heard that the ancient Hebrew alphabet consisted only of consonants," I said. "Is this correct?" "Yes," replied Robert Gordon. "When we write English today we use an alphabet of twenty-six letters; twenty-one of them are consonants and five are vowels. However, the ancient Hebrew alphabet consisted only of consonants, and it had no signs for vowels, perhaps because no word in ancient Hebrew began with a vowel sound."

So the original written Hebrew text of the Old Testament was a series of consonants. However, when the manuscripts were read, clearly vowel sounds had to be used. Somewhat similarly, in text messages today on mobile phones, the word *text* is often written as the consonants *txt,* but all mobile phone users know from experience that this is read as *text*. But I was still puzzled. "So how do people know how to read the consonants of the Old Testament text?" I asked. "A good question," replied Alan Millard. "Early in the Middle Ages (about A.D. 800–900), Jewish scholars who copied the Old Testament added small marks, called vowel signs, to the consonants to preserve the pronunciation they had received from their ancestors. Those scholars are known as the Masoretes, which is Hebrew for 'transmitters of tradition,' and their text is called the Masoretic Text, which is the basis for the text of the Old Testament normally used today and which has been translated into hundreds of other languages, including English. The vowels that the Masoretes marked show how Hebrew was read in their tradition, and that certainly went far back in history. However, there is no way of knowing with certainty how Hebrew was pronounced in biblical times."

Having learned about consonants in ancient Hebrew, let's now return to the question of whether it is possible to locate the ancient town of Adam after three thousand years. When we try to locate places mentioned in the Bible and other ancient literature, one course of action is to look for modern names that are similar to the ancient ones. Over the course of time as peoples have moved and languages have changed, names have altered, too. However, the consonantal core of the name sometimes survives, and there are known patterns by which modern Arabic names can be traced back to ancient Hebrew names.

In the original Hebrew text, the word the Masoretes represented as Adam was simply the consonants *'dm*. The symbol ' may seem strange to us, but we use a similar symbol today, although with a different significance, when we write *it's* instead of *it is* or *let's* instead of *let us*. The symbol ' is in fact the first mark of the Hebrew word *'aleph,* which is the name of the first letter of the Hebrew alphabet (the first letter of the Greek alphabet, alpha, is derived from aleph).

The symbol ' is the breathing sound we make when we say *a* as in *add*. When modern Arabic words replace Hebrew words, the initial ' is usually no longer sounded and an Arabic ending is added. In order to try to find ancient Adam on a modern map of the state of Jordan, I therefore looked on a map to see if there is a suitable town on the river Jordan containing the consonants *dm,* and indeed there is! On modern maps of the state of Jordan, a town appears on the eastern side of the river Jordan called Damiya, about seventeen miles north of where the river Jordan passes closest to Jericho. Not only that, but on the 1989 Bartholomew World Travel Map of Israel with Jordan, the same town is actually marked *Damiya (Adamah).* This strongly suggests that the ancient town of Adam is modern Damiya. I was later to find that many scholars agreed on this, which is why the Bartholomew map states it. Of course, the consonantal form of an ancient place-name does not always survive to the present day, but sometimes it does, and this will form a key part of our reconstruction of the route of the Exodus later in this book.

The Clue of the Earthquakes

So far we haven't really proved anything. We have simply suggested that the town called Adam in the book of Joshua could be the modern town of Damiya. But can we prove this beyond reasonable doubt after three thousand years have elapsed? I believe we can, and science provides the critical evidence. On July 11, 1927, a well-documented earthquake shook the town of Jericho, causing cracks in the buildings and panic in the local population. The earthquake was detected in seismological stations as far apart as Europe, South Africa, North America, and Russia and was measured at a magnitude of about 6.5 on the Richter scale, which means that it was a large earthquake. (By comparison, the earthquake that struck Kobe, Japan, on January 17, 1995, and killed over five thousand people was of a magnitude 7.2 on the Richter scale. The San Francisco earthquake of October 17, 1989, which killed sixty-two people and collapsed a section of the San Francisco–Oakland Bay Bridge, was of a magnitude 7.1 on the Richter scale.) Various people, including the world-renowned geophysicist Amos Nur, who is the Wayne Loel Professor of Earth Sciences and professor of geophysics at Stanford University, have made a detailed study of the 1927 Jericho earthquake and found that it was due to slippage along a geological fault called the Jericho fault, which runs approximately north-south under the Jordan River. The Jericho fault forms the boundary between two tectonic plates, with the Arabia plate to the east and the African-Sinai plate to the west. This boundary has produced the Great Rift Valley, which we will get to know in a later chapter.

Professor Nur has written to me about this earthquake:

During the 1927 earthquake, several ground cracks appeared, together with an outpouring of ground water. This soil liquefaction phenomenon has been well observed in earthquakes elsewhere. *During the earthquake, mud slides occurred along the Jordan near Damia, about 30 kilometres [about eighteen miles] north of Jericho; these temporarily stopped the river's flow* [my italics].

The photograph (2.2) shows a more recent landslide of the bank of the Jordan River near Damia that did not quite make it to the other bank.

Note that Nur, and some modern maps, spell the name *Damia*, whereas other modern maps spell it *Damiya* or *Damiyeh*. There is often more than one way of transliterating these Middle Eastern names. *Damia, Damiya,* and *Damiyeh* sound the same, and they are the same place. This can be very confusing. What has happened is that travelers to the Middle East invented English spellings of Hebrew and Arabic place-names based on how they sounded. So a particular Hebrew or Arabic place-name can have a variety of English spellings. I

2.2. Landslide off the bank of the River Jordan in 1957.

will try to be consistent in this book and give the most accepted English spelling.

Amos Nur then searched historical records and found that the river Jordan had been temporarily stopped on a number of occasions, all because of mud slides induced by an earthquake. The earliest historical record of this that Nur found occurred in 1160. Nur recognized the relevance of these earthquakes to the passage in the book of Joshua quoted above. He writes,

Adam is now Damia, the site of the 1927 mud slides which cut off the flow of the Jordan. Such cut-offs, lasting typically one to two days, have also been recorded in 1906, 1834, 1546, 1534, 1267, and 1160. *The stoppage of the Jordan is so typical of earthquakes in this region that little doubt can be left as to the reality of such events in Joshua's time* [my italics].

We therefore have a scientific explanation of the crossing of the Jordan in terms of a natural mechanism: an earthquake-induced mud slide behind which the waters of the Jordan piled up until they broke through, typically one to two days later. While the flow of the Jordan was temporarily stopped, the Israelites were able to cross over. I believe this enables us to identify Adam, the place of the earthquake-induced mud slide, with modern Damiya beyond reasonable doubt.

Was the Crossing a Miracle?

Some readers may raise an objection to this scientific explanation, because it is clear from the Bible that the Israelites regarded the crossing of the river Jordan as a major miracle straight from the hand of God, and we have explained it as being caused by a natural mechanism: an earthquake. Well, let's try to think as the ancient Israelites would have thought. Most ancient civilizations believed that god(s) controlled the forces of nature. For example, the ancient Egyptians had a god who they believed controlled the annual flooding of the river Nile, another god who they believed controlled the rain, and so on. Most ancient civilizations had many gods like this, but ancient Israel was different: the people had one God who, they believed, controlled all the forces of nature. If an earthquake temporarily caused the river Jordan to stop flowing and enabled them to cross into the promised land, the ancient Israelites would have seen this as just as much the hand of God as if they had seen an angel holding the waters back.

I think we can demonstrate that this was indeed the case by considering the biblical description of another major miracle in the Exodus account, the crossing of the Red Sea. The Israelites undoubtedly regarded this as one of the greatest miracles that happened to them, and the book of Exodus describes it as follows: "Then Moses stretched out his hand over the sea, and all that night the Lord drove the sea back with a strong east wind and turned it into dry land" (Exodus 14:21). The Bible is explicit that this miracle was caused by a natural mechanism, a strong east wind, but the Bible also states that this wind was the agent of the hand of God (here represented by the hand of Moses stretched out over the sea). We will consider the crossing of the Red Sea in detail later in the book. It is an even more remarkable event than the crossing of the river Jordan.

Another major factor with regard to miracles is timing. In our modern world, our lives are dominated by deadlines, and industry operates on a just-in-time philosophy. Some years ago the best-selling management book was called *The One-Minute Manager.* We want things, and we want them fast! In the ancient world, life was more leisurely and there was a time for waiting as well as a time for action. I believe that there can be little doubt that the ancient Israelites would have regarded the earthquake-induced stoppage of the river Jordan as a major miracle of timing. After forty years of waiting in the wilderness, the Israelites were now opposite Jericho, but the Jordan River, which was in flood, separated them from their promised land. Just at this time, when the Israelites were gathered on the banks of the Jordan, the earthquake-induced stoppage of the river occurred. What a great climax to the Exodus journey!

The Israelites realized that the Red Sea crossing was enabled by a natural mechanism, a strong wind, but did they realize that the crossing of the Jordan was also enabled by a natural mechanism, an earthquake? This is not clear from the description in the book of Joshua quoted at the start of this chapter, but I suggest that they probably did know this. When they stood beside the river Jordan they must have felt the ground trembling beneath their feet from the earthquake that induced the landslide at Adam, 17 miles away. They were sufficiently interested in the cause of the river Jordan stopping that they located and recorded where this happened: at Adam. A visit to Adam would have revealed the earthquake-induced landslide. This is possibly hinted at in the Old Testament Psalm 114: "When Israel came out of Egypt . . . the sea looked and fled, the Jordan turned back, the mountains leaped like rams, the hills like lambs. . . . Tremble, O earth, at the presence of the Lord."

Although the psalm is clearly using poetic language, just what is being described by this language? It seems clear to me as a scientist that mountains moving and the earth trembling can only be descriptions of one thing: an earthquake. Indeed, nonscientists might well use similar language today. Note how this description of an earthquake is associated with the presence of God.

The concept that for the ancient Israelites the miracles of God involved God displaying his power through control of natural events like earthquakes is so important for this book that I would like to give one further Old Testament quotation that makes this matter absolutely clear. This comes from Psalm 77:

You are the God who performs miracles;
you display your power among the peoples . . .
Your thunder was heard in the whirlwind,
your lightning lit up the world,
the earth trembled and quaked.
Your path led through the sea,
your way through the mighty waters,
though your footprints were not seen.
You led your people like a flock
by the hand of Moses and Aaron.

The above passage specifically associates miracles with thunder, lightning, and earthquakes, which belong to God ("your" lightning, and so forth). It is remarkable that the text says, "though your footprints were not seen." In other words, the ancient Israelites' view of miracles did not normally involve directly seeing the footprints of God, left behind like a celestial visiting card saying "God was here" after a miraculous event. The miracles of God, for the ancient Israelites, instead involved God displaying his power through natural events like earthquakes occurring at the right time. We should therefore first seek natural events to explain the many miracles described in the Exodus account, using the power of modern science to throw light upon what really happened. I have no doubt that the ancient Israelites would have approved of this approach. They would have seen a modern scientific explanation as being fully compatible with their concept of a miracle.

Let me finish this chapter by returning to place-names, because they are so important in reconstructing the Exodus route. I have suggested that ancient Adam is now modern Damiya. Various arguments support this conclusion. First, both Adam and Damiya have the same core consonants *dm*. Second, modern Damiya is on the Jordan River and north of Jericho, and the Old Testament records that ancient Adam was on the Jordan River and north of Jericho. Third, and most important, historical records show that earthquakes at Damiya have stopped the flow of the river Jordan on a number of occasions, and the Old Testament states that in the time of Joshua the flow of the Jordan stopped at ancient Adam. As a scientist looking at this evidence, I am happy to agree beyond reasonable doubt that ancient Adam is modern Damiya.

Picture the Scene

At the start of this chapter I wrote, "So what really happened at the crossing of the Jordan? Picture the scene. The Israelites are standing on one side of the river Jordan in flood." Unfortunately, if you visit the Jordan River, as I have done, or if you look at a modern photograph of it, you don't get a true picture of this river in ancient times. In recent years the river Jordan has been used for irrigation, with large quantities of water being taken from it, which has greatly diminished the volume of water flowing in it. To know what the Jordan really looked like we need an old photograph, taken before the recent (since 1940) irrigation works, and taken at the right time of the year.

So what was the time of year when the Israelites crossed the Jordan? The ancient book of Joshua tells us exactly. Joshua 4:19 states, "On the tenth day of the first month the people went up from the Jordan." The ancient Israelites had a lunar calendar, in which each month was a lunar month, the first day of each month being determined by the sighting of the new crescent moon in the sky. So the new light from the new moon signified a new month—a nice piece of symbolism. Incidentally, the new moon is first seen in the sky shortly after sunset, which is why the Jewish day runs from sunset to sunset. Modern Jews still use this ancient lunar calendar for religious purposes. The first month in this lunar calendar starts in the spring, and it is now called the month of Nisan. The first day of Nisan usually falls in our March, but sometimes it is in early April. So the ancient Israelites crossed the river Jordan in the spring.

Where does the river Jordan start? The main sources of the river are on the slopes of Mount Hermon, a snowcapped mountain on the Lebanon-Syria border and close to the border with modern Israel. Each spring the snow melts and the sudden volume of extra water turns the Jordan into a fast-flowing river with treacherous currents. Because of irrigation, the effect is not nearly as great now as it used to be. However, a British expedition sailed down the river Jordan in the

2.3. Photograph from the nineteenth century showing the River Jordan overflowing its banks in the springtime.

nineteenth century and estimated that the Jordan in flood was half a mile wide. This is huge! Imagine the barrier the Israelites faced.

On my one-week vacation to Israel and Egypt in the spring of 2001, to revisit some of the route of the Exodus, I was browsing in a bookshop in Eilat when I picked up a book by Leen and Kathleen Ritmeyer called *From Sinai to Jerusalem: The Wandering of the Holy Ark*. In this book the authors reproduce a rare photograph from the nineteenth century showing the Jordan River overflowing its banks in the springtime, and with their permission I reproduce this photograph here (2.3). So this was the river in flood that the Israelites needed to cross. Picture the scene! Imagine you were there! Isn't it amazing to be able to reconstruct ancient events in detail as we have in this chapter? And not just any ancient events: events that have changed the course of history.

In this chapter we have used a combination of science (in particular earth science and geophysics), historical records, geography, ancient Hebrew, and the Old Testament writings to reconstruct what happened in the final stage of the Exodus from Egypt at the crossing of the river Jordan. I believe the evidence fits together so well that we can say, beyond reasonable doubt, how and where the crossing occurred. I find it quite remarkable that we can now do this after over three thousand years have elapsed.

Only one main point is missing from our reconstruction of the crossing of the river Jordan. How many years ago did it occur? This depends upon the date of the Exodus, which scholars have been hotly debating for many years. In the next chapter we will try to solve this great controversy; it is another fascinating puzzle.

In the rest of this book we will try to reconstruct what really happened in the complete Exodus story, starting at the birth of Moses and ending with the Israelites at Mount Sinai (the real one!). This is a much more difficult problem to solve than the problem of crossing the Jordan, which may be why it has never been solved before. However, the best way to solve all major problems, whether in life, science, or history, is to break them down into bite-sized chunks, and that is what we shall do in each chapter. The story is even more extraordinary than the crossing of the Jordan. I believe it to be one of the greatest stories ever told.

THREE

THE DATE OF THE EXODUS

So they [the Egyptians] put slave masters over them [the Israelites] to oppress them with forced labor, and they built Pithom and Rameses as store cities for Pharaoh.

Exodus 1:11

In the four hundred and eightieth year after the Israelites had come out of Egypt, in the fourth year of Solomon's reign over Israel, in the month of Ziv, the second month, he began to build the temple of the Lord.

1 Kings 6:1

The date of the Exodus is one of the longest-running chronological controversies in the Bible. Historians and biblical scholars are totally divided on the answer, and the causes of their dispute are the two texts quoted above. On the one hand, Exodus 1:11 says that the Israelite slaves in Egypt built Pithom and Rameses, as store cities for Pharaoh, and Egyptologists believe that the building of Rameses started in about 1300 B.C. On the other hand, 1 Kings 6:1 says that the Exodus occurred 480 years before the building of King Solomon's temple, which dates the Exodus to about 1446 B.C. If the Exodus from Egypt occurred in 1446 B.C., then the Israelite slaves wouldn't still have been in Egypt in 1300 B.C. What a puzzle!

The authoritative multivolume *Cambridge Ancient History* writes about the date of the Exodus, "The statements in the Old Testament are self-contradictory." The modern translation of the Bible called the *New International Version,* which has sold millions of copies and which is the translation I'm quoting from in this book, has in the front a time chart called "Old Testament Chronology." Because of the controversy over the date of the Exodus it shows two different time charts up to 1050 B.C.: one dates the Exodus at 1446 B.C., the other gives a date range of 1300 to1200 B.C. The former it calls the "traditional date," the latter the "date accepted by many scholars." However, in its preface to the book of Exodus it declares its hand and states, "There are no compelling reasons to modify in any substantial way the traditional 1446 B.C. date for the Exodus of the Israelites from Egyptian bondage."

So which date is correct, 1446 B.C. or later than 1300 B.C.? Are the Old Testament texts quoted at the start of this chapter really self-contradictory? Can we tell after three thousand years? In this chapter I'm going to try to solve this problem.

It is a key part of understanding the Exodus story to know roughly when it occurred. What I discovered is a fascinating historical puzzle that hinges on the meaning of certain numbers in the Bible. By the end of this chapter we will have answers not only on the date of the Exodus but also on whether the Bible really does contradict itself about this date.

When Was Rameses Built?

If you look at a map of modern Egypt you will find no place called Rameses. For many years the location of Rameses was unknown, but modern archaeology has revealed that ancient Rameses is modern Qantir (see map 3.1 on the next page).

Egyptian records show that Rameses was Egypt's capital in the Nile Delta, started by an Egyptian pharaoh called Sethos I but built mainly by his son, the famous Ramesses II, sometimes called Ramesses the Great. The city of Rameses was named after this pharaoh. (It is conventional to spell the name of the city slightly differently from the name of the pharaoh, and I will follow this convention in this book.) Archaeology shows that Rameses was an absolutely magnificent city, and I will describe it further in a later chapter.

No pharaoh had built a capital in the Nile Delta since invading pharaohs from foreign lands, called the Hyksos pharaohs, had settled there in the period 1648 to 1540 B.C., much earlier than any possible date for the Exodus. The Egyptian pharaoh Ramesses I reigned for only one year (1295 to 1294 B.C.), then Sethos I ruled from about 1294 to 1279 B.C., and his son Ramesses II from about 1279 to 1213 B.C.

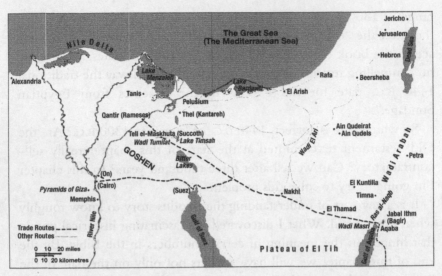

3.1. Map showing the location of Rameses (modern Qantir) and showing ancient trade routes from Egypt to Arabia.

How accurately do we know the above dates? David Rohl in *A Test of Time* has reanalyzed Egyptian chronology and controversially places the dates of Sethos I and Ramesses II about three hundred years later than the conventional chronology. In particular, he has Ramesses II reigning in Egypt in 950 B.C. at the time Solomon was the king of Israel. Very few Egyptologists believe Rohl's revised chronology, and having looked at the evidence, I don't either, although his book is stimulating and interesting to read. There is an interlocking network of evidence supporting the conventional Egyptian chronology, and the maximum likely error in the dates at this time is about twenty years. The dates I've given above for Sethos I and Ramesses II are from Kenneth Kitchen's article on the chronology of the Old Testament in the *New Bible Dictionary*. These dates are known as the "low chronology" because they are the latest possible dates. There is another school of thought that gives somewhat earlier dates than these (they are known as the high chronology), and this is the chronology that *The Cambridge Ancient History* uses. In this "high chronology," Sethos I ruled from 1318 to 1304 B.C. and Ramesses II from 1304 to 1238 B.C. We don't yet know with certainty whether the high chronology or the low chronology, or something in the middle, is correct. So the very earliest the building of Rameses could have started was 1318 B.C. The book of Exodus records that Moses killed an Egyptian slave master supervising the building work. Moses then feared for his life, fled to Midian, and then returned to Egypt when the pharaoh who wanted to kill him, probably Sethos I, had died. He then led the Israelites out of Egypt in the Exodus, so the most likely pharaoh at the time of the Exodus is Ramesses II, and the earliest possible date for the Exodus from Egypt is 1304 B.C., though it probably took place some years later than this.

So, if Exodus 1:11 is correct, and the Israelite slaves did indeed build Rameses, it is very difficult to see how the Exodus could have taken place earlier than 1304 B.C. This is the view of most modern scholars, but a substantial number support the traditional date of 1446 B.C. Both can't be right!

The 480 Years

As we've seen, 1 Kings 6:1 says that Solomon began to build the temple in the fourth year of his reign, which was 480 years after the Exodus from Egypt. So when was Solomon's temple built? By comparing and synchronizing events in the reigns of Israelite kings with known dated records from Assyria, we can fix the start date of the building of Solomon's temple as 966 B.C. This is probably accurate to within five years either side. Counting back 480 years gives the date of the Exodus as 1446 B.C.

The above argument seems clear and convincing. Indeed, had this Old Testament book of Kings been written today, then 480 years would have meant a literal 480 years. But the book of Kings was written over two thousand years ago, and the key questions to ask are what the author meant by 480 years and what the original readers would have understood by 480 years.

I would like to emphasize that I'm not saying that 480 years is inaccurate, but I am saying that it might have had a different meaning over two thousand years ago than it has today, and I want to explore what the writer may have meant by it. Clearly it may mean literally 480 years, but is there another equally valid meaning?

Today, we take our calendar almost for granted. If we've forgotten when President Kennedy died we can go to a computer, type *President*

Kennedy into a search engine, and seconds later the date of his death pops up on the screen. Now let's go back to events that occurred five hundred years ago. When did Christopher Columbus discover America? I pulled down a book from my bookcase and found that he landed on one of the Bahama Islands in 1492, and he discovered Honduras in Central America in 1502. I could just as easily have found this information on a computer. Today it's straightforward to find out about historical dates from computers and books.

Let's now go back to the time of Solomon, to the year we call in our calendar 966 B.C., when Solomon started to build his temple. How would the writer of Kings have known the date of the Exodus? In those days there was not a written-down calendar, going both forward and back in time, as we have today. One reason for this was that the Jewish calendar was an observational calendar, with the first day of each lunar month being determined by the first sighting of the crescent of the new moon. So the Jewish calendar wasn't a calculated one, like our modern calendar.

So how did the ancient Israelites date past events? We know that the ancient Egyptians and Greeks dated past events by counting generations, and this would have been the simplest method for the Israelites to have used as well. So they would have dated key events by reference to whether they happened in the time of their father or grandfather or great-grandfather, and so forth, or in the time of certain kings. For example, the Old Testament prophet Isaiah dates a life-changing vision he had to "the year that King Uzziah died" (Isaiah 6:1). That's why ancient Egyptian records contain so many lists of kings, generation by generation, and why the Bible has so many genealogies.

So how was the dating of past events done in practice? We know that the ancient Phoenicians and Carthaginians often reckoned time by counting each generation to be a nominal forty years, even though a real generation (from birth of father to birth of son) was likely on average to have been less than forty years. Somewhat similarly, the length "one foot" was originally the length of a human foot, even though most people's feet are significantly less than twelve inches long. There is evidence that in the Old Testament forty years is often a round number meaning a generation. For example, Psalm 95:10 writes of the Exodus wanderings, "For forty years I was angry with that generation." The kings Saul, David, and Solomon are each said to have reigned for forty years. Moses is said to have been forty when he killed the Egyptian slave master and fled to Midian, eighty when he saw the burning bush, and one hundred twenty when he died. The number forty is used so many times in the Bible that it seems clear it is often meant to be taken as a round number, and that in particular forty years often means a generation.

So a possible interpretation of 480 years is that this refers to twelve generations, each of a nominal forty years, instead of a literal 480 years. The Hebrew text of the Old Testament was translated into Greek in the third century B.C. by scholars living in Alexandria in Egypt. This Greek version is called the Septuagint, and I'll give further details about it in a later chapter. What I find fascinating is that the Septuagint version of 1 Kings 6:1 says that there were 440 years (not 480 years) between the Exodus and the building of Solomon's temple. This difference of forty years is easily explained if the reckoning is by generations of a nominal forty years, that is, twelve generations in the Hebrew text and eleven generations in the Greek Septuagint, with one of these texts miscounting by a generation. I suggest the "missing generation" of forty years in the Septuagint text strongly supports the interpretation of 440 and 480 years in terms of generations. (We do not know in detail why the Greek Septuagint text differs here, and elsewhere, from the Hebrew Old Testament text. One possibility is that in the third century B.C. some Hebrew manuscripts had 480 years and others had 440 years, and the Septuagint writers decided to use 440 years. The Hebrew manuscript[s] with 440 years were then lost or destroyed, so we no longer possess them. Whatever the reason, I think it likely that 440 years means eleven generations of a nominal forty years.)

The Genealogy of the High Priests

Wouldn't it be good if we could prove the generation interpretation to be either right or wrong by counting the number of generations from the Exodus to the building of Solomon's temple? I think we would have then solved the problem of whether 480 years was intended to be taken as literal years or as twelve generations of forty years (or as eleven generations of forty years, if the Septuagint is correct). We therefore need to look at lists of genealogies in the Bible.

I quickly found that genealogies in all ancient literature, including the Bible, must be handled with great care, for a variety of reasons. First, it is easily demonstrated that certain genealogies in the Bible omit some generations. For example, in the New Testament, Matthew 1:8 calls Jehoram the father of Uzziah, but it is clear from the Old Testament, in 2 Chronicles 21:4–26:23, that there were several generations between Jehoram and Uzziah. So *father* is used in the sense of "forefather" here. Perhaps it is like my CV (curriculum vitae) at work. I have a full CV and a short CV because I give many invited scientific lectures, and some people ask me to send them my full CV, which is three pages long, and others ask for a short CV, which is half a page long. My short CV is not less accurate; it is simply less detailed, and it concentrates on the most relevant issues. I think some biblical genealogies are like this: there are shortened forms that deliberately leave out the less well known names. Second, some genealogies appear to be schematic, often for reasons that are not very clear to us now. Third, genealogies in all ancient literature are known to be particularly susceptible to copying errors by scribes. Fourth, some genealogies in ancient literature are known to have been deliberately falsified to create desired links with famous ancestors.

So, remembering these strong warnings about genealogies, I decided to try to reconstruct the genealogy of the high priests from the time of the Exodus to the building of Solomon's temple. The high priests were particularly important to the Israelites, and if any genealogy can be reconstructed accurately and in detail from the Old Testament, this one is the most likely.

I'm well aware that many people find genealogies boring. If you are one of these people, then please fast-forward to the end of this section because I'm going to have to take a reasonably detailed look at genealogies in order to see whether 480 years does mean twelve generations of a nominal forty years or not. However, I hope some readers will stay with me because I think a fascinating story emerges.

Who was the high priest at the time of the Exodus? The answer is Aaron, who is called the chief priest in Ezra 7:5. The chief priest in Solomon's temple was Azariah, who succeeded the famous priest

Zadok. 1 Chronicles 6:10 makes a point of saying that Azariah was the priest in the temple Solomon built in Jerusalem. So we need to reconstruct the sequence of priests from Aaron to Azariah.

This genealogy is given in three places in the Old Testament: in Ezra 7:1–5, 1 Chronicles 6:3–13, and 1 Chronicles 6:50–54. Unfortunately, each of these genealogies differs slightly in a manner that suggests copying errors. I've set them out in the genealogy table below. I've also tried to reconstruct the "original" genealogy, which is consistent with the three slightly different genealogies, and I give this in the left-hand column of the table.

The Genealogy of the High Priests

Reconstruction	Ezra 7:1–5	1 Ch. 6:50–53	1 Ch. 6:3–13	
Aaron	Aaron	Aaron	Aaron	
Eleazar	Eleazar	Eleazar	Eleazar	
Phinehas	Phinehas	Phinehas	Phinehas	
Abishua	Abishua	Abishua	Abishua	
Bukki	Bukki	Bukki	Bukki	
Uzzi	Uzzi	Uzzi	Uzzi	
Zerahiah	Zerahiah	Zerahiah	Zerahiah	
Meraioth	Meraioth	Meraioth	Meraioth	
Azariah	Azariah			Azariah
Amariah	Amariah	Amariah	Amariah	Amariah
Ahitub	Ahitub	Ahitub	Ahitub	Ahitub
Zadok	Zadok	Zadok	Zadok	Zadok
Ahimaaz		Ahimaaz	Ahimaaz	
Azariah			Azariah	
			Johanan	
	Shallum			Shallum
	Hilkiah			Hilkiah
	Azariah			Azariah

Let me explain what I've done in order to reconstruct the "original" genealogy. In the genealogy of 1 Chronicles 6:3–13, the sequence Amariah, Ahitub, and Zadok appears twice, in verses 7–8 and again in verses 11–12. This suggests a copying error, and the genealogy is made clearer if set out as shown. The revised form of this genealogy is then fully consistent with Ezra 7:1–5. My reconstruction in the left-hand column is then consistent with all three genealogies.

If we look at this reconstructed genealogy we see that Azariah is thirteenth in line from Aaron; that is, there are thirteen generations from the birth of Aaron to the birth of Azariah. However, for two reasons this is not the number of generations from the Exodus to Solomon's temple. First, Exodus 7:7 states, "Moses was eighty years old and Aaron eighty-three when he spoke to Pharaoh," which was shortly before the Exodus. I think the meaning of this text is that Aaron was three years older than Moses but that both were about two generations old at the time of the Exodus. Thus to get from the date of the Exodus to the birth of Azariah, we subtract two from thirteen generations to arrive at eleven generations.

However, Azariah would not have been the high priest of Solomon's temple as a baby; typically he would have been about one generation old, so we have to add one generation to account for this. Thus from the Exodus to the building of the temple, there were exactly twelve generations. This deduction requires careful counting, and it is easy to see how the writer of this part of the Septuagint could have miscounted and arrived at only eleven generations.

Some biblical scholars have suggested that the number of names in the genealogies listed above from Aaron to Azariah have been carefully selected to fit the 480 years of 1 Kings 6:1. I think this is unlikely in view of the careful counting required, but if it is correct, then it reinforces the idea that 480 years meant twelve generations to the Old Testament writers. So either way, the evidence is strong that the 480 years of 1 Kings 6:1 means twelve generations of a nominal forty years each.

The Meaning of a Generation

As we've seen, a generation is from the birth of a father to the birth of his son, and various ancient civilizations reckoned this to be a nominal forty years. But what is the average length of a true generation? A colleague told me that antique dealers estimated the ages of objects passed

3.2. Massive statue of Ramesses II from the Luxor temple.

down through a family from generation to generation in terms of the average life of a generation, so I went into an antique shop in Cambridge and asked if this was true. "Yes," the man in the shop replied, "and antique dealers take the length of a generation to be thirty years: it's a very good average length." In addition, the *Oxford English Dictionary* defines *generation* as "30 years as a time measure."

So in the last few hundred years, the time length of a generation has been about thirty years. Twelve generations is therefore about 360 years. If a generation was thirty years at the time of the Exodus, then the date of the Exodus, according to 1 Kings 6:1, was therefore about

360 years before the building of Solomon's temple in 966 B.C., so that the Exodus took place in about 1326 B.C. (966 + 360). However, Bright in *A History of Israel* states that in ancient civilizations a generation was about twenty-five years, presumably because people had children when they were younger. If Bright is correct, then twelve generations were about 300 years, and the Exodus took place in about 1266 B.C. This places the Exodus squarely in the reign of Ramesses II.

We can now return to the questions we asked at the start of this chapter. First, which date for the Exodus is correct: 1446 B.C. or somewhat later than 1300 B.C.? I believe we can say with reasonable certainty that 1446 B.C. is wrong and that the evidence strongly supports a date of around 1300 B.C., probably between 1300 and 1250 B.C., when the pharaoh was Ramesses II. We know what this pharaoh looked like from the many statues of himself he had carved from rock (photograph 3.2).

Second, are the Old Testament texts quoted at the start of this chapter self-contradictory? The answer to that question is clearly no when the texts are properly understood. Thus the *Cambridge Ancient History* view that "the statements in the Old Testament are self-contradictory" seems not to be substantiated.

Having solved the problem of the date of the Exodus, we now turn, in the next chapter, to the start of our story, to the birth of one of the greatest men who has ever lived, Moses, and his journey to the mysterious land of Midian. Midian is largely ignored by biblical scholars. As we will see, this is a big mistake: Midian is absolutely central to the events of the Exodus, just as Moses is the central character in these events.

PART TWO

MOSES AND MIDIAN

FOUR

MOSES AND MIDIAN

She [Moses' mother] got a papyrus basket for him ... and put it among the reeds along the bank of the Nile. ... Pharaoh's daughter went down to the Nile to bathe. ... She saw the basket among the reeds and sent her slave girl to get it. She opened it and saw the baby. He was crying and she felt sorry for him. "This is one of the Hebrew babies," she said. ... She named him Moses. ... One day, after Moses had grown up ... he saw an Egyptian beating a Hebrew. ... He killed the Egyptian and hid him in the sand. ... When Pharaoh heard of this, he tried to kill Moses, but Moses fled from Pharaoh and went to live in Midian.

Exodus 2:3, 5, 6, 10, 11, 12, 15

How do you visualize Moses? Many people see him as just another biblical character. So let me tell you how one of the greatest artists in the world saw him. Michelangelo carved Moses as a marble God. This superhuman statue, in the church of San Pietro in Vincoli in Rome, symbolized for Michelangelo the pivotal significance of Moses in world history. Moses was one of those rare leaders who changed the course of history. So who was this remarkable man? And where was the ancient land of Midian, where he spent many years and where I believe Mount Sinai is located? This chapter seeks to answer these basic questions. It is a foundational chapter upon which the rest of this book builds.

Moses was born to parents who were slaves, when the Israelites were in captivity in Egypt. They had been there for several hundred years and had bred so rapidly that the Egyptians feared they would be a formidable fighting force if there were an uprising. So the king of Egypt decided to reduce their numbers, and he ordered the Hebrew midwives to kill every newborn Israelite boy but to let the girls live. The midwives cunningly avoided doing this, so the king of Egypt gave this command to his own people: "Every Hebrew boy that is born you must throw into the Nile, but let every girl live" (Exodus 1:22). Try to picture the scene: Pharaoh is demonstrating his power and killing human babies as if they were unwanted animals. Think of the grief of the Hebrew parents. Since Egyptian kings had immense power, we have every reason to believe this really happened. Amid all this culling and carnage, Moses was born. Amazingly, he survived. Even more remarkably, he was brought up not as a slave child, but as a prince in a palace. How could this be?

The passage from the second chapter of Exodus quoted above describes simply yet vividly how the mother of Moses preserved his life by hiding him for three months after he was born, but when she could hide him no longer, she devised a desperate plan and placed him in a papyrus basket in the reeds along the bank of the river Nile. As Moses' mother must have hoped, no doubt based on previous observations, a daughter of the king of Egypt went down to the Nile to bathe and found the baby in the basket. The baby's crying filled her with compassion, so she didn't kill him, as ordered by her father, but instead adopted him as her own son. So a daughter's special pleading got around her father: the world doesn't change. And that's how Moses came to be brought up in an Egyptian royal palace. Isn't it remarkable that in the male-dominated societies of ancient Egypt and Israel, the Exodus story starts with the brave and loving actions of two women: Moses' mother and Pharaoh's daughter? Isn't it even more remarkable that one of these women was a foreigner?

Moses would have known from an early age that he was someone special. He would have been very well educated in the Egyptian knowledge of the time concerning geography, history, astronomy, desert plants and animals, and so forth. He would also have been able to read and write Egyptian hieroglyphs. What an amazing story! The abandoned slave baby Moses, plucked from the Nile, became one of the best-educated people in the ancient world.

The above story reminds me of an event from my childhood that is etched in my memory. My father was visited at work by a German businessman he had never met before who said that he would like to see some British castles and palaces. So my father drove my mother, the German, and me to the nearest impressive palace he could find on the map: Blenheim Palace, near Oxford. My father had never been there before. We entered this hugely imposing palace to find inside a special exhibit commemorating Winston Churchill and the victory of England and America over Germany in the Second World War. The great British leader, Winston Churchill, had been born and brought up in Blenheim Palace, and the exhibit was full of photographs of destroyed German aircraft and victorious British soldiers. Our German visitor asked to be excused and went to the lavatory.

When he had gone my father said to my mother, "This is terrible. I had forgotten that Churchill was born here. What shall we do? Shall we apologize to the German and leave?" They decided, in typical British fashion, that it was best to say nothing. So for at least an hour (it seemed much longer!) we continued walking around Blenheim Palace, but a tense silence descended: my parents said nothing because they did not know what to say, the German also said nothing because presumably he wondered why, out of all the castles and palaces in Britain, he had been brought to this one. As we left the palace, our German visitor turned to us and graciously said, "This is a wonderful palace. I now understand why Churchill was such a great leader. To be brought up in a place like this must make you feel really special." So it must have been with Moses.

The book of Exodus recounts that when Moses became an adult, he went out to where the Israelite slaves were laboring and saw an Egyptian beating an Israelite, one of his own people. Moses killed the Egyptian and hid his body in the sand. Moses must have been strong, fearless, and capable of intense righteous anger. But unfortunately for Moses, his impulsive act had been seen. In the eyes of Pharaoh Moses was now a murderer, and the furious Pharaoh wanted him captured and killed, so "Moses fled from Pharaoh and went to live in Midian" (Exodus 2:15). Thus Moses, who had been living a life of luxury in Pharaoh's palace, and who was destined for a very comfortable future, suddenly became a hunted man who feared for his life and who fled Egypt to the safety of the land of Midian. This event, from riches to rags, was a critical turning point in Moses' life. But where was the land of Midian to which he fled?

I believe there is an interesting parallel between Moses' journey to Midian and the later Exodus of Moses and the Israelites from

Egypt. The third chapter of the book of Exodus describes how Moses fled Egypt, went to Midian, and then went to Mount Sinai. Ten chapters later, the book of Exodus describes how Moses led the Israelites out of Egypt (the famous Exodus event) and brought them to Mount Sinai. The rather obvious question is this: Could Moses have taken the same route on both occasions? Curiously, most books on the Exodus of the Israelites from Egypt totally ignore this earlier journey of Moses to Midian. I believe this is a big mistake. As we will see, this earlier journey is a precursor of the Exodus journey. That's why we are now going to spend some time extracting information about Midian from the Bible and other sources. This detective work is a necessary preparation if we are to solve one of the greatest unsolved problems in history: what really happened at the Exodus from Egypt.

The Land of Midian

So where was Midian, and what sort of land was it? Few people know where it was, very few people know about its geography and history, and extremely few people have visited it in recent centuries. Although some biblical commentaries mention Midian, they do so only in passing, and no real details about the land are given. In a sense it is a "lost land." In order to make progress with solving the problems of the Exodus, we are going to have to discover what we can about the lost land of Midian. I never expected, when embarking on this project to reconstruct what happened at the Exodus, to be faced with the challenge of discovering a lost land!

For many reasons, information about the land of Midian is difficult to obtain. In recent years it has been hard to obtain a visa to travel to northwest Saudi Arabia, where the ancient land of Midian is located. In earlier years the local tribesmen often vigorously defended their territory against visitors, so it was dangerous to travel. Thus the number of archaeological excavations in northwest Saudi Arabia have been limited. Also, biblical scholars and ancient historians in general have not appreciated the importance of the land of Midian.

To learn about the land of Midian, I therefore needed to consult not only the rather few recent articles about its archaeology, but also the books written by intrepid explorers of the last two centuries who risked their lives to visit this amazing place. Many of these books are rare and difficult to find, and I have accumulated them slowly from secondhand bookshops throughout the world.

How did the land of Midian get its name? The Old Testament book of Genesis tells us that a person called Midian was one of the sons of Abraham (Genesis 25:2). The descendants of Midian were, not surprisingly, called the Midianites, and they lived in the land of Midian, which was east of the Gulf of Aqaba and east of the northern part of the Red Sea. The location of the land of Midian is shown on the map (4.1, pg. 46). The land of Midian was in the northwest of ancient Arabia (modern Saudi Arabia) and it also contained the southern part of modern Jordan. Its borders started roughly at Aqaba at the northern head of the Gulf of Aqaba, then ran down the eastern side of the Gulf of Aqaba, down the eastern side of the Red Sea, to the bottom of the map, then east along the bottom of the map, north up the eastern side of the map to a point roughly opposite Aqaba, then west across to Aqaba, as shown in map 4.1. Midian was a sizable territory, spanning over two hundred miles from east to west and also over two hundred miles from north to south. The Midianites lived in towns and settlements in the land of Midian. The land of Edom was to the north of Midian, the boundary running roughly east-west through the head of the Gulf of Aqaba.

Many biblical scholars claim that Midian also encompassed all or part of the Sinai Peninsula. As we will see later, the Bible hints strongly that Mount Sinai is in Midian. Most biblical scholars are tied to the idea that Mount Sinai is in the Sinai Peninsula; thus it is convenient for them to claim that the Midianites occupied both northwest Arabia and all or part of the Sinai Peninsula. What are the facts?

Many ancient tribes, including the Midianites, were seminomadic: they lived in towns and settlements, but they also traveled large distances in search of pasture for their flocks and for trading purposes. We know that the Midianites were seminomadic from references to them in the Old Testament and other ancient literature. For example, the book of Genesis records that Joseph was sold by his brothers to passing Midianite traders who took him to Egypt (Genesis 37:28), presumably along with their trade of frankincense and gold from Arabia. However,

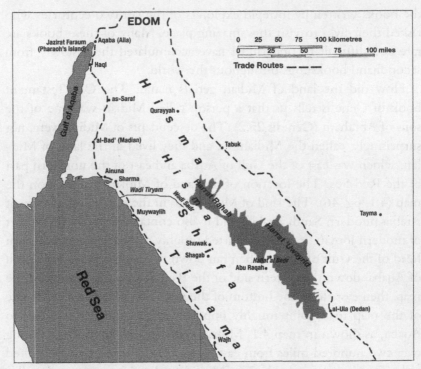

4.1. The land of Midian showing two major ancient trade routes that ran through it. The Sinai Peninsula is to the west of Midian, with Edom to the north.

where was the home base of the Midianites at the time of the Exodus, and can we know after three thousand years have elapsed?

Questions like these are notoriously difficult to answer, and I found the writings of biblical scholars about Midian to be of little help. So I turned to a colleague of mine at Cambridge, the well-known Egyptologist John Ray, for advice. "John," I said, "I'm really struggling to find out anything about the land of Midian. Who do you suggest I ask?" John replied, "William Facey, the director of the London Centre of Arab Studies, is your man. He has a very wide knowledge of ancient Arabia." So I contacted William Facey, who has been extremely helpful in advising me and photocopying for me various articles about the archaeology and plant and bird life of Arabia.

Archaeological work by Peter Parr and others published in various journals (see the bibliography, pg. 343), William Facey's book *Riyadh: The Old City,* and Winnett and Reed's *Ancient Records from North*

Arabia all enable a clear and fascinating picture to be built up about life in ancient Midian. First, they reveal that the Midianites did indeed live in northwest Arabia, as defined in the map 4.1 on page 46.

On the other hand, no Midianite settlement in the Sinai Peninsula has been found by archaeologists, so we can conclude that Midianites did *not* live in the Sinai Peninsula.

When did the Midianites live in settlements in northwest Arabia? This is a key question, because if the Midianites were not settled in Midian at the time of the Exodus, this clearly throws doubt on the Exodus story of Moses living with the family of Jethro in the land of Midian. Two Midianite towns, Qurayyah and Tayma, have been excavated by archaeologists, and what has been found is fascinating. Both of these sites contain distinctive painted pottery, called Midianite pottery, which appears to have been made on a slowly turning wheel, rather like a modern potter's wheel. The clay body is very light in color, unlike most ancient pottery from elsewhere, where iron-rich clays resulted in darker colors. The most distinctive feature of this Midianite pottery is the painted decoration: shades of yellow, brown, red, and black appear on a creamy white painted background. A variety of geometrical shapes and animals were painted on the pottery: bulls, birds, and camels; sticklike humans; spirals and other curves. Open bowls, dishes, and large and small jugs were made by these skillful Midianite potters.

But where and when was this Midianite pottery made? Kilns for firing Midianite pottery have been found at Qurayyah by archaeologists, thus confirming that this pottery was indeed made in Midian. But how can we date it? The archaeologists Rothenberg and Glass describe in *Midian, Moab, and Edom* their spectacular discovery of Midianite pottery mixed in with Egyptian objects from the Nineteenth Dynasty at the Egyptian copper mines at Timna in the Arabah (see map 3.1, pg. 30), thus enabling Midianite pottery to be dated to the thirteenth to twelfth centuries B.C., or precisely the time of the Exodus, as we've seen in the previous chapter. So the really important conclusion we can make is that there were major occupied settlements in Midian at the time of Moses and the Exodus.

How did Midianite pottery find its way to Timna in the Arabah? As Parr and others point out, there would have been routes connecting major settlements such as Qurayyah and Timna, and Midianites may well have been involved in the metallurgical mining activities at Timna. Archaeology reveals that Qurayyah was an extensively fortified town with an elaborate system of irrigation for farming, many stone structures, and masonry tombs. Parr dates all of these to the main period of occupation of Qurayyah: to the thirteenth to twelfth centuries B.C. Midianite pottery has been found at a number of other sites in Midian, so we have clear archaeological evidence that there were occupied towns and settlements in Midian in the thirteenth to twelfth centuries B.C.

Why did Moses flee to Midian rather than somewhere else? The educated Moses would have known about the trade route from Egypt to Midian, and he may well have met Midianite traders bringing gold and incense to Egypt. Hence Moses could expect a friendly reception in Midian. Moses would also have known that the area of land we now call the Sinai Peninsula was effectively under Egyptian control, although it was not formally part of Egypt. We know this, too, because the Egyptians owned copper and turquoise mines at various sites in the peninsula (for example at Serabit el-Khadim; see map 1.3, pg. 10).

The ancient Egyptians also left many inscriptions in the Sinai Peninsula, and the famous Nineteenth Dynasty pharaoh Ramesses II (approx. 1290–1224 B.C.) erected a temple to Hathor at the copper mines there. Egyptian control of the Sinai Peninsula ceased after the reign of Ramesses III (approx. 1194–1163 B.C.). However, since the most probable date for the Exodus was in the reign of Ramesses II (see the previous chapter), we can be sure that at the time of Moses the Sinai Peninsula was under Egyptian control, being essentially part of greater Egypt.

The Egypt-Arabia Trade Route

The great British explorer Richard Burton, in his famous two-volume book *The Land of Midian,* first published in 1879, calls the trade route from Egypt to Arabia "one of the oldest in the world." As Rothenberg, Parr, and others point out, this trade route would have existed at the time of Ramesses II in order to transport copper from the mines at Timna to Egypt, and spices and gold from Arabia to Egypt. The original trade route linking Egypt to Arabia went from the head of the Gulf of Suez to the head of the Gulf of Aqaba. When the capital of Egypt shifted to Rameses (modern Qantir), we can expect that a branch of this trade route went up to Rameses (see map 3.1, pg. 30).

After my first visit to Mount Sinai (the traditional one in the Sinai Peninsula) in 1995, I traveled to the Nile River in Egypt in 1996 and visited the Sinai Peninsula and the Red Sea in 1999 and 2001. Our annual one-week vacations have been spent at Easter time in the Middle East, researching and studying the territory. I know firsthand just how barren the Sinai Peninsula is and how easy it is to get lost there. Some biblical scholars have suggested that three thousand years ago, in the time of Moses, the rainfall was higher in the Sinai Peninsula than it is now, but I know of no evidence to support this. Alfred Lucas, a chemist who lived in Egypt for forty years from about 1900 to 1940, states in his book *The Route of the Exodus of the Israelites from Egypt,* "The rainfall and wells in the Sinai Peninsula are now probably much as they were at the time of the Exodus, and since the routes across the desert are conditioned by the water supply, desert traveling only being possible when there is drinking water at fairly short intervals, the present routes until recently were probably much the same as they had been for several thousands of years." The Middle Eastern expert Kenneth Kitchen, referred to above, also states in his article "Wilderness of Wandering" in the *New Bible Dictionary* that in the Sinai Peninsula "there has apparently been no fundamental climatic change since antiquity."

Thus we can reasonably assume that at the time of Moses the Sinai Peninsula was as dry as it is now. When traveling in desert regions such as this, three things are absolutely necessary: water, water, and water! It is possible to survive for more than fifty days without eating, but you can live only a few days without water. When I was at a scientific conference in Jerusalem a few years ago, a group of us hired a taxi to drive through the desert to the Dead Sea. We passed a Bedouin on the way, and he ran out into the road in front of us looking totally exhausted. The Israeli taxi driver stopped, opened the trunk of his car, and filled up the Bedouin's water bag from a huge plastic container he carried in the trunk. The Bedouin held the water bag at some distance from his mouth and drank copiously, the water traveling in a rainbow-curved arc from bag to mouth. Then the driver refilled the water bag, and the Bedouin's camel drank. A third time the driver filled the Bedouin's water bag, and then he gratefully left, revived by the precious gift of water. Moses would have known all about the importance of water in the desert.

The track of the ancient trade route between Egypt and Arabia would have been chosen to minimize the journey time between those two countries while maximizing the supply of drinking water. The great Czech explorer Dr. Alois Musil, professor of Oriental Studies at Charles University in Prague, undertook an expedition to Midian in 1910. In his book, *The Northern Hegaz,* he describes how along this trade route in the spring there are rain pools in various riverbeds, although these usually dry up at other times of the year. Major Claude Jarvis, the former British governor of Sinai, in *Yesterday and Today in Sinai,* states that at Nakhl, about halfway along this trade route (see map 3.1, pg. 30), "Water is plentiful but unpleasant, though not harmful to health." Thus this ancient trade route did have supplies of water at intervals. (Incidentally, Hegaz is usually written as Hijaz on modern maps.)

Trade routes were vital to travelers because of the water supplies along them. To stray off a trade route in the desert heat was to dice with death. Hence I believe that when Moses traveled from Egypt to Midian, in northwest Arabia, we can be virtually certain that he used the ancient trade route between Egypt and Arabia shown in map 3.1; there was no realistic alternative. How did people travel in the thirteenth to twelfth centuries B.C., the time of Moses? It was before camels were used for travel, and it is well documented that donkeys were the main means of transport: they carried water, food, and people. Although camels were painted on some of the Midianite pottery found at Qurayyah from the thirteenth to twelfth centuries B.C., it is believed that camels were only slowly being domesticated, used for milk in this time period and only later used for travel.

Moses would have taken with him as much water and food as he could carry. He may even have attached himself to a trade caravan going from Egypt to Arabia or taken with him a donkey or one or more servants; we do not know. What we do know is that this ancient trade route linking Egypt and Arabia was an ideal escape route for Moses.

Where Did Moses Go to Live in Midian?

The book of Exodus does not reveal the name of the place where Moses lived in Midian, but it provides some useful clues. Can we use these clues, together with our knowledge of the local geography and ancient trade routes, to discover where Moses probably lived in Midian? It's a fascinating detective story. Moses lived with the family of a priest of Midian called Reuel (Exodus 2:18). Apparently the same priest is called Jethro in Exodus 3:1, and it has been suggested that Reuel may be the clan name to which Jethro belonged. In addition, it is known from pre-Islamic inscriptions from Arabia that the inhabitants sometimes had two names, as indeed we often do today, so there is no problem in taking Reuel/Jethro to be the same person: and for simplicity we will refer to Reuel/Jethro by his more commonly used name, Jethro. He appears to have been an important person (Exodus 3:1 calls him "the priest of Midian"); therefore, it is likely that he lived in an important place in Midian, for example, the capital city. According to Exodus 2, Jethro was both a priest and a shepherd. Moses drew water from a well near where Jethro lived (Exodus 2:15), and there were also other shepherds living there (Exodus 2:17). So we can deduce that the place where Moses lived with the family of Jethro in the land of Midian was probably a major settlement with water and pasture for sheep.

So we've seen that Moses probably traveled from Egypt to the northern head of the Gulf of Aqaba using the ancient trade route linking the two. When he arrived at the head of the Gulf of Aqaba he had two main options if he stayed on a trade route: he could either go north up the trade route leading to Gaza or Damascus or south down the trade route leading to southern Arabia (see map 4.2, pg. 52).

Since the book of Exodus states that he went to the land of Midian, which was in Arabia, then he must have gone south. It is worth repeating that for a traveler to leave a trade route in an inhospitable country was to risk death. We have therefore deduced from the book of Exodus, combined with our knowledge of geography, that Moses probably traveled from Egypt to the head of the Gulf of Aqaba using the ancient trade route between them. He then probably continued south along the trade route that led to southern Arabia until he met

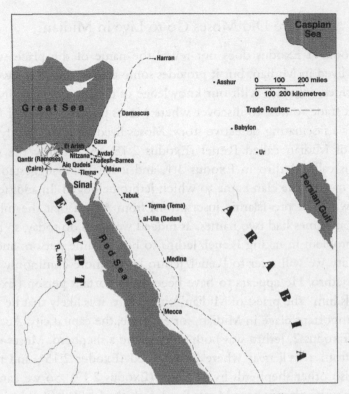

4.2. *Some major trade routes in the ancient Middle East.*

Jethro and his family at a major settlement on or near this trade route.

What would have been the first major settlement Moses would have come to on this trade route? Musil, in *The Northern Hegaz,* lists the places along this route. After Musil leaves the head of the Gulf of Aqaba, the first place he mentions is Hakl (usually spelled Haql; see map 4.1, pg. 46), but he says the water there is not fit for human consumption, so Moses wouldn't have stopped there. The next place is as-Saraf, but the archaeologist David Hogarth, in *Hejaz before World War I,* says that there is no water there. The next place is a major oasis called Madian, modern al-Bad', where Musil says there is plenty of excellent water. (The symbol ' in *Bad*' sounds in Arabic like someone saying "a" and being strangled at the same time!) So ancient Madian would have been the first place Moses would have found along this trade route with good drinking water.

Some ancient writings as well as some strong traditions indicate the actual place where Jethro lived in the land of Midian. Ancient traditions may or may not correspond to historical fact, but they sometimes do and thus they are always worth exploring. As we will see, the ancient traditions regarding the place where Moses and Jethro lived come from a range of sources, but, unusually, they all point to the same location, which, interestingly, is on the ancient trade route from the head of the Gulf of Aqaba to south Arabia. This is just as we've deduced from the Old Testament and from geography. The ancient writings are summarized below.

The first-century A.D. Jewish historian Flavius Josephus wrote in his *Antiquities* that Moses fled Egypt and went to the city of Madiana, opposite the Red Sea. The second-century A.D. Egyptian astronomer and geographer Ptolemy, in one of the earliest geography books to have survived (fittingly called *Geography*), records a settlement, Madiama, on the northwestern border of Arabia. The letters *m* and *n* are frequently misheard by foreigners because they often sound similar when spoken, and all the famous explorers of Arabia I will refer to in this book (Burton, Doughty, Musil, Philby, and Wallin) identify Madiama with Madiana. The third- to fourth-century A.D. Christian writer Eusebius locates a town called Madiam to the east of the Red Sea. According to the Koran (11:85, 22:43, 29:35f., 50:13), the preacher Shu'ayb came to the inhabitants of Madjan. Shu'ayb appears to be identical with the biblical Jethro, for reasons given below, and Madjan is the same place as Madian in Arabic since *i* and *j* are sometimes interchangeable in transliteration. Thus a wide variety of ancient writings all locate Jethro and Moses in the town or city of Madian (or equivalently Madjan, Madiam, Madiama, or Madiana). Interestingly, as we've just seen, ancient Madian would have been the first place in Midian that Moses would have found with good drinking water, so it makes sense that he would have stopped here.

It is worth noting again how a place-name in Arabic can have a variety of similar-sounding names when transliterated into English. Lawrence of Arabia, in his famous book *The Seven Pillars of Wisdom*, recounts how his publisher despaired because he refused to use consistent spellings for place-names throughout the book. Hence great care is needed when studying ancient place-names.

The Czech explorer Alois Musil, in his book *The Northern Hegaz,* refers to many ancient Arabian writings and traditions about Moses and Madian. Some traditions state that Moses traveled from Egypt to Madian and that this was a distance of nine nights' encampments. Another tradition states that the ancient town of Madian had cultivated gardens and date palms irrigated by many wells and streams. A further Arabian tradition says that there used to be exhibited at Madian a stone that Moses lifted (presumably from a well) when he wished to water the flocks of sheep and goats belonging to Shu'ayb (Jethro).

The explorers Musil, Burton, and Wallin all report that near modern al-Bad' (also spelled al-Bed'), on the ancient trade route from Egypt to southern Arabia, and seventy-five miles south of Aila (modern Aqaba) at the northern head of the Gulf of Aqaba, is a place called Mughayir Shu'ayb, which means the "Caves of Shu'ayb" (Jethro), and nearby there are indeed many natural rock caves. The traditional "Well of Moses" is also located near there. Musil, Burton, and Wallin all agree that this site is ancient Madian and that it contained several ancient settlements (see map 4.3. pg. 55).

The British explorer H. St. John Philby describes in detail his visit to ancient Madian in his book *The Land of Midian,* published in 1957. He believes that Madian was the ancient capital of the land of Midian, and this has been confirmed by articles in the *Journal of Saudi Arabian Archaeology.* In addition to the many natural caves, there are also rock tombs, similar in style but less grand than the magnificent rock tombs carved out by the Nabateans at Petra. Thus Philby believes the Nabateans carved out the rock tombs in Madian (Mughayir Shu'ayb) about two thousand years ago. The caves of Jethro are in the same location as these Nabatean tombs. Philby believes that the Well of Moses near Mughayir Shu'ayb is of Turkish construction but that the Turks may have redug and rebuilt an earlier well. An article by the archaeologist M. L. Ingraham, published in 1981 in *Atlal: The Journal of Saudi Arabian Archaeology,* reports finding substantial quantities of Midianite pottery at al-Bad', so this site was occupied in the thirteenth to twelfth centuries B.C. In summary, I think the evidence is rather strong that Moses and Jethro lived in ancient Madian, modern al-Bad'.

If we accept that Moses probably lived in ancient Madian, we can then suggest the most probable route taken by Moses when he fled

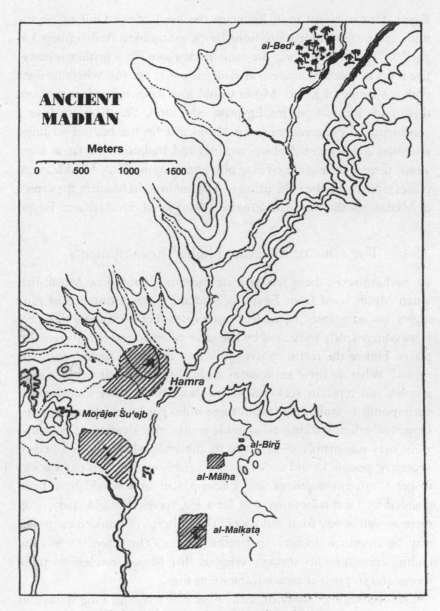

4.3. *Map of the site of ancient Madian, from Musil's*
The Northern Hegaz, *p. 110.*

Egypt. First eastward from Egypt to the head of the Gulf of Aqaba, using the ancient trade route from Egypt to southern Arabia (map 3.1, pg. 30). Then south along the same trade route for a further seventy-five miles to Madian, modern al-Bad' (map 4.1, pg. 46), where he lived with the family of Jethro. Moses would have known in advance about these trade routes from his Egyptian education. We therefore have a consistent and coherent route for Moses that fits the biblical writings, Josephus, and ancient Arabian writings and traditions. As far as I am aware, there is no ancient writing or tradition against this. In addition, it makes sense that Jethro, the priest of Midian, lived in Madian, the capital of Midian, on the major trade route linking southern Arabia to Egypt.

The Clue of the Nine Nights' Encampments

As we have seen, there are Arabian traditions, quoted by Musil, that when Moses went from Egypt to Madian, it was a distance of nine nights' encampments. In ancient times maps didn't exist and distances were conveniently measured by the time taken to travel between two places. Hence the terms "a day's journey" or "three nights' encampments." What do these expressions mean? In the ancient world, a day's journey was typically reckoned to be about twenty-five miles, which corresponds to walking at about three miles per hour for eight hours. However, when walking along trade routes, the location of encampment sites was mainly determined by the availability of water, and, if necessary, people would walk for considerably longer than eight hours to get to an encampment site. Encampment sites would have been guarded by local tribesmen, and for a fee, travelers could safely sleep there as well as buy food and water. The concept of modern campsites may be based on ancient encampment sites! The reference to nine nights' encampments strongly suggests that Moses traveled on trade routes and stopped at nine encampment sites.

Concerning the ability of ancient peoples to go on long walks and marches, I would like to make a short digression to comment on the health and fitness of ancient populations because there seems to be a widespread belief that three thousand years ago people were riddled with disease and were unfit and unhealthy. I believe this to be untrue. Let me start with some quite remarkable figures. Recently in the U.K.

old graves have been dug up and the height of skeletons has been measured. In A.D. 1000 the average height of a man was 5 feet 9 inches; by A.D. 1800 it had dropped to 5 feet 3 inches, and today it is 5 feet 9.5 inches, only slightly greater than in A.D. 1000. The explanation of this is that in A.D. 1000 nearly everyone lived in rural villages, and although they were poor and had little medical care, they had fresh milk, meat, and vegetables to eat, and so they were healthy and grew to a good height. By A.D. 1800 many people had moved away from rural farming and into cities because of the Industrial Revolution. Food was now less fresh and there was no refrigeration. So even though people were better off financially, their diet was poor and the average male height dropped. Today, with a much more healthful diet, the average male height in the U.K. has risen again, but only slightly more than it was in A.D. 1000.

Some people think of the Israelite slaves in Egypt as being like emaciated prisoners-of-war, poorly fed by their captors. I believe this is almost certainly wrong. The ancient Israelites in Egypt kept their own cattle, sheep, and crops (see Exodus 9:4), so even though they were slaves they would have been well fed with their own fresh meat and vegetables. After the Exodus from Egypt, when the Israelites were in the desert and short of food, they complained to Moses and said, "If only we had died by the Lord's hand in Egypt. There we sat round pots of meat and ate all the food we wanted" (Exodus 16:3). We can therefore expect the ancient Israelites in Egypt to have been well fed and healthy. The slaves were engaged in manual labor, and we can expect them to have had considerable physical strength and stamina, just as modern laborers on construction sites are very fit, or indeed just as modern Bedouin are very fit.

Concerning length of life, a surprisingly durable modern myth is that today we can expect to live into our seventies or eighties whereas our ancestors mostly died in early middle age. Although the first part of this sentence is true, I believe the last part is false, as a visit around an old graveyard will show. A major difference between the modern and ancient world is that in the ancient world many children died at birth or in the first month of life. Even one hundred years ago in the U.S., 15 percent of babies died before their first birthday. Think of how this dramatically lowers the average life expectancy. Infant mortality has greatly improved with modern hygiene and medical care. I think this explains why when Moses, after leaving Egypt, counted the numbers of priests of the tribe of Levi, he counted only those over one month old (Numbers 3:15). So many people died in the first month of life that to have included those less than a month old would have made the figures meaningless. (I am reminded of a poster in a maternity hospital depicting a beautiful baby above which a caption read, "The first month of life is the most dangerous." Underneath someone had written, "The last month is pretty dodgy as well.")

If you survived childbirth and the early years of life in the ancient world, then I believe you could expect to live to be seventy or eighty, unless you were killed in a war or mishap. (Psalm 90:10 says, "The length of our days is seventy years—or eighty if we have the strength.") In other words, if you did not die as a child, then your life expectancy was only slightly less than it is today. For example, the Greek playwright Sophocles, who was born in about 496 B.C., was eighty-five when he died. We know from Egyptian records that Ramesses II, probably the pharaoh at the time of the Exodus, lived to be ninety-six years old, even though he had two hundred wives and concubines (or perhaps because he had them)!

Hence, the Israelites in Egypt would have been well fed, healthy, and physically strong, with lots of stamina. In fact, they would have been far fitter than most of us are today. An Israelite three thousand years ago no doubt could have walked at three miles an hour, carrying water and food, for many hours at a stretch with no problem at all, just as a modern Bedouin can.

Let's now return from our digression to talk about encampment sites. Musil, in *The Northern Hegaz,* gives evidence that the ancient trade routes from Egypt to Arabia and from Syria to Arabia later became pilgrim routes to the Arabian cities of Mecca and Medina. It is extremely likely that the campsites on the ancient trade routes became the campsites on the pilgrim routes because in both cases these sites would have been determined by the availability of water. Although some of the pilgrims traveled on camels (once camels were domesticated), the front camel in a camel train was guided by a man on foot, and pilgrim camel trains thus traveled at walking speed.

As we've seen, Arabian texts state that when Moses traveled from Egypt to Midian it was a journey of nine nights' encampments. Is this consistent with Moses going from Egypt to Madian in Midian along trade routes? Richard Burton, in *The Land of Midian,* says that a famous Arab geographer called al-Ya'qubi wrote a book called the *Book of Countries* in A.D. 1210 that al-Ya'qubi states was based on earlier Arab traditions. In this book al-Ya'qubi says that there are six desert marches from the Gulf of Suez to Aila at the head of the Gulf of Aqaba. This makes sense because the distance along the trade route from the Gulf of Suez to the Gulf of Aqaba is one hundred fifty-five miles, so to cover this in six marches means walking on average just over twenty-five miles per day. So there were six nights' encampments in going from Egypt to the head of the Gulf of Aqaba along the trade route.

What about the journey down from the head of the Gulf of Aqaba to Madian? How many nights' encampments was this? Burton doesn't tell us, but Musil, in *The Northern Hegaz,* does. It was a journey of three nights' encampment along the trade route. The distance involved is seventy-five miles, so three nights' encampment corresponds to walking at twenty-five miles per day, which is consistent with what we know about daily marches on this trade route.

So if Moses did indeed go to Madian, then the total distance he traveled from Egypt was six plus three, or nine nights' encampments. This is precisely the distance given by the Arabic sources referred to above. It is reasonable to conclude, therefore, that when Moses left Egypt he traveled by the direct trade route linking Egypt with the head of the Gulf of Aqaba, a distance of six nights' encampments, and that he then traveled a further distance of three nights' encampments along the trade route to Madian. If Moses had traveled by any other route from Egypt to Madian, the journey would have been longer than the one suggested here and inconsistent with the figure of nine nights' encampments in Arabic sources. In addition, if Moses had stayed at a place different from ancient Madian, then the figures again would not add up correctly.

This analysis give us some confidence that our proposed route for Moses is probably correct: it is consistent with the biblical text, consistent with the known trade routes, and consistent with a variety of ancient Jewish, Arabic, and Christian traditions. In particular, all the information we have supports the old tradition that Moses stayed with Jethro at Madian, modern al-Bad'. It is also reassuring to know that archaeology reveals that al-Bad' was a Midianite settlement in the thirteenth to twelfth centuries B.C., precisely at the time Moses stayed there, according to the arguments in this book.

In the next chapter we will consider the fascinating problem of what kept the burning bush burning. Our investigations will lead us to study stories of fire from the ground from around the world. As we will see, this chapter also provides a key clue to solving the mystery of the location of Mount Sinai, and reveals an error in translation that biblical scholars have made that may place Mount Sinai in the wrong country.

FIVE

THE BURNING BUSH

Now Moses was tending the flock of Jethro his father-in-law, the priest
of Midian, and he led the flock to the far side of the desert and came to
Horeb, the mountain of God. There the angel of the Lord appeared to
him in flames of fire from within a bush. Moses saw that although the
bush was on fire it did not burn up. So Moses thought, "I will go over
and see this strange sight—why the bush does not burn up."

Exodus 3:1–3

Zsa Zsa Gabor once famously said, "Husbands are like fires:
they go out if unattended." So what kept the burning bush
burning? This three-thousand-year-old mystery will be considered later in this chapter; first we place the event in its context.

Moses was about to have his routine life shattered. After the luxury
of his royal upbringing in Egypt and the excitement of his escape to
Midian, he had settled down as a shepherd in Midian, where he married Zipporah, a daughter of Jethro, and had two sons called Gershom
and Eliezer. He had become a family man with a steady job. What
happened next would change his life and change the course of history.
His encounter with the burning bush is described above in the quotation from the book of Exodus.

So much information is packed into these few verses. For the first
time in the Bible, Horeb, the mountain of God, is mentioned. As we
will see later, elsewhere in the Old Testament the same mountain of
God is called Sinai, and Horeb and Sinai seem to be used interchangeably to refer to the same mountain. It is not unusual for two different
names to be used for the same mountain. For example, the famous
Greek volcano Santorini is also known as Thera. Later, in chapter 19,

I will say more about the fascinating meanings of the names Horeb and Sinai.

However, let us return to the story of the burning bush. Three key questions spring from the verses above: Why did Moses go to the far side of the desert; where was the burning bush; and what kept the burning bush burning? The answers to these questions are fundamentally important to understanding the Exodus story, and I believe the traditional answers given are largely wrong. In this chapter we will see how modern science provides some key new insights. A rare illustration of what one artist thought the burning bush looked like is given in figure 5.1 on the next page, photographed from the 1469 Cologne Bible. Notice that the artist thought that Moses had a dog!

The Far Side of the Desert

Why did Moses go to the far side of the desert? The first point to note is that he did not go alone, as he might have done if visiting a friend, but "he led the flock to the far side of the desert." It appears that he went for the benefit of the sheep! This puzzled me for some time until I went for five days' vacation in Syria in the spring of 2000. As our small tour group approached the amazing ruins of Palmyra in Syria, we passed Bedouin leading their flocks from Palmyra to Tartus, on the Mediterranean coast of Syria, a distance of about 125 miles. Our knowledgeable local tour guide said that the Bedouin had been traveling this route with their flocks for thousands of years in order to find better pasture. Each spring the Bedouin take their sheep from Palmyra to Tartus, and each autumn they bring them back to the desert steppe country around Palmyra, where the sheep can survive from November to April because of winter rain. Our guide said that the Bedouin with their flocks of sheep walked typically twenty-five miles per day. Interestingly, this figure for "a day's journey" for modern Bedouin is consistent with the figure given in the previous chapter for pilgrims and the Israelites several thousand years ago.

There are many records in ancient texts of Bedouin migrating with their flocks to find better pasture, either annually or in years of drought. For example, Bedouin from Jordan used to bring their flocks

*5.1. Moses at the burning bush. Reproduced from a woodcut illustration in the
Cologne Bible, first printed in Cologne in 1469, and probably the first
Bible printed in a monastery.*

each year to Bosra in southern Syria because the volcanic soil there
was very fertile and supported many sheep. In addition, William Facey
tells me that all around the fringes of the Fertile Crescent, Bedouin
have been migrating with their flocks each year for thousands of years
to find better pasture. We can deduce from this traditional behavior of
Bedouin shepherds that when the book of Exodus states that Moses
led the flock of Jethro to the far side of the desert, he did this to find
better pasture for the sheep.

As we have seen, when Moses fled Egypt he went to Midian and
stayed with the family of Jethro, probably in the coastal region of Midian to the east of the Gulf of Aqaba, at ancient Madian (modern al-
Bad'). Do we have any specific evidence that the Arabs in Midian
migrated with their flocks to find better pasture? The answer is yes.
The British explorer Philby states in his beautifully written book *The
Land of Midian:* "The local Arabs send their flocks down to the Tihama valleys in the winter to avoid the intense cold of the Hisma up-
lands which, though not very extraordinary as thermometers measure

it, has a peculiar quality of penetration which has to be experienced to be credited. The minimum temperature of this night [the night Philby spent there] was 36°F [2°C—just above freezing point]."

Where are the Tihama valleys referred to by Philby? They are the hot, relatively low-lying coastal regions in Midian, east of the Gulf of Aqaba and east of the Red Sea (see map 4.1).

This is clear, for example, from the explorer Charles Doughty's map in his book *Arabia Deserta* (note that Doughty spells Tihama as Tehama: the vowel change in the English is unimportant, as we have already seen). From Doughty's map, ancient Madian is clearly in the Tihama along with the rest of the coastal region. The *Cambridge Atlas of the Middle East* gives the mean July temperature in the coastal region of Arabia as greater than 86°F (30°C). On some days the temperature exceeds 104°F (40°C). It is definitely not the place to be in summer when you can escape to the cooler hills to the east. The Hisma, in the above quotation from Philby, is the high desert region to the east of the coastal plains (see map 4.1, pg. 46). It is a barren desert except in oases, where it is relatively fertile. Thus, according to Philby, the Arabs used to lead their flocks eastward from the coastal region to the high plain of the Hisma in the spring to avoid the intense summer heat of the coastal plains, and lead them back in the autumn to avoid the winter cold in the Hisma. We can reasonably expect this annual migration to have been happening for thousands of years, and I suggest that Moses was following this traditional practice. So when we read that Moses led the flock to the far side of the desert, we can reasonably conclude that he went to higher land east of the coastal region.

But surely something must be wrong! We have just deduced that when Moses "led the flock to the far side of the desert and came to Horeb, the mountain of God" (Exodus 3:1), he traveled *east* from the coastal plain of Midian; that is, he traveled east from the Gulf of Aqaba. Yet all the atlases in the world place Mount Horeb, which is Mount Sinai, in the Sinai Peninsula, which is *west* of the Gulf of Aqaba. This is not just a small difference in location: the atlases are placing Mount Sinai in a different country! We have just deduced that Mount Sinai is in Arabia, whereas all the maps in the world place it in the Sinai Peninsula.

What do biblical commentaries say? The scholarly standard commentary on the book of Exodus, *Exodus,* by James Philip Hyatt, commenting on Exodus 3:1, interprets "the far side of the desert" as "the west side of the wilderness." Many other major commentaries agree. Not only this, but at least one major translation of the Bible, the Revised Standard Version, translates Exodus 3:1 as: "he led his flock to the west side of the wilderness." So world-class biblical scholars have Moses leading his sheep west from Midian to Mount Sinai in the Sinai Peninsula. But surely this makes no sense. If Moses lived with the family of Jethro in Midian and he then traveled west to the Sinai Peninsula, he and his sheep would have had to swim across the Gulf of Aqaba! Even if they had taken the long journey west to the Sinai Peninsula by walking up and around the top of the Gulf of Aqaba and then down the other side, what was the point? The pasture in the barren Sinai Peninsula is very poor, and in all the books I have read about the land of Midian there is no record of Bedouin ever having taken their flocks from Midian to the Sinai Peninsula. It would be pointless to do so. In my opinion, all the major biblical commentaries have Moses going in the wrong direction, presumably because of the preconception of the writers that Mount Sinai has to be in the Sinai Peninsula, so Moses has to travel west from Midian to get there.

West Side Story: Fact or Fiction?

It is one thing for biblical commentaries to be mistaken, but is it really likely that the international team of thirty-two world-class scholars who translated the biblical texts to form the widely respected Revised Standard Version (RSV) would have made a major factual error in translation? Surely not! However, let's look more closely. The RSV was first published on September 30, 1952, and has met with wide acceptance throughout the world and among both Protestants and Catholics. It has been reprinted many times and must have been read by literally millions of people. If the RSV translates Exodus 3:1 as "He [Moses] led his flock to the west side of the wilderness," then these millions of readers could reasonably expect that the Hebrew text really does say "west side." But is this "west side story" correct, or, like the musical, is it fictional?

The Hebrew word the RSV translates as "west side" is *'achar.* But what does *'achar* really mean? A major standard reference book that seeks to give all possible meanings of Hebrew words in the Bible is the authoritative *Dictionary of Classical Hebrew,* edited by David Clines. According to this dictionary, *'achar* principally means "behind, to rear of." Not only is this the main meaning of *'achar,* but the dictionary specifically gives this meaning for Exodus 3:1; *'achar* may occasionally mean a westward direction (because if a person is looking at the sun rising in the east, then "behind" is to the west), but the principal meaning of *'achar* is "behind, to rear of." Clearly the New International Version rendering of *'achar* as "the far side" is in line with the meanings given in the *Dictionary of Classical Hebrew.* Whether "behind, the rear of, the far side" means north, south, east, or west is then a matter of interpretation depending on the context. The world-class Hebrew scholars who translated the RSV appear to have been so convinced that Mount Sinai was to the west of Midian that they allowed this belief to influence their translation, so they translated *'achar* as "west" in Exodus 3:1 rather than the more literal "behind" or "the rear of." In doing so, they misled a large number of people into thinking that Exodus 3:1 explicitly states that Moses went west from Midian to Mount Sinai, when in fact the Hebrew text does not say this at all.

The RSV was updated in 1989, and the new version was called, not surprisingly, the New Revised Standard Version (NRSV). Interestingly, the NRSV translates Exodus 3:1 as "He [Moses] led his flock beyond the wilderness," a much better translation. So the new translators have corrected the RSV here and not let their preconceptions of where Mount Sinai is color their translation. However, another widely read modern version of the Bible, the New American Standard Bible (NASB), first published in 1971, still renders Exodus 3:1 as "west side of the desert," which I believe continues to mislead large numbers of readers. Let us hope that when this version is revised, a more accurate translation will be made of this verse. Reputable translations of the Bible normally agree closely with one another, and we can have considerable confidence in them. It is only occasionally that differences occur, as with the meaning of *'achar* in Exodus 3:1.

In the first chapter of this book we said that solving the problem of the Exodus was like a complex detective story. In a really complex story there are false clues that lead you along the wrong trail. I believe the RSV and NASB translation of *'achar* as "west" is a false clue that leads in the wrong direction—indeed, in the literally wrong direction: west instead of east. This misinterpretation also indicates the strength of the mind-set of biblical scholars that Mount Sinai is in the Sinai Peninsula. So convinced of this were many of the leading biblical scholars in the world that they collectively agreed to a less-than-accurate translation of *'achar.* I believe this demonstrates the magnitude of the task we face in this book. If we are to convince people with this mind-set that Mount Sinai is not in the Sinai Peninsula, we will need a mass of evidence and a really convincing story. I ask you, the readers, to come to this book with an open mind on where Mount Sinai might be and a willingness to believe in the possibility that the leading biblical scholars in the world might be wrong on this issue. We shall see! I promise you that this will be a story you will never forget.

I am reminded of a remarkable incident that happened some years ago when I was driving in America. I knew I was on the correct route since I kept seeing the route number displayed by the road, but I recognized none of the place-names. I gradually realized I was lost, so I stopped at the next toll booth and asked directions. The toll collector roared with laughter and stepped outside her booth. "You're from England?" she inquired. "Yes," I replied. "I like the English. Just watch what I'm gonna do," she said. She went inside her toll booth, and suddenly all the traffic lights above the toll booths on the six lanes on my side of the road went red, and all the lights on the six lanes on the other side of the highway went red. All the traffic stopped in both directions. She said, "You're on the right route, but you're going in the wrong direction. Drive around where I'm pointing and onto the opposite lanes, and you'll be going in the right direction." So I drove around as she said, got onto the opposite highway, and drove away. It's just possible that biblical scholars were going in the wrong direction, too!

Of course, we haven't yet proved that biblical commentators and the translators of the RSV and the NASB have all got Moses traveling in the wrong direction. We have simply suggested that it makes much more sense, and is consistent with our knowledge of the traditional routes of Arabian shepherds, for Moses to have traveled east to the far side of the desert and not west to the Sinai Peninsula. We will need much more evidence if we are to demonstrate conclusively that all the atlases in the world and all the major biblical scholars in the world have placed Mount Sinai in the wrong country. In addition, there may be counterevidence later in the Exodus story that Mount Sinai really is in the Sinai Peninsula. We must keep an open mind on this, to let the evidence speak for itself and see if a consistent story emerges. All we can say so far is that the first piece of evidence we have analyzed on the location of Mount Sinai would seem to place it somewhere in Arabia, east of the Red Sea, and not in the Sinai Peninsula.

The Far Side: A Closer Look

Since it is important to know if the mountain of God is east or west of the Gulf of Aqaba, let's look more closely at what is meant by "the far side of the desert" in Exodus 3:1: "Now Moses was tending the flock of Jethro his father-in-law, the priest of Midian, and he led the flock to the far side of the desert." "Far side" with respect to what? There are various possibilities. Moses had traveled east to come from Egypt to Midian. Hence the "far side" viewed from where Moses had come from would be farther east, that is, farther east from the coastal plains of Midian (see map 4.1, pg. 46). An alternative interpretation is to recognize that Moses was probably living at ancient Madian. On the west side of Moses was the Gulf of Aqaba; on the east side was the desert. If Moses led his flock to the far side of the desert, then it seems clear that he must have gone east. Thus with either of the above interpretations, the "far side" means east of the Gulf of Aqaba.

For completeness, we should explore one further possible interpretation: that "the far side" could mean the far side of the desert as viewed by the writer of Exodus 3:1 from where he was writing. A huge amount has been written on the authorship of the book of Exodus, and I will make only a few brief comments here. Traditionally, all or most of the first five books of the Old Testament were written by Moses. However, most modern scholars believe that the book of Exodus had various sources, one of which could have been Moses, whose words were later put together by an editor into the book we have today. Hence the words *the far side of the desert* were written either by Moses or by a different source or editor probably writing from Jerusalem. If the writer was in Jerusalem, then from his perspective the far side of the desert from the Red Sea coast of Midian, which was southeast of Jerusalem, would have been farther southeast of the coastal plains of Midian. Thus, whichever of the above interpretations we adopt, when Moses went to the far side of the desert he would have traveled east, or southeast, of the Gulf of Aqaba. This is consistent with what we have deduced from the traditional behavior of Arabian shepherds migrating with their flocks. This is the first clear indication that the true Mount Sinai/Horeb could not have been in the Sinai Peninsula.

The famous book *The Seven Pillars of Wisdom,* by T. E. Lawrence, better known as Lawrence of Arabia, includes a delightful passage that indicates just how hot it gets in the summer on the coastal plain of Midian and how much relief from the heat one can gain by traveling east to higher ground:

> By May the ninth [not yet the hottest part of summer!] all things were ready and we left Feisal's tent [in Wejh on the Red Sea coast of Midian (see map 4.1, pg. 46), where Wejh is given the alternative spelling Wajh]. . . . We rose with the sun. . . . We plodded soberly on [riding camels] for six hours in great heat. The summer sun in this country of white sand behind Wejh could dazzle the eyes cruelly and the bare rocks each side of our path threw off waves of heat which made our heads ache and swim.

Lawrence then traveled east to higher ground, and he writes, "The air on the high tableland was not so warm, and morning and evening there blew across us a free current which was refreshing after the suspended stillness of the valleys." I believe this is why Moses led his flock east or southeast to the far side of the desert: to escape the searing heat of summer in the coastal region and to find better pasture that had not been withered by the intense sun. Incidentally, going west into the barren Sinai Peninsula around the traditional Mount Sinai would have achieved neither of these objectives.

What Kept the Burning Bush Burning?

We now turn to the question "What kept the burning bush burning?" The book of Exodus simply says,

> There the angel of the Lord appeared to him [Moses] in flames
> of fire from within a bush. Moses saw that though the bush was
> on fire it did not burn up. So Moses thought, "I will go over to
> see this strange sight—why the bush does not burn up."

Try to imagine the scene: Moses sees a bush on fire with flames
leaping out. He probably thinks, as we would today, that someone has
set fire to the bush and that the fire will soon die out when all the
wood has burned up. But, amazingly, the fire does not go out, the
bush just keeps on burning, and the flames keep leaping out.

I am reminded of an incident in my home a few years ago. In my
lounge we have a coal-effect gas fire. Some Japanese scientists had
come for dinner, and we gathered in the lounge before dinner. It was
a cold evening outside, and the Japanese warmed their hands in front
of the fire. We then went to our separate dining room for dinner, after
which we returned to the lounge. One very observant Japanese said in
amazement, "The fire is still burning, yet you did not put on any
more coal. How is it possible?" The other Japanese were equally
amazed. It turned out that they had never seen a coal-effect gas fire
before, in which it appears that the coal is burning, but in reality it is
the gas supplied from below the coals that is burning. Then they all
took photographs of the fire!

In the same way as there is a scientific explanation for the fire in
our lounge, which burns although the coal is not consumed, is there a
scientific explanation for the burning bush? The commentary on the
book of Exodus by Hyatt says, "All naturalistic explanations of this
narrative [about the burning bush] are vain," and this is the general
view of biblical scholars. However, we have seen how a naturalistic explanation accounts remarkably well for the crossing of the Jordan, and
we have also seen how the ancient Israelites regarded miracles as God
demonstrating his power through his control of natural events, so I'm
now going to tentatively explore the possibility that there may be a
scientific explanation for the burning bush.

According to Exodus 3:1–2, the burning bush was at the mountain
of God, also called Mount Horeb and Mount Sinai. Traditionally, as
we have seen, Mount Sinai is on the Sinai Peninsula, and some people
believe you can see this "burning bush" today at St. Catherine's

Monastery, which lies between Mount Catherine and Mount Sinai on the Sinai Peninsula. I visited this marvelous old monastery in the spring of 1995, which was the start of my quest for the real Mount Sinai. It is the oldest working monastery in the world and was built between A.D. 527 and 565 on the orders of the Roman emperor Justinian. The monastery is named after St. Catherine, an Alexandrian martyr who died in A.D. 307 after being tortured on a chariot wheel; Catherine Wheel fireworks are named after this gruesome event. The monks at the monastery cultivate a bush, *Rubus collinus,* a type of bramble, that visitors are told is the burning bush, which has been propagated continuously by the monks and which, we were told, goes back to the original burning bush (see photograph 5.2, pg. 72). However, as various commentaries on Exodus point out, *Rubus collinus* is a cultivated variety of bramble, not a wild variety, and there is no evidence that *Rubus collinus* grows wild in the region. Hence it is extremely unlikely that it was growing wild anywhere three thousand years ago. We can therefore effectively rule this out as being the burning bush.

Some biblical commentaries suggest that the burning bush could have been a bush with red berries or red leaves or leaves that reflected the bright sunlight, but surely the well-educated Moses wouldn't have been taken in by this so as to think that the bush was on fire! Moses was living in the Midian countryside as a shepherd; he would have been knowledgeable about the local plants. It is clear from the Exodus account that the burning bush was an amazing sight that Moses had never seen before. There is a somewhat similar story in a famous book, *The Pilgrim's Progress,* written by John Bunyan when he was in jail in Bedford, England, in 1672. The main character, Christian, saw a fire burning against a wall. When water was poured on the fire, amazingly it did not go out but burned even brighter. Christian was then shown the other side of the wall, where a man with a container of oil in his hand was secretly and continually pouring oil onto the fire. Is there a similar explanation for the burning bush—an explanation that has a scientific basis?

One scientific possibility for the burning bush is that it was a bush with blossoms that emitted a volatile gas. If such a bush is large, with many blossoms open at the same time, and there is no wind to disperse

5.2. The traditional burning bush in St. Catherine's Monastery.

the gas, then a high concentration of volatile gas can gradually build up around the bush. If the temperature is very high, then what is called the flash point of the gas can be reached and the gas surrounding the bush catches fire spontaneously. The gas burns and the bush itself may also catch fire. This spontaneous catching fire of a bush can be produced in a laboratory, for example, with the plant *Dictamnus albus,* but it occurs rarely in nature. Such an event could be described as a bush being on fire but not burning up, and it appears to be an attractive candidate for the burning bush seen by Moses.

However, I believe there are two problems with this theory. First, wherever the real Mount Sinai might be, we would need to show that *Dictamnus albus,* or a similar plant emitting volatile gas, could grow there. Second, even if the plant could have grown there, and even if the temperature was high enough to cause spontaneous combustion, the flames would not have lasted for very long. As soon as the gas emitted by the blossoms had burned up, the fire would have gone out. I do not know how long such a fire would last, and I can find no record of this, but I believe the volatile gas would burn off very quickly and the fire would probably last for no more than one minute. But the account in the book of Exodus strongly suggests a long-lasting fire that Moses went to investigate, not a fire that flares up and then rapidly goes out. So I think we can rule out this explanation of the burning bush because it does not really fit the Exodus account.

Natural Gas from the Ground

Is there another scientific mechanism to explain the burning bush? I believe there is: gas coming up from the ground under the burning bush to keep it burning, rather like the natural gas that keeps my coal-effect gas fire burning. You may think this is incredible, but read on!

There are two main sources of gas from the ground: natural gas and gas from volcanic vents. Natural gas is well known. It is the product of the underground decay of organic matter (plants and animals). The main constituent of natural gas is methane. Natural gas deposits are usually deep underground, or far below the seabed, and the gas is extracted by drilling into these deposits. However, occasionally natural gas deposits lie very close to the surface. For example, over three thousand years ago the Chinese extracted gas from shallow wells by using hollow bamboo poles, and they then burned the gas to boil seawater to obtain salt!

Will o' the wisp is a curious name for a fire that burns over marshes and swamps throughout the world. In Wales, will o' the wisp is known as "corpse candles" because the flames are sometimes seen in graveyards. Such flames were once thought to be supernatural, but we now know they are due to a form of natural gas released from decaying plants and animals (including humans!), and the gas then spontaneously catches fire. I used to live in Abingdon, near Oxford in England, and close to my home was a gravel pit into which the local council dumped household waste. The household refuse was then covered with soil. Frequently the landfill would spontaneously catch fire, due to the gases emitted by the decaying waste. Flames would shoot up into the air, and the children of the neighborhood would all watch as fire engines arrived and the local firefighters sprayed water from fire hoses to put out the fire.

Fire from the ground sometimes occurs in earthquakes. For example, in the earthquake that destroyed parts of San Francisco on April 18, 1906, there are many eyewitness reports of flames issuing from the ground. Although some of these were caused by broken gas mains in the streets of the city, many people also reported seeing flames in neighboring areas where no gas mains existed. The flames are due to natural gas emissions from the ground that spontaneously ignited. There are many reports of sheets of flames arising from earthquakes around the world.

America's "father of natural gas" is William Hart, who in 1821 observed gas bubbles streaming up to the surface of Candaway Creek in Fredonia, New York. So he deduced this natural gas deposit must be close to the surface. He dug a well alongside this creek to extract the gas, and so the first natural gas company in America was formed: the Fredonia Gas Light Company. So we know that natural gas deposits lying close to the surface of the earth are an observable fact. The gas can seep out through the ground, particularly if there are cracks in the rocks, be ignited either spontaneously or by lightning, and create burning springs of flame. In a number of countries in the ancient world such "eternal flames" were regarded as sacred, and in ancient India and Persia (modern Iran) temples were built around them.

The most famous example of such a temple comes from Greece, and I want to spend a little time describing this because, like the story of burning bush, the story of this temple is often thought to be a legend. While he was leading his goats to new pasture, so the story goes, a goatherd discovered a burning flame of gas on Mount Parnassus in Delphi in Greece. The local people then regarded the spot as sacred and built a temple to the god Apollo around the burning flame. Animals were sacrificed to Apollo on an inner altar where the eternal flame burned. The priestess at the Temple of Apollo was called the Pythoness, or Pythia; she went into trances and predicted the future, and she was said to be the medium through which the god Apollo spoke. The fame of the Pythia spread far and wide, and people came from all over the world to consult her. She foretold the fates of kings and of nations and became so famous that she was called the Oracle of Delphi. In return for a fee she would go into a trance and answer questions ranging from whom a king should marry to whether he should go to war. Different women filled the role of the Pythia from about 700 B.C. to A.D. 380, a very long period of time, after which Christianity displaced Apollo worship in Delphi.

Ancient Greek writers describe in some detail the prophetic performances of the Pythia. Beneath the Temple of Apollo, near the inner altar with the eternal flame, there was a small enclosed chamber called the *adytum,* which was located above a chasm in the rock. To commune with the god Apollo, the Pythia entered this small room and fell into a trance. The Athenian playwright Aeschylus wrote in 458 B.C. that the Pythia inhaled fumes he called *pneuma* (which means "breath") coming up from a crack in the ground. The Greek writer Plutarch, who was a priest of Apollo in the temple at Delphi, also attributed the Pythia's prophetic powers to vapors coming up from deep in the ground. Another Greek writer, Pausanias, describes how the Pythia drank water from a nearby spring that ran into the adytum. He attributed Pythia's powers to this special water.

For many years the story of the naturally burning flame of gas, and of vapors coming up from the ground, was regarded as a legend. This seemed to be confirmed when, in 1927, a team of French geologists surveyed the Temple of Apollo in Delphi and found no evidence of rising gases. Most history books and travel guide books to Greece therefore call the story a legend (although the temple, of course, is a reality and its ruins are still there today).

However, a new four-year-long study, reported in the August 2001 issue of *Geology*, has revealed that two geological faults intersect directly below this Temple of Apollo. The research has been performed by archaeologist John Hale from the University of Louisville in Kentucky; geologist Jelle de Boer of the Wesleyan University in Connecticut; and geochemist Jeffrey Chanton of Florida State University. This multidisciplinary team has found that movement of the geological faults under the Temple of Apollo has left the rocks beneath the temple full of cracks, through which gases and water springs can rise up from deep in the earth's crust. They also found that some of the temple walls are coated with a mineral called travertine. When the research team analyzed the spring water and the travertine they found they contained methane (the main constituent of natural gas), ethane, and ethylene (also called ethene). Ethylene is a known hallucinogenic if inhaled, and in high doses it can be fatal.

Interestingly, Plutarch describes how a prophetess once died after inhaling the fumes in the adytum, and he says that the gases had a sweet smell like perfume—just like ethylene smells. Dr. Jelle de Boer, a coauthor of the paper in *Geology*, stated in a National Geographic news interview on August 14, 2001: "Plutarch made the right observation; indeed, there were gases that came through the fractures." As we have seen, according to tradition, the Pythia made her prophecies in a small enclosed chamber in the basement of the temple. Dr. de Boer stated that if the Pythia went to the chamber once a month, as tradition says, she could have been exposed to concentrations of the narcotic gas that were strong enough to induce a trancelike state. We can therefore say with reasonable certainty that the "legends" of the vapors from the ground and of the burning flame of gas on Mount Parnassus are based on fact.

Just as the ancient Greek herdsman in about 700 B.C. was amazed by the burning flame he saw on the slopes of Mount Parnassus, so Moses the shepherd in about 1300 B.C. was amazed by the burning flame he saw coming from within a bush on the slopes of Mount Sinai. What a remarkable parallel! If the burning flame seen by the

Greek herdsman has a natural explanation, as suggested strongly by scientific observation, and the story is therefore based on historical fact, is there a similar natural explanation for the flames coming from the burning bush that attracted the attention of Moses?

The burning bush was probably located in Midian, part of modern Saudi Arabia. So are there natural gas deposits in Saudi Arabia? As is well known, the answer is yes. Saudi Arabia's natural gas reserves are the fourth largest in the world, but they are mainly located in the East Province. However, interestingly, the U.S. Department of Energy Country Analysis Brief dated June 8, 2001, and available on the Web, states, "Gas also is located in the country's extreme northwest, at Midyan [which we are spelling Midian in this book]. In early 2000 Saudi Arabia reportedly decided not to move ahead with development of [the gas fields of] Midyan." So there is natural gas in Midian, where I believe the burning bush should be located, but as far as I am aware, no natural gas has been discovered in the Sinai Peninsula. In addition, there are historical records of many earthquakes in Midian, so we can expect many rocks to be cracked, enabling natural gas in deposits close to the surface to escape.

We therefore have a possible natural explanation for the burning bush. It was growing on top of a region containing natural gas, which is known to exist in Midian. The natural gas came up from under the bush through cracks in the rocks, was ignited either spontaneously or by lightning, and gave rise to what the book of Exodus describes as "flames of fire from within a bush" so that "although the bush was on fire it did not burn up." This is clearly a possible natural explanation for the burning bush. There is, however, another possible explanation, a volcanic vent.

A Volcanic Vent

Gas escaping from volcanic vents is relatively common. For example, more than five hundred volcanic vents have been identified in the state of California. At least seventy-six of these vents have erupted, some repeatedly, during the last ten thousand years. The "smoke" from volcanoes is actually volcanic gas naturally released from both active and dormant volcanoes. The gases come from the molten rock, called magma, that lies beneath volcanoes. Volcanic gas is a complex mixture of gases and contains water vapor, carbon dioxide, sulfur dioxide, hydrogen, and other gases, and the gas composition varies considerably from one volcano to another.

Volcanic vents can vary in size from a tiny hole or crack in the ground to a large hole or fissure. Both lava and hot gases can be emitted from volcanic vents. In the spring of 2002 I visited the famous volcano Mount Etna, in Sicily. I was walking on the black lava on the slopes of Mount Etna when suddenly I saw the air shimmering by my side. I looked down and saw an almost invisible hole in the lava, only about two inches across: truly a black hole. I carefully felt the lava rocks close to the hole; they were very, very hot. Colorless, invisible hot gases were coming out of the vent, heating the surrounding lava and the air above and causing it to shimmer. I had some sheets of paper in my pocket, so I rolled these up and placed them over the vent. In only about a second they burst into flames. It was clear to me that if a volcanic vent opened up under a bush then the bush would catch fire.

Since the land of Midian (modern northwest Saudi Arabia) contains many volcanoes, I believe that a volcanic vent is a possible source of the gas that ignited the burning bush and kept it burning. The March 2000 issue of *Volcano Watch,* a weekly feature provided by scientists at the Hawaiian Volcano Observatory, states,

> Large and colorful flames sometimes play from vents on Kilauea volcano. These flames, which range from yellowish orange to greenish blue and reach a height of 1 meter (3 feet), result from hydrogen gas burning in air. . . . The large flames sometimes persist for several hours and then slowly diminish and disappear.

Thus a possible scientific mechanism for the burning bush is that a small volcanic vent opened up under the bush. As we will see in a later chapter, a common bush in Midian is a species of acacia, *Acacia seyel.* The Finnish explorer Georg Wallin, in *Travels in Arabia,* says that this bush, when burned, makes excellent charcoal instead of turning to ashes. So if *Acacia seyel* was the burning bush, then initially it would catch fire and then the flames would continue to come out from within the charred and glowing charcoal framework of the bush for as long as the gas was supplied, or until the bush finally disintegrated. As with the natural gas hypothesis I suggested above, the volcanic vent mechanism also fits well the description in the book of Exodus that there were "flames of fire from within a bush" and that "though the bush was on fire, it did not burn up." The effect would be like the coal-effect gas fire in my lounge described earlier: an even better analogy would be a log-effect gas fire. The logs appear to be burning and not consumed, whereas in reality it is the gas coming up from below the logs that is burning.

It is interesting to note that nowhere in the Exodus story is the burning bush called a holy bush. On the other hand, the ground on which the burning bush grew is called holy ground: "Do not come any closer," God said. "Take off your sandals, for the place you are standing on is holy ground" (Exodus 3:5). The fact that the book of Exodus calls "holy" the ground on which the burning bush stood, but not the burning bush itself, is consistent with my suggestion that the fire came from the ground (either due to natural gas or volcanic gases) and not from the bush itself, and Moses recognized this.

So as well as the natural gas hypothesis, we have another tentative theory that fits well the description in the book of Exodus: the burning bush could have been due to a volcanic vent. Earthquakes are common in volcanic regions, both because of the movement of tectonic plates and because magma (molten rock) under high pressure is seeking a way up to the earth's surface. There are often many networks of cracks in the ground around volcanoes through which natural gas, if present, or volcanic gases can easily emerge.

But are there volcanic regions in Midian that have been active in the last four thousand years? As we will see in later chapters, the answer is yes. These regions are in higher territory to the east and southeast of the coastal plains of Midian, consistent with our deduction earlier of the direction in which Moses led the sheep. However, there are no volcanic regions in the Sinai Peninsula that have been active in the last four thousand years. Thus a tentative picture is starting to emerge: the burning bush could be in a volcanic region in Midian, east or southeast of the Gulf of Aqaba. We will need much more evidence, of course, for this to be convincing; however, the seeds of a theory have been sown.

If it is correct that the burning bush was growing on top of a volcanic vent, or on top of a natural gas source in a volcanic region, this volcanic area had to have been inactive for at least one hundred years prior to Moses. The reason is that plants do not grow on fresh volcanic lava, which takes many years to break down. However, broken-down lava yields very fertile soil, which is why farmers live and work around volcanoes such as Vesuvius even though they know that one day Vesuvius will erupt again and possibly kill them. There is a famous volcano in Mexico called Paricutin, which started life as a vent in a field of corn (some textbooks state a field of lettuce). Hot gases and lava started emerging from a vent in this cornfield on February 20, 1943. After a year of activity all the corn was burned, and a volcanic cone 1,066 feet high had built up in the middle of the cornfield. The fissure marked the start of volcanic activity, which continued until 1952, when it simmered into silence.

If our tentative theory so far is correct, then the region containing the burning bush would not have been volcanically active in the years just prior to Moses, or else the bush would not have been there. We can expect the pastureland to have been very good in this region of fertile volcanic soil, consistent with Moses' taking the sheep there, but do we have any evidence of this? In the previous chapter I referred to the handbook of the archaeologist David Hogarth, *Hejaz Before World War I*, which contains a chapter describing the Hejaz (or Hijaz, Hegaz) tribes. (Hejaz is a large region in northern Arabia that contains Midian.) This is what he says about the Moahib tribe: "They inhabit the southern part of the 'Aweiridh, a rugged mass of volcanic rock upon a platform of sandstone. They are sheep breeders. . . ." So Arab sheep breeders do indeed live in the volcanic regions of Midian (see map 4.1, pg. 46, for the 'Aweiridh volcanic region, which is usually spelled 'Uwayrid). Hogarth then goes on to write about the Sihamah Arabs, who form a clan of another Midianite tribe called the Billi: "In summer the Sihamah come up with their flocks into the harrah." Now *harrah* is the Arabic name for volcanic lava fields, so Hogarth is saying that in the heat of summer these Arabian tribespeople bring their sheep up into cooler and fertile volcanic territory, just as we have deduced Moses did three thousand years ago. Again, a consistent story has emerged as to why Moses led the flock of Jethro to the far side of the desert: he led them to a cooler, fertile volcanic region where he witnessed the extraordinary sight of the burning bush that kept burning because there was a source of natural gas, or a volcanic vent, underneath. Without further information it is not possible to say whether the natural gas or the volcanic vent mechanism is more likely to be correct, but both are certainly possible natural explanations of the burning bush.

In the next chapter we will explore the characteristics of the mountain of God, Mount Sinai, described in the book of Exodus, and in particular we look into the exciting possibility that Mount Sinai was a volcano, a mountain of fire. As we will see, the evidence for this is strong, and I believe the biblical description of Mount Sinai is the world's oldest description of an erupting volcano, yet it has gone unrecognized by both scientists and biblical scholars.

SIX

THE MOUNTAIN OF GOD, THE MOUNTAIN OF FIRE

You came near and stood at the foot of the mountain [Mount Sinai] while it blazed with fire to the very heavens, with black clouds and deep darkness.

Deuteronomy 4:11

Recently I was traveling in Japan on the famous bullet train from Tokyo to Kyoto when suddenly all the passengers on my side of the carriage stood up and looked out the windows on the other side. My very polite Japanese neighbor said to me, "Please excuse me. Yesterday there was a typhoon here that swept all the pollution out of the sky, and you can now see the whole of Mount Fuji, right up to the top. Normally this is impossible. Mount Fuji is a very special mountain for Japanese people. It is very beautiful." So I, too, stood up and saw the magnificent characteristic cone shape of the volcanic Mount Fuji, the summit sprinkled with sparkling snow. I could well understand why this mountain was special for the Japanese.

For Moses a different mountain, called "the mountain of God," was special, but why? Let's look again at the first mention of this mountain in the Bible. "Now Moses was tending the flock of Jethro his father-in-law, the priest of Midian, and he led the flock to the far side of the desert and came to Horeb, the mountain of God" (Exodus 3:1). As I said in chapter 5, Horeb and Sinai seem to be used interchangeably in the Bible to refer to the same mountain, and in this chapter I will use the more common name, Sinai, for the mountain of God. Many biblical commentaries assume that Moses happened to come across Sinai, the mountain of God, by chance. But anyone who has walked in the blisteringly hot deserts in the Middle East knows that you do not undertake a journey there without knowing precisely where you are going. In addition, Moses had in his care not his own sheep, but the flock of his father-in-law, Jethro, which probably amounted to his life's savings. In ancient times a person's wealth and food supplies, both present and future, were largely measured by the number of animals they possessed. The reality surely is that Moses and Jethro would have discussed in advance where Moses would take the sheep to find better pasture at a higher elevation, and both would have agreed that Moses would take the sheep to Sinai, the mountain of God. If this was an annual event, and it seems for the reasons given in the last chapter that it probably was, then Moses would have been there before, and probably Jethro would have gone with Moses the first time to show him precisely the location of Sinai, the mountain of God.

Why was Sinai called the mountain of God? The obvious answer, which is also supported by most commentaries, is because of events that occurred there later, especially the giving of the Ten Commandments. This is of course a valid viewpoint.

However, I would like to explore the interesting possibility that Sinai was already called the mountain of God before Moses visited it, because I believe that is the natural meaning of the text. In addition, elsewhere in the book of Exodus the writer is careful to explain when a place-name is being used because of events that happened there *after* Moses had arrived. For example, Exodus 17:7 states, "He [Moses] called the place Massah and Meribah because the Israelites quarreled there and because they tested the Lord [*Massah* means testing, and *Meribah* means quarreling]." Since this explanation of naming because of subsequent events is not given in Exodus 3:1, I believe it is therefore likely that this mountain was *already* called Sinai, the mountain of God, before Moses visited it.

In the final chapter of this book I will argue that Jethro, the priest of Midian, may have been the priest of the Moon-god, since this is known to have been one of the principal gods of Arabia at this time. In addition, as we will see at the end of this book, the real Mount Sinai would have been a mountain holy to the Moon-god before the arrival of Moses and the Israelites. So I suggest that Jethro, the priest of Midian, would have visited this holy mountain regularly, and he would have known about the quality of the pastureland there. I believe this explains why Jethro and Moses agreed that Moses should take Jethro's flock to this special mountain rather than to another mountain, and it could well be that Jethro planned to join Moses there later. In addition, if the mountain of God was already well known to Jethro, this explains how Jethro was easily able to find Moses at this mountain at a later date, as recorded in Exodus 18:5: "Jethro, Moses' father-in-law, together with Moses' sons and wife, came to him in the desert, where he was camped near the mountain of God."

Why should a mountain be given the awe-inspiring title "the mountain of God"? Are there other examples of this name being used in ancient literature? In my search through ancient writings I found a whole class of special mountains that always seemed to be called holy mountains by virtue of what they were: active volcanoes. The ancient Greeks called magnificent Mount Etna, on the island of Sicily, the mountain of God because they believed the god of fire, Hephaistos, dwelled there and was responsible for its fiery eruptions. They believed that the mighty god Hephaistos forged the weapons of the gods in a furnace beneath Mount Etna and when he hammered on his anvil, smoke and sparks emerged from the top of the mountain. Sometimes he would beat iron into shape with such force that huge flames leaped out of the mountain and annihilated nearby villages. The ancient Romans had similar beliefs but called their god of fire Vulcan. They believed this Fire-god dwelled in a fiery mountain on the island called Vulcano, named after Vulcan, off the southwest coast of Italy. In fact, this is where we get our English word for volcanoes.

There is evidence that the ancient Greeks, Romans, Indonesians, Japanese, Icelanders, and Hawaiians all called volcanoes "mountains of God." Japan's great volcanoes are all sacred, and temples and shrines surround them. Mount Fuji has two Shinto shrines dedicated to the god of the mountain, one near the bottom of the mountain and the other at the top, close to the volcanic crater. Given the evidence for "mountains of God," when we find the designation in the book of Exodus, we should explore the possibility that this mountain was also a volcano, particularly since, as we shall see later, volcanoes that have been active in the last few thousand years exist in the land of Midian (but not in the Sinai Peninsula). For the rest of this chapter we will examine the descriptions of the mountain of God (Mount Horeb or Mount Sinai) given in the Old Testament and see if these descriptions are consistent with a volcano. We have already seen in the previous chapter that the phenomenon of the burning bush, located at or near the mountain of God (Exodus 3:1–2), is consistent with volcanic activity.

In the last few years I have walked up two famous volcanoes: Vesuvius in Italy and Etna on the island of Sicily. Both were in a semi-quiescent state and not erupting. However, wreaths of white smoke drifted up from the summit of Vesuvius, and at Mount Etna large columns of white cloud arose from three craters, with dark cloud being emitted from a fourth (see photograph 6.1, pg. 86). How would superstitious tribespeople have interpreted the smoke emitted from volcanoes, even when they were dormant? Perhaps as the smoke rising up from a burned sacrifice, offered by invisible hands to the god of the volcano? It takes little imagination to see why volcanoes were called mountains of God.

Exodus 19:16–19 describes Mount Sinai as follows:

On the morning of the third day there was thunder and lightning, with a thick cloud over the mountain, and a very loud trumpet blast. Everyone in the camp trembled. Then Moses led the people out of the camp to meet with God, and they stood at the foot of the mountain. Mount Sinai was covered with smoke, because the Lord descended on it in fire. The smoke billowed up from it, like smoke from a furnace, the whole mountain trembled violently, and the sound of the trumpet grew louder and louder.

Exodus 24:17 states, "To the Israelites the glory of the Lord looked like a consuming fire on top of the mountain." Deuteronomy 4:11 states, "You came here and stood at the foot of the mountain while it blazed with fire to the very heavens, with black clouds and deep darkness." The key question is whether these dramatic descriptions were meant to be taken literally or whether they are poetic language describing an ordinary, nonvolcanic mountain.

6.1. Mount Etna in a semiquiescent state.

Let's compare these vivid descriptions of Mount Sinai in the Old Testament books of Exodus and Deuteronomy with historical descriptions of the volcano Vesuvius. In A.D. 104 Pliny the Younger wrote to the Roman historian Tacitus about the eruption of Vesuvius in A.D. 79.

> There had been for several days before some shocks of earthquake, but that night they became so violent that one might think that the world was not being madly shaken, but turned topsy-turvy. . . . [Coming out of Vesuvius was] a black and dreadful cloud bursting out in gusts of igneous serpentine vapor now and again split open to reveal long fantastic flames, resembling flashes of lightning but much larger. . . . Soon afterwards the cloud I have described began to descend to the sea. . . .

Note the similarities of this description of Mount Vesuvius with the earlier Old Testament writings about Mount Sinai: thick black cloud, lightning, the land trembling, fire on top of the mountain. Here is the description of a later eruption of Mount Vesuvius in 1767 by Sir

William Hamilton, British ambassador to the Court of Naples, who was on the mountain when it erupted:

> About noon I heard a violent noise within the mountain, and at about a quarter of a mile off the place where I stood, the mountain split and with much noise from this new mouth a fountain of liquid fire shot up many feet high. . . . The explosions from the top of the mountain were much louder than any thunder I ever heard. . . . After having taken breath, as the earth still trembled greatly, I thought it most prudent to leave the mountain. . . .

Spoken like a true British ambassador! Note the description of the noise as being like thunder, just as in the Exodus description of Mount Sinai, in addition to the trembling of the mountain and the fire shooting out from it.

The descriptions of Mount Sinai in the books of Exodus and Deuteronomy are so similar to eyewitness descriptions of the eruptions of Vesuvius that I believe there can be little doubt that Mount Sinai was an active volcano. As we will see in chapter 19, I am not the first person to say this: a few people before me have suggested that Mount Sinai was a volcano, but they have not made a strong case, and they also have not agreed on which volcano it was! But why have all the leading biblical scholars and historians in the world rejected the idea that Mount Sinai was a volcano? There are three main reasons.

First, some scholars argue that Moses could not have walked up an active volcano, as recorded further on in the book of Exodus. However, as we will see in a later chapter, there are different types of volcanoes, of varying degrees of volcanic intensity, and people do walk up even intensely active volcanoes like Vesuvius. For example, the explorer Doughty makes a digression in his book *Arabia Deserta* to describe standing on the top of Vesuvius during an eruption:

> In the year 1872 I was a witness of the great eruption of Vesuvius. Standing from the morning alone upon the top of the mountain, that day in which the great outbreak began, I waded ankle-deep in flour of sulfur upon a burning hollow soil of lava:

in the midst was a mammal-like chimney, not long formed, fuming with a light corrosive breath; which to those in the plain had appeared by night as a fiery beacon with trickling lavas. . . .

If Doughty can stand on the top of the mighty Vesuvius when it is erupting, then surely Moses could have stood on the top of a less intensely active volcano, particularly if the lava flow was down one side and Moses walked up the other side. So I think we can dismiss this objection.

Second, most commentaries on the book of Exodus argue that the writer is not really describing a volcano but instead is using poetic and metaphorical language to describe an ordinary mountain. Clearly, we must recognize that ancient literature, including the Bible, sometimes uses poetical and metaphorical language, but in most cases it is obvious when this is happening. In some cases it is not clear whether the writer intends a description to be taken literally or not, but I would then argue that the correct approach is tentatively to take the description literally and see if this makes sense and fits the facts. If a literal interpretation does not make sense, then we are justified in a metaphorical interpretation.

The third and main reason scholars do not believe Mount Sinai to be a volcano is because there are no active volcanoes in the Sinai Peninsula. However, once it is realized that Mount Sinai may be in Arabia, as we have already argued, and that there are active volcanoes in Arabia, as we will see in detail in a later chapter, then we are free to accept the exciting possibility that Mount Sinai, the mountain of God, was indeed a mountain of fire, a spectacular volcano, that erupted exactly as described in the Old Testament. Why do we take Pliny's description of Vesuvius literally? Because we know that volcanoes exist in Italy. I suggest that we should similarly take the biblical description of Mount Sinai literally because we know that volcanoes exist in Arabia.

Although most readers of this book will never have witnessed a live erupting volcano, most of us will have seen volcanoes on television, in films, and in photographs, and we have a good idea of what a volcano is like. Moses and the Israelites almost certainly had never seen a volcano before because there are no volcanoes in Egypt or in the Sinai

Peninsula. Just imagine being with the Israelites in Midian and seeing a volcano for the very first time: a mountain that quakes and shakes, that emits a noise like thunder, that throws out huge flames of fire and clouds of smoke reaching far up into the sky. What a magnificent, awe-inspiring sight! What a setting for Moses to receive the Ten Commandments!

Finally, let's look at the biblical description of Mount Sinai through the eyes of modern-day science. Apart from the fire and the clouds of smoke, which we all know are associated with volcanoes, there are two details in the account that I find fascinating. First the reference to lightning: "On the morning of the third day there was thunder and lightning, with a thick cloud over the mountain, and a very loud trumpet blast" (Exodus 19:16). Lightning occurs in only some volcanic eruptions, and it is due to static electricity on ash particles in an eruption cloud discharging. Here is how two geologists, Keith and Dorothy Stoffel, flying in a light plane over the summit of Mount St. Helens in Washington when it erupted on March 20, 1980, described what they saw:

> To the east of the volcano the ash cloud separated into billowing mushroom-shaped clouds and a higher overhang of cirrus-type clouds. Ashfall from the mushroom-shaped clouds was heavy. Lightning bolts shooting through the clouds were tens of thousands of feet high. (Decker and Decker, *Mountains of Fire*)

The book by the Deckers omits the information that the flight over Mount St. Helens was a birthday treat for Dorothy Stoffel organized by her husband before the eruption occurred. Mount St. Helens blew when their plane was overhead, and it almost cost them their lives.

The second detail that attracted my attention was the reference to "a very loud trumpet blast" (Exodus 19:16) coming from the mountain. Molten volcanic rock, called magma, contains dissolved volcanic gases, such as water vapor and carbon dioxide. If these gases are forced out through cracks in the solid rocks of the volcano surrounding the erupting hot zone, then the sound of a very loud trumpet blast is indeed sometimes heard. (A normal trumpet blast is similarly produced by blowing air through a narrow opening in the mouthpiece of a trumpet.) For example, the Roman historian Dio Cassius reported that the sound of trumpets was heard during the eruption of Vesuvius.

Somewhat more recently, T. A. Barnes wrote an article in the *Illustrated London News* of March 15, 1930, describing his visit to a sacred volcano 125 miles west of Kilimanjaro. He writes that the Masai tribesmen call this volcano Oldonyo-lengai, meaning the "Mountain of God." He further writes, "The internal rumblings of 1917 [which preceded an eruption] were put down to bellowings of cattle [from inside the volcano]." The sound of trumpets and the bellowings of cattle from volcanoes are both due to the same source: volcanic gases being forced under pressure through cracks in rocks.

Now for a really important point. If asked to describe an erupting volcano, most of us would refer to the fire (see photograph 6.2, pg. 91) and clouds of smoke (see photograph 6.3, pg. 91). But how many of us would also refer to lightning and trumpet blasts (or cattle bellowing)? I know that I wouldn't. It takes an eyewitness to know these details about erupting volcanoes. So in these details from the books of Exodus and Deuteronomy, I believe we have remarkable evidence not only that Mount Sinai was an active volcano, but also that the account of its eruption was written down by an eyewitness, perhaps by Moses himself since his royal Egyptian education would have taught him to write.

Finally, note the description of the erupting Mount Sinai in Exodus 19:18: "The smoke billowed up from it like smoke from a furnace." This is precisely the imagery we saw was used by the ancient Greeks and Romans when they described their gods as having furnaces below volcanic mountains, but the description in the book of Exodus is much earlier. If we are correct that the book of Exodus is describing a volcano, then as far as I am aware, this is the world's oldest description of a volcano. Yet it has gone unrecognized by scientists, historians, and biblical scholars alike. There is so much that is amazing about the extraordinary Exodus journey! Just think about this again: here in the Old Testament we probably have the oldest description in the world of a volcano, yet it receives no mention in any books on volcanoes, which frequently start with a chapter on historic volcanoes, and it receives no mention in the many TV programs on volcanoes.

Let me summarize the evidence that Mount Sinai was a volcano. The Old Testament descriptions we have quoted above contain no

6.2. *Volcanic fire.*

6.3. *Volcanic smoke.*

fewer than seven characteristic features of an explosive volcanic eruption: (1) it blazed with fire to the very heavens (Deuteronomy 4:11);
(2) smoke and clouds billowed up from it (Deuteronomy 4:11 and Exodus 19:18); (3) the noise of explosions—thunder (Exodus 19:16); (4)
the sound of hot escaping gases—a very loud trumpet blast (Exodus
19:16); (5) electrical discharges in the eruption cloud—lightning (Exodus 19:16); (6) volcanic earthquakes—the whole mountain trembled
violently (Exodus 19:18); (7) a summit cloud and darkness (Deuteronomy 4:11). Here we have a remarkable description of an erupting
volcano based on careful observation. I suggest it is inconceivable that
the author(s) of Exodus and Deuteronomy could combine these seven
characteristic features of an active volcano unless they had seen one
and unless, in addition, they really intended to describe Mount Sinai
as an active volcano. Surely this was no poetic description of an ordinary mountain.

Only one feature of an erupting volcano is missing from the biblical
account: lava. Lava, which is molten rock, usually flows down only one
side of a volcano, and Moses and the Israelites obviously would have
camped on the other side of the mountain for safety reasons. In addition, as I've said above, when Moses climbed Mount Sinai either he
would have waited for the lava flow to cease or else he would have
climbed on the other side, to avoid it. Pliny the Younger, in his description of the eruption of Vesuvius in A.D. 79, doesn't mention lava
flow either. The reason is that from a distance, when both Pliny and the
Israelites first saw their erupting volcanoes, the lava flow was not visible;
and even close up, if the lava flow was on the other side of the volcano,
it was not visible. It is therefore easy to see why the writers of Exodus
and Deuteronomy and also Pliny do not mention lava flow.

Intriguingly, however, another biblical writer appears to. Here is
how the Old Testament book of Judges describes Mount Sinai: "The
mountains melted from before the Lord, even that Sinai from before
the Lord God of Israel" (Judges 5:5). A melted mountain can mean
only one thing: molten rock, or in modern language, lava, flowing
down the side of a mountain. Here we see that the Bible itself possibly
associates lava with Mount Sinai. Now for an interesting point of detail. The quotation above from the book of Judges is from the original
King James Version (KJV) of the Bible, translated into English in 1611.

The much more recent New International Version (NIV), translated in 1978 and revised in 1983, which we are mainly using in this book, translates Judges 5:5 thus: "The mountains quaked before the Lord, the One of Sinai before the Lord, the God of Israel." The Hebrew word translated "melted" in the KJV and "quaked" in the NIV is *nazal*. So what does *nazal* mean? Its main meaning is "to flow," and it is used with this meaning in fifteen other places in the Old Testament. Clearly this meaning of *nazal* applied to a mountain is consistent with describing flowing lava. The reasons the modern Hebrew scholars who translated the NIV rendered *nazal* as "quaked" are complicated and beyond the scope of this book, but, briefly, the consonantal form of *nazal* is *n-z-l*, and the NIV translators took the text to represent a verb *z-l-l*, which means "to shake." This interpretation is used in two other places in the Old Testament. Clearly a shaking mountain is consistent with the tremors volcanoes make before and during eruptions, but I suggest the more usual translation of *nazal* as "to flow" when applied to a mountain can mean only one thing: lava flows.

Most biblical scholars are not scientists and so are unaware of the powerful arguments I have presented in this chapter that Mount Sinai was a volcano. I believe this illustrates clearly why reading ancient texts through the lenses of scientific knowledge is so important: science can provide new insights into what the original authors intended. In this case I believe it is beyond reasonable doubt that the writers of the Old Testament were describing Mount Sinai as an active volcano.

We have made some remarkable discoveries in part 2 about Moses and the land of Midian. But the best is yet to come! We move now to the extraordinary story of the Exodus of the Israelites from Egypt. This will involve more fascinating historical detective work, with science again playing a key role. In particular, we will see that the ten plagues of Egypt all have scientific mechanisms, and the crossing of the Red Sea has a wonderful scientific explanation, never before revealed, that enables us to pinpoint exactly where this miracle occurred.

In the next chapter we will see how Moses received his momentous mission to lead the Israelites out of Egypt as he stood by the burning bush at the mountain of God. Moses was given three instructions that were to change the course of history, and he received a brilliant game-plan to enable him to overcome the mighty pharaoh.

PART THREE

OUT OF EGYPT

SEVEN

MISSION IMPOSSIBLE:
THE EXODUS STRATEGY

*I [God] am sending you [Moses] to Pharaoh to bring my people the Is-
raelites out of Egypt. . . . When you have brought the people out of
Egypt you will worship God on this mountain [Sinai]. . . . I have
promised to bring you up out of your misery in Egypt into the land of
the Canaanites . . . a land flowing with milk and honey.*

Exodus 3:10, 12, 17

M*ission Impossible* screams a striking sign across an image of
Tom Cruise currently outside a Cambridge cinema. I look
closer, and almost hidden in the tangled hair of Tom
Cruise is the number 2. So the film is really *Mission Impossible 2*, the
sequel to the 1996 film in which Tom Cruise also starred. The 1996
film was itself the sequel to one of the most successful television series
ever made, also called *Mission Impossible,* which had 168 episodes,
starting way back in September 1966. There is something about impossible missions that grips our imagination and stirs our spirit.

In *Mission Impossible 2,* Tom Cruise plays agent Ethan Hunt, who
leads an Impossible Mission Force team to recapture a deadly German
virus before it falls into the wrong hands. It is a good plot, but it pales
by comparison with the second mission impossible of Moses. In
Moses' original mission impossible he twice defied death at the hands
of one of the most powerful men in the world, the pharaoh of Egypt,
first at his birth and then again after he killed an Egyptian slave master.
In Moses' sequel, he masterminds the great escape of the Israelites
from Egypt in the face of overwhelming odds. Tom Cruise's sequel involves deadly viruses; Moses' sequel involves deadly viruses and much,

much more (see chapter 9, on the plagues of Egypt). Tom Cruise's *Mission Impossible 2* uses some astonishing special effects; Moses' *Mission Impossible 2* includes a real-life special effect, the crossing of the Red Sea, which is so awesome that it totally dwarfs anything in the Tom Cruise film.

I have called part 3 of this book "Out of Egypt." In this opening chapter of part 3, we analyze the impossible mission of Moses to lead the Israelites out of Egypt.

Standing before the burning bush, with flames leaping out, at the volcanic mountain of God, whose flames did not yet leap out, Moses received his mission. Picture the dramatic scene. All around was black volcanic soil, upon which stood the towering black basalt volcanic cone of Mount Sinai: in the foreground was a blackened burning bush with brilliant tongues of fire leaping out, constantly renewed as if there were a divine furnace below. In this awe-inspiring setting Moses heard the voice of God coming from the bush. Not surprisingly, Moses was terrified, and he hid his face (Exodus 3:6).

God then gave Moses three clear instructions that changed the course of history and that formed the basis of the extraordinary journey to be undertaken by Moses and the Israelites. These instructions are fundamental to our understanding of the Exodus route. The first instruction was: "So now, go. I am sending you to Pharaoh to bring my people the Israelites out of Egypt" (Exodus 3:10). The second instruction was: "When you have brought the people out of Egypt, you will worship God on this mountain" (Exodus 3:12). The third instruction was in the form of a promise: "I have promised to bring you up out of your misery in Egypt into the land of the Canaanites, Hittites, Amorites, Perizzites, Hivites, and Jebusites—a land flowing with milk and honey" (Exodus 3:17).

Moses was instructed to bring the Israelites out of Egypt and take them to "this mountain," Mount Sinai. Some time after that the Israelites would enter the "promised land," a land flowing with milk and honey, but it is of interest to note that God does not say that this would occur under Moses, and indeed Moses died before this happened. Moses' mission was to take the Israelites to Mount Sinai and then to lead them in the right direction after leaving Mount Sinai, but it was his successor, Joshua, who led the Israelites across the river Jordan into the promised land, as we saw in chapter 2.

Before we go further let's pause and consider the magnitude of the three tasks set for Moses. First, Moses was to go to the king of Egypt and persuade him to let the Israelites leave Egypt. This was at a time when Egypt was one of the most powerful nations in the world, probably in the period 1300–1250 B.C. The pharaoh Moses was going to talk to was probably Ramesses II, who was arguably the greatest Egyptian pharaoh of all time. I have visited Egypt many times and marveled at the magnificent temples built by Ramesses II; he built many more temples than any other pharaoh. Figure 7.1, below, shows the entrance to Abu Simbel, a temple built by Ramesses II in ancient Nubia. The entrance has not one but four colossal statues of him, each one 65 feet high (one statue fell in ancient times). In Egypt, importance was measured by the size of one's statue, so Ramesses II must have had a huge ego.

Ramesses II needed slave labor to achieve his massive building plans. The number of Israelite men twenty years old and over whom Moses led out of Egypt was in excess of six hundred thousand, according to the books of Exodus and Numbers. In fact, I think the ancient Hebrew text has been misinterpreted and this number should be

7.1. Abu Simbel temple built by Ramesses II.

about five thousand (see chapter 8), but five thousand male slaves is still a substantial workforce. Those Israelite slaves would have been a significant part of the total slave labor force of Ramesses II (we know from Egyptian writings that Egypt had slaves from various other countries).

So God asked Moses to go to the most powerful king of one of the most powerful nations in the world and persuade him to give up five thousand of his slave labor force, which played a key role in his massive building plans. It is rather like a foreigner going to the president of the United States and asking if he could take away from Silicon Valley in California five thousand scientists and their families and transport them to another country. The whole idea is preposterous. It is, I believe, totally clear that Ramesses II would never, ever let his Israelite slaves leave Egypt permanently.

So Moses was given what I call the Exodus strategy to achieve his mission. God says to Moses, "You and the elders of Israel are to go to the king of Egypt and say to him, 'The Lord, the God of the Hebrews has met with us. Let us take a three-day journey into the desert to offer sacrifices to the Lord our God'" (Exodus 3:18). In other words, Moses did not ask Pharaoh the impossible request that the Israelites should leave Egypt permanently. Instead, he made the almost impossible request that they leave temporarily for a three-day journey into the desert to make sacrifices to their God. Some biblical scholars have inferred from this that Mount Sinai was a three-day journey away from Egypt, but this interpretation is wrong: no mountain was mentioned by Moses. Instead, this request to make a temporary three-day journey into the desert for religious purposes was a clever strategy to get the Israelites out of Egypt. Moses would have known that if he could persuade Pharaoh to agree to a three-day journey, then the Israelites would be allowed to take out food and water to last for about a week (supplies for three days out plus three days back plus one day for sacrifices). In addition, the Israelites would be allowed to take out animals for sacrifices and for food. So this "three-day journey for sacrifices" strategy would in fact enable the Israelites to take out of Egypt substantial quantities of food, water, and animals without arousing the suspicion of the Egyptians that they really planned a permanent exit.

However, clearly it would be almost impossible to persuade

Pharaoh to let the Israelites leave for a three-day journey. Why should a powerful king grant such a request to mere slaves, and lose their labor for a whole week? So God provided another part of the Exodus strategy. He said to Moses, "I know that the king of Egypt will not let you go unless a mighty hand compels him. So I will stretch out my hand and strike the Egyptians with all the wonders that I will perform among them. After that, he will let you go" (Exodus 3:19–20). So God sent ten plagues upon the Egyptians, of increasing severity, until the Egyptians in desperation let the Israelites go on their three-day journey. Thus Moses was able to bring the Israelites out of Egypt.

Moses was then instructed to bring the Israelites to Mount Sinai. But again, this was a near impossibility. How could he lead five thousand men plus their wives and children across barren deserts? The provisions they would have taken with them from Egypt would have lasted at most one week, although the animals would last longer for food. Even if they carefully chose routes with freshwater wells and springs, there would be times when they would need to buy food and water from the local inhabitants. In addition, it can be cold in the desert at night. How were the Israelites to survive? This brings us to the third part of the Exodus strategy. God said to Moses, "I will make the Egyptians favorably disposed towards these people, so that when you leave you will not go empty-handed. Every woman is to ask her neighbor and any woman living in her house for articles of silver and gold and for clothing, which you will put on your sons and daughters. And so you will plunder the Egyptians" (Exodus 3:21–22).

We should remember that the Egyptians were the richest nation in the Near East. The implication of the above passage is that the Egyptian people would be so glad to be rid of the plagues that they would give the Israelites plenty of gold, silver, and clothing to adorn themselves when they made their sacrifices in the desert. In fact, the Israelites used some of the gold and silver to decorate the Ark of the Covenant, which they later made at Mount Sinai, and some to purchase food and water when necessary, as recorded in Deuteronomy 2:6: "You are to pay them in silver for the food you eat and the water you drink."

So God provided three enabling mechanisms for Moses to achieve his mission. First, there was a brilliant game plan for the Israelites to

escape from Egypt: tell Pharaoh you want to go on a three-day journey into the desert to make sacrifices to your God. Second, there was
a tough strategy to achieve this: to strike the Egyptians with plagues
until the Egyptians gave in. Third, to make the Egyptians so relieved
that the plagues have ended that they happily give the Israelites gold
and silver to use as currency and clothing to keep them warm. Thus
the Exodus from Egypt was carefully planned in advance. Moses had a
strategy to achieve the seemingly impossible.

The American anthropologist and writer Margaret Mead once said,
"Never doubt that a small group of thoughtful committed citizens can
change the world: indeed, it's the only thing that ever has." In fact,
that "small committed group" can be just one person with a vision.
Moses was such a person, inspired by his vision of God in the burning
bush to have a vision for the future of his people and to lead them out
of Egypt on an absolutely extraordinary journey. How many people
did Moses lead out of Egypt? This has been a puzzle for many years.
The solution hinges on the real meaning of some very large numbers
in the Old Testament. As we will see, a key Hebrew word has been
misinterpreted and the numbers of Israelites at the Exodus is very different from what is generally believed. All will be revealed in the next
chapter.

EIGHT

HOW MANY PEOPLE
WERE IN THE EXODUS?

*And so he [Moses] counted them in the Desert of Sinai. . . . All
the men twenty years old or more who were able to serve in the army
were listed by name. . . . The number in the tribe of Reuben was
46,500. . . . The total number was 603,550.*

Numbers 1:19, 20, 21, 46

As we saw in chapter 3, we have to be careful when interpreting large numbers in ancient literature. The 480 years
between the Exodus and building Solomon's temple could
have meant a literal 480 years, but it could also have meant twelve
generations of a nominal forty years each. By considering other evidence we were able to show that the latter interpretation is almost
certainly the correct one.

What about the very large number of people the Old Testament
says were involved in the Exodus? According to the passage from the
book of Numbers quoted above, there were 603,550 men twenty
years old and older. This implies a total number of men, women, and
children of at least two million. This is a huge number of people, particularly three thousand years ago when populations were a lot smaller
than they are today. In addition, this very large number of people
seems to be inconsistent with other biblical statements that imply a
much smaller number of Israelites at the Exodus. So we have another
puzzle to solve involving Old Testament numbers. As with the 480
years we looked at in the earlier chapter, 603,550 men can clearly be
interpreted literally, but is there another interpretation that is equally

valid? Unlikely as it may seem, I think there is, and the answer is fascinating. First, however, let's look at the problems involved if we try to interpret 603,550 men literally.

Problems with the Very Large Numbers in Numbers

Let me list some of the problems involved:

1. "The Israelites went up out of Egypt armed for battle" (Exodus 13:18). Over 600,000 Israelites armed for battle would have been an incredibly formidable army. For example, it would have been nine times as great as the whole of the Duke of Wellington's army (69,000 men) at the famous battle of Waterloo in 1815. According to the ancient Greek historian Herodotus, 600,000 Israelites would have outnumbered the total number of soldiers in the Egyptian army. Why then should such a mighty Israelite army have been "terrified" by the Egyptian army that pursued them when they left Egypt, as described in Exodus 14:10? Why should such a huge Israelite army have struggled to defeat some tribesmen called the Amalekites, as described in Exodus 17:8?

2. The clue of the midwives. Exodus 1:15 states, "The king of Egypt said to the Hebrew midwives, whose names were Shiphrah and Puah . . ." I think this phrase clearly implies that there were only two Israelite midwives, particularly since they are named. But only two midwives would be hopelessly inadequate for a population of over two million people.

3. In various places in the Exodus account the impression is given that the number of Israelites was not large. For example, when Moses was speaking to them at Mount Sinai he said, "The Lord did not set his affection on you and choose you because you were more numerous than other peoples, for you were the fewest of all peoples" (Deuteronomy 7:7). In addition, the Bible states that initially the Israelites were too few to occupy the promised land (Exodus 23:30). Yet two million Israelites would easily have filled the promised land, and until the relatively recent

Jewish immigration into Israel the total population of Israel was only about one million.

4. Now for a point involving the size of families. The book of Numbers states, "The total number of first-born males a month or more old was 22,273" (Numbers 3:43). However, if the number of Israelite men aged twenty and over was 603,550, then very roughly the total number of Israelite men of all ages would have been about one million, because in ancient civilizations roughly half the population was under twenty. So what was the average family size? This was the total number of men divided by the total number of firstborn men, that is one million divided by 22,273, which is about fifty. So the average mother must have had fifty sons. But we've forgotten about the women. The average mother must have had about fifty daughters as well! In fact, if we interpret the numbers in the book of Numbers as being literally true, then the average mother must have had about a hundred children. This is unlikely!

For these reasons, it is difficult to believe that the very large numbers in the book of Numbers should be interpreted literally. In fact, most biblical scholars believe they are fictitious numbers that shouldn't be taken seriously. But we saw in chapter 3 that the number 480 wasn't fictitious, and it was to be taken seriously. In 1 Kings 6:1, 480 years has a real meaning: twelve generations of a nominal forty years, which when properly understood enables us to date the Exodus. Are the very large numbers in Numbers like that? Do they have a meaning that has been forgotten, and can we discover the real meaning? Can we find out how many people were involved in the Exodus from Egypt? To do this we are going to have to understand the meaning of a certain Hebrew word that holds the key to unlocking this puzzle.

Words with Several Meanings

In the English language the same word can sometimes have a range of different meanings. Let's take the word *crab* as an example. This can mean a sea creature, a zodiacal constellation, a famous nebula called the crab nebula, a wild apple, or something that can be caught when rowing. (To "catch a crab" means that a rower leaves the oar too long in the water before repeating the stroke. The rower is then struck by the handle of the oar and falls backward in the boat.) The context usually makes clear the particular meaning intended, but there is obviously the potential for misunderstanding.

Similarly, in Hebrew the same word can sometimes have more than one meaning, and I was fascinated to find that this is the case for the Hebrew word 'eleph, which is the word translated "a thousand" in the Numbers texts quoted in this chapter.

The word 'eleph does indeed mean "a thousand." It has this meaning in "I am giving your brother a thousand shekels of silver" (Genesis 20:16), for example. I also believe it has this meaning in some texts in Numbers, for example, "He [Moses] collected silver weighing 1,365 shekels" (Numbers 3:50). In both these cases, and in many others in the Old Testament, it is correct to translate 'eleph as "a thousand."

However, 'eleph has another meaning, which is "group" (as in family, clan, or troop). It has this meaning in "My clan ['eleph] is the weakest in Manasseh." (Judges 6:15) and in "So now present yourselves before the Lord by your tribes and clans ['eleph]" (1 Samuel 10:19). The word 'eleph has carried these two meanings in Hebrew, "thousand" and "group," since ancient times, and Professor Alan Millard tells me that the equivalent word in ancient Assyrian has the same two meanings.

The possibility of misinterpretation arising because of the different meanings of 'eleph can be seen from different English translations of the same biblical texts. For example, the KJV and the RSV translate 1 Samuel 23:23 as, "All the thousands ['eleph] of Judah," whereas the more recent NIV reads, "All the clans of Judah." Similarly, in Joshua 22:14 the KJV translates 'eleph as "thousand," whereas the RSV and NIV have "clans." In both cases, interpreting 'eleph as "clans" seems correct. However, the important point is this: if expert Bible translators can misinterpret 'eleph as "thousand" when "clan" was intended by the original writer, then there is clearly scope for a scribe, or an editor, working on an ancient Hebrew text to interpret 'eleph as "thousand" when "group" (or family, clan, or troop) was intended. Since the numbers in Numbers refer to "all the men twenty years old or more who were able to serve in the army," I propose we use the word troop for a group of these military men.

The Clue of the Number 273

How do we decide in a particular text whether *'eleph* means "a thousand" or "troop"? Usually, the context makes this clear, so there is no problem. However, as we've seen, at times it will be unclear. This set me thinking: Could it be that the very large numbers in the book of Numbers, and possibly elsewhere, arise because of a misinterpretation of *'eleph?* In some of these large numbers has *'eleph* been interpreted as "thousand" when it should have been "troop"? How can we possibly know after three thousand years?

I was rereading the book of Numbers when suddenly one figure leaped off the page: the number was 273. This is where it occurs: "The 273 firstborn Israelites who exceed the number of the Levites" (Numbers 3:46). Why was I so forcibly struck by this number? First, because of its precision: 273 is clearly not a rounded number. Second, because it is *small:* amid all the large numbers in Numbers, 273 really stands out for its smallness, like a dwarf among giants. Third, 273 does not look like a "symbolic" number in the way that 3, 7, and 40 are sometimes symbolic numbers in the Bible. So I think there are good grounds for believing that the number 273 literally means 273.

I then performed a mathematical analysis of all the large numbers in Numbers based on the very reasonable assumption that the number 273 was factual. Don't worry, I'm not going to present the equations here, but if you want to see this, I have published it in the leading Old Testament journal *Vetus Testamentum* (vol. 48 [1998], pp. 196–213). Incidentally, the paper generated huge interest, including letters from scholars to the journal to which I replied in print, and many more letters to me personally. The response from nearly everyone was very positive. A leading British newspaper, the *Sunday Times,* even picked this up and ran a large article on my new interpretation.

Essentially, I argue in the paper, what the book of Numbers tells us is that there were 273 more firstborn Israelite men than the total number of Levite men, who were the priests. This may seem a very obscure clue, but it enabled me to write down and solve some mathematical equations. This enabled me to test which interpretation of *'eleph* is correct.

If *'eleph* is translated "thousand," then as we've seen, there were 603,550 Israelite men twenty years of age and older at the Exodus.

However, this figure is totally inconsistent with my mathematical analysis. On the other hand, if *'eleph* is translated as "troop," then the total number of men over twenty is 5,550 (a huge difference!). This means that the total number of men, women, and children at the Exodus was probably about 20,000.

Let me explain how my new interpretation works. The text quoted at the start of this chapter states, "The number in the tribe of Reuben was 46,500" (Numbers 1:21). The Hebrew text essentially says 46 *'eleph* and 500 men. The traditional interpretation of this is 46 thousand and 500 men, that is, 46,500 men. My suggested interpretation is 46 troops and 500 men. Thus there were 500 men in the tribe of Reuben over twenty years old, not 46,500 men. So interpreting *'eleph* as "troop" instead of "thousand" gives large differences in the numbers. In my new interpretation, the numbers in the tribes of Israel add up consistently to a total of 5,550 men twenty years of age and older.

Only one thing puzzled me. As we've just seen, my interpretation of the numbers in the tribe of Reuben is that there were 46 troops and 500 men. This means that there were only about ten men per troop. Isn't this much too small? Well, in a modern army it would indeed be much too small, but what about in 1300 B.C.? Do we know what troop sizes were like then?

In 1887, 380 clay tablets were discovered in Egypt by the local inhabitants at a place called Tell el-Amarna. They have come to be known as the Amarna tablets. The tablets are letters from foreign kings to the Egyptian pharaoh of the time, and they were written in the fourteenth century B.C., only slightly earlier than the date of the Exodus. In one of these tablets, King Rib-Addi of Byblos (in modern Lebanon) asked the king of Egypt for a contingent of troops of twenty men each. In another letter he asked for a troop of ten men from Nubia (in southern Egypt). This is remarkable confirmation that at the time of the Exodus, troop sizes were about ten men, just as I deduced from the book of Numbers when *'eleph* is interpreted as "troop." I believe this is a powerful argument in favor of this interpretation.

Near the start of this chapter I asked several questions. Do the numbers in Numbers have a meaning that has been forgotten? I believe the answer is yes. Can we discover the real meaning of these very large numbers? Yes again. Can we find out how many people were involved in the Exodus from Egypt? Yes, about twenty thousand.

In this chapter I've given a new interpretation of the very large numbers recorded in the book of Numbers. The much smaller numbers resulting from this new interpretation are consistent with other numbers in the text, which they weren't before, and also credible, which again they weren't before. In the new interpretation, *'eleph* is interpreted as "troop" instead of as "thousand," which is a known and valid interpretation.

Many people have had great difficulty in believing that the Exodus from Egypt as recorded in the Bible could have been a factual, historical event because of the impossibility of two million Israelites surviving in the desert for forty years. There is simply not enough drinking water to have supported this many Israelites in their travels. However, as we will see, I believe that twenty thousand Israelites could have survived. An important feature of this chapter, therefore, is that it has removed a major obstacle to belief in the Exodus and greatly added to the plausibility of the biblical account of the Exodus being a factual account. Of course, we will need more evidence if we are to claim that the Exodus really happened, but this chapter has removed a significant problem.

When Were Exodus and Numbers Written?

I've just argued that the numbers in Numbers had an original meaning that has been forgotten. So when was the book of Numbers written, and who wrote it? As we've seen in chapter 5, the traditional view is that Moses was the author of the first five books of the Old Testament. These books are often called the Pentateuch, meaning "five-volumed book." If Moses was the author, then they would have been written in the thirteenth century B.C., according to our date for Moses and the Exodus (see chapter 3).

However, during the last two hundred years, many scholars have come to believe that there are four underlying sources of the Pentateuch. These sources are called J, E, D, and P, and they are usually dated from the tenth to the fifth centuries B.C. So what are the facts?

First, nowhere does the Bible claim that Moses wrote all of the Pentateuch, but it does claim that he wrote some of it. For example, "At the Lord's command Moses recorded the stages in their [the Israelites'] journey" (Numbers 33:2). However, since the book of

Deuteronomy records the death of Moses (Deuteronomy 34), it is clear that Moses could not have written all of the Pentateuch.

Second, we can look at the style and the language used in the Pentateuch. If we read a Shakespeare play, for example, then it is obvious from the spelling and grammar used that this wasn't written today. Or look at the writing in figure 1.2, pg. 8, made in 1680. It is very clear that this wasn't written today. Similarly, experts can look at the spelling and grammar used in the standard Hebrew text of the Pentateuch we have today and deduce that it was written much later than the thirteenth century B.C. It is impossible to say with our present state of knowledge exactly when it was written, but scholars like Professor Alan Millard date the text to somewhere between the tenth and sixth centuries B.C., and some other scholars date it even later.

As I've said above, many scholars believe there were four main sources of the Pentateuch, the earliest of which comes from the tenth century B.C. Throughout this book I will give evidence that suggests that at least some of the book of Exodus was written by an eyewitness, and I see no reason why this could not have been Moses himself. Therefore, my very tentative conclusion is that although an editor may have put together the text of the first five books of the Bible some time in the tenth to sixth centuries B.C., the original source(s) of this text may be much earlier, and go back to Moses. This would explain the factual reliability I keep finding in the books of Exodus and Numbers. It would also explain how the original meaning of the numbers of Israelites recorded by Moses in the Desert of Sinai has been misinterpreted by an editor hundreds of years later and incorrectly transmitted, because the editor incorrectly understood the meaning of 'eleph.

In the next chapter we look at the plagues of Egypt. Were these a series of independent events? Or did one plague lead to another in an escalating sequence of natural events? Can modern science explain the plagues? Can we tell if the order of the plagues has been faithfully preserved since the time of Moses? Come with me to learn how the water of the Nile was turned to blood, why this was followed by a plague of frogs, and much, much more.

NINE

THE PLAGUES OF EGYPT

Moses struck the water of the Nile, and all the water was turned into blood. The fish in the Nile died, and the river smelled so bad that the Egyptians could not drink its water. . . . Aaron stretched out his hand over the waters of Egypt and the frogs came up and covered the land. . . . Aaron struck the dust of the ground, gnats came upon men and animals. . . . Dense swarms of flies poured into Pharaoh's palace and into the houses of all his officials. . . . All the livestock of the Egyptians died. . . . Festering boils broke out on men and animals.

Exodus 7:20–21; 8:6, 17, 24; 9:6, 10

For British farmers, mad cow disease has been a recent plague of biblical proportions. A U.K. government-commissioned report states that 200,000 cows have died from it, and over 3 million cattle have been deliberately slaughtered and incinerated to remove them from the food chain. Hundreds of farmers have lost their jobs, and over one hundred humans have died a slow and terrible death from the human form of mad cow disease. We do not know how many more people in the U.K. will die from this dreadful disease, but many people ate BSE-infected beef, and the incubation period is very long: between ten and forty years. Mad cow disease has now spread to many other countries, and as I write this chapter, hundreds of thousands of cattle are being slaughtered in Germany. Various countries, including the U.S., are refusing to accept blood from the U.K. for transfusions because of the risk that the blood may be infected with the human form of mad cow disease.

The spread of mad cow disease has some interesting parallels with the plagues of Egypt, so we will explore its origins further. Mad cow disease is believed to have started when infected cow and sheep remains were made into a feed for cattle. The cows then developed a fatal brain disease called BSE (bovine spongiform encephalopathy), which is slowly progressive. The cows foam at the mouth and stagger about uncontrollably, hence the popular name "mad cow disease." Many (but certainly not all) scientists believed that BSE in cows could not cross the species barrier and affect humans. The minister for agriculture in the U.K. government appeared on television and deliberately fed his daughter a hamburger in front of millions of surprised viewers in a desperate attempt to protect the livelihood of farmers and reassure the British public that beef was safe to eat. He was like a latter-day pharaoh trying to persuade his people that the plague of mad cow disease would go away and not affect them.

Tragically, the U.K. government was wrong. Eating BSE-infected meat can cause a related human brain disease, vCJD (variant Creutzfeldt-Jakob disease), which eventually kills humans in a terrible form of death. Fortunately, scientists now know enough about the spread of this dreadful disease (although we still don't fully understand this complex brain disorder) that we can limit its progression around the world. However, if we did not have this scientific knowledge about how BSE spreads to humans, then undoubtedly many more people would have died throughout the world from vCJD and it would have become a worldwide plague.

In 1990 the students at my college in Cambridge, Selwyn College, were very concerned that beef was still being fed to them. "You don't need to worry," said the college bursar, "your beef is cheap beef from the Czech Republic that has no reported cases of BSE. Only the college fellows [that is, the professors] are given British beef." A quick-witted student responded, "But is mad cow disease transmittable from fellows to humans?"

What happened in the U.K. mad cow disaster was a connected chain of events. The remains of sheep and cows were fed to cattle, which developed the plague of mad cow disease, which killed the cattle. Humans ate infected beef, which led to a plague of vCJD, which killed the humans. The exact sequence of events is important. It appears that if the same infected remains of sheep and cows are fed to pigs and poultry instead of to cows, then the pigs and poultry do not become infected, and the humans who eat the pigs and poultry do not develop vCJD. It appears that humans develop vCJD via cows and not via pigs.

There is, therefore, a specific biological route for humans to become infected with vCJD. In this chapter we are going to travel back three thousand years and ask the following fascinating question: Did the plagues of Egypt, like the modern infection of humans with vCJD, follow a biological sequence in which one plague led to another?

In chapter 7 we left Moses in Midian at the burning bush, having received his orders and strategy. The book of Exodus records that Moses then returned to Jethro, collected his wife and two sons, put them on donkeys (the known means of transport at the time), and headed back for Egypt, no doubt using the same ancient trade route linking Egypt and Arabia that he had used when coming to Midian after fleeing for his life from Egypt. Moses knew it was safe to return to Egypt since he had heard that the pharaoh who had wanted to kill him was now dead.

The Plagues of Egypt

Moses, with the help of his brother Aaron, then commenced his cut-and-thrust contest with the king of Egypt, probably Ramesses II, trying to persuade him to temporarily release the Israelites to make a three-day journey into the desert to offer sacrifices to their God. The mighty pharaoh refused, and the plagues followed, of increasing severity, as described in detail in Exodus 7–11.

The famous Egyptologist Flinders Petrie observed in 1911, "The order of the plagues was the natural order of such troubles on a lesser scale in the Egyptian season, as was pointed out long ago." In other words, it has long been realized that the plagues follow a natural connected sequence. A number of scholars have tried to identify the scientific causes underlying each plague and to show how one plague led to another. The most detailed study, published in 1957–58, is by Greta Hort, a professor of English literature at Aarhus University in Denmark, who consulted widely with scientists in her research. The most recent work, in 1996, is by Marr and Malloy in the U.S. Dr. John S. Marr was for many years the principal epidemiologist for the New York City Department of Health. He has published many papers on infectious diseases and lectured throughout the U.S. Curtis Malloy is a research associate with the Medical and Health Research Association of New York City whose research specialties include infectious diseases and epidemiology. Their work has received considerable publicity in the press and on TV (see, for example, the booklet *The Ten Plagues of Egypt* by Platt, published to accompany a TV program). In this chapter we build upon, and in some cases correct, the work of Hort and also Marr and Malloy, and we will give the most up-to-date reconstruction yet of what happened in the plagues of Egypt. As we will see, it is a fascinating story.

The First Plague:
A River of Blood

I will describe each plague in the words of the Old Testament. In the first plague, "Moses struck the water of the Nile, and all the water was turned into blood. The fish in the Nile died, and the river smelled so bad that the Egyptians could not drink its water" (Exodus 7:20–21).

This was not the first time the water of the Nile had "turned into blood." An ancient Egyptian text, *The Admonitions of Ipuwer*, states, "Lo, the Nile overflows yet none plough for it. . . . Lo, the river is blood. As one drinks of it one shrinks from the people and thirsts for water." The date of this Egyptian text is uncertain, with some Egyptologists dating it at around 1600 B.C., but almost certainly it was written well before the time of the Exodus from Egypt (about 1300 B.C.; see chapter 3). Hence the Nile had "turned into blood" on an earlier occasion from that described in the book of Exodus. However, the Exodus event seems more severe because "the Egyptians could not drink its water," whereas in the writings of Ipuwer, it appears that they did drink the water, although with great distaste.

"Red tides" in saltwater seas are not uncommon. They are due to what are called algal blooms. Algae are microscopic single-celled plants that live in the sea and estuaries (coastal bodies of water where freshwater from rivers flows into saltwater from the ocean) and occasionally in freshwater lakes and ponds. There are many thousands of species of algae, but only about one hundred of these are harmful. Sometimes the algae grow very fast, or "bloom," accumulating into dense visible patches near the surface of the water (there can be 60 million cells per quart of water) and giving the water an intense color—another reason the algae are said to "bloom." *Red tide* is the popular name given to this because certain algae species contain red pigment. Red tides, in fact, are not associated with tides at all, and red tides are usually not harmful. There are also brown-colored algae that give rise to "brown tides," green- and blue-colored algae, and colorless algae. The U.K. national newspaper the *Independent* wrote on April 14, 1998,

> It looks like a biblical plague. The waters around Hong Kong have succumbed to a scourge known as the red tide, which is gobbling up marine life. This lethal build-up of toxic microscopic organisms has occurred before but never with the vengeance with which it has hit Hong Kong in recent weeks. Sham Cunhung, Assistant Director of Agriculture and Fisheries, said yesterday that it had wiped out 150,000 tons of fish, half of Hong Kong's fish stock, in just four weeks.

Although red tides in saltwater seas are relatively well known, they are unknown in flowing freshwater rivers, although they can occur in static freshwater lakes and ponds. So was the first plague of the Nile (a *freshwater* river) turning blood red due to a red tide? Most previous investigators of the plagues have thought so, but they have not fully appreciated the subtleties of the science. For example, Hort identified two organisms, *Euglena sanguinea* and *Haematoccus pluvialis,* as being responsible. These are indeed red, but they do not produce toxins to kill the fish. So what turned the river Nile red and killed the fish in it? I would like to spend some time on this because it is a fascinating story.

The famous ancient historian Herodotus called Egypt "the gift of the Nile," because if it were not for the Nile, Egypt would have been a barren desert land supporting a very small population. If we are to understand about life in ancient Egypt, we therefore need to know something about the properties of the life-enabling river Nile. In particular, we need to know why and when the Nile floods each year because, as we will see, the first plague is connected with the Nile flooding.

The Nile has three main sources: the White Nile, the Blue Nile, and the Atbara, all of them lying south of Egypt in central Africa. The Nile therefore flows from south to north, coming up through Egypt into the Mediterranean Sea (see map 3.1, pg. 30). The White Nile originates at Lake Victoria on the equator, where the daily rains of the tropics give the river a fairly constant flow. The Blue Nile rises in the mountains of Abyssinia. Here the summer rainfall is greater than in winter, and also the snow on the high mountains melts in the summer. The Atbara also originates in Abyssinia and has similar characteristics to the Blue Nile. Hence the water flow in the Blue Nile and Atbara is much greater in summer than in winter.

This large increase in water in the Blue Nile and Atbara is responsible for the annual flooding of the Nile in Egypt. The Nile begins to rise in late June and reaches its maximum height in September, after which it begins to subside. The Nile was vital for ancient Egypt, not only because it provided almost the only source of freshwater for the Egyptians, but also because the annual flooding deposited organic matter and nutrients that helped to fertilize the fields. Near Cairo the Nile branches off into the delta region, and in ancient times it flowed into the Mediterranean at seven points. The English word *delta* is derived from the Greek letter delta because capital delta in Greek is the shape of a triangle. From the map of the Nile Delta (see map 3.1, pg. 30) it is obvious why the Nile Delta is so called.

The Nile River has changed dramatically in recent years due to the building of the Aswan High Dam in 1970 in order to generate electricity using hydroelectric power. Therefore, since 1970 there has been no natural annual flooding of the Nile north of Aswan, although water is sometimes released from the dam, and the seven branches of the Nile in the Nile Delta region (map 3.1 shows the three main branches) have been reduced to two. However, the state of the Nile River before the building of the Aswan High Dam is well documented, and I will return to this later.

In the summer, as the swollen waters of the Blue Nile and Atbara travel in torrents through the steep gorges of Abyssinia, they pick up large quantities of the red earth in those regions. The red earth is so striking it is given a special name, *Roterde* (which is German for "red earth"): particles of this red earth suspended in the water do indeed give the Nile River a reddish color. Some people have claimed, therefore, that the Nile was "turned to blood" because it was carrying this red silt in the water at the time of the annual

Nile flood. Indeed, it is interesting to note that the Egyptian sage Ipuwer appears to link the river's turning to blood with the Nile overflowing since he writes, "The Nile overflows yet none plough for it . . . ; the river is blood."

However, red soil particles don't cause huge quantities of fish to die, so was there a natural mechanism for the first plague? I believe that recent research on harmful algal blooms provides the answer. Harmful red tides are due to toxic red algae called dinoflagellates. Dinoflagellates (also known as "whirling whips") are minute single-celled organisms having two whiplike flagella by which they move. Various kinds of toxic dinoflagellates produce powerful neurotoxins that can kill fish and other animals. The algae that bloom and contain toxins are called by scientists "harmful algal blooms." We still do not know a lot about them, but we do know that three factors are required to make algae bloom and produce toxins: long hours of daylight, warm temperatures, and water that is rich in nutrients.

As we saw above, harmful algae live in the saltwater sea and in estuaries. In estuaries, the fresh river water is blocked from streaming into the open sea by surrounding land or fringing salt marshes or barrier islands. In the U.S., Puget Sound, Chesapeake Bay, and Indian River Lagoon are all estuaries. In the U.K. we have the Severn Estuary, for example. Intriguingly, there is an estuary in Egypt—the Nile Delta (see map 3.1, pg. 30), which I described above. The Nile Delta is formed from the branches of the Nile that feed the marshlands that separate the Nile from the Mediterranean Sea. The mixing of fresh and saltwater in estuaries throughout the world creates a unique environment that brims with many kinds of life. The estuary holds nutrients from both the land and the ocean.

It is in this estuary environment that a number of harmful algae live. Some of them have been discovered only since 1985 following investigations into the deaths of millions of fish in estuaries in the U.S., but they have probably existed for thousands of years. As far as I am aware, no one has looked to see what toxic algae exist today in the Nile Delta, but whether they do or not tells us little because the Nile Delta has changed so much since pharaonic times, largely due to the building of the Aswan High Dam. According to the celebrated oceanographer

Jacques Cousteau, the algae that lived in the silt of the Nile Estuary have disappeared since the building of the dam, as have the larger fish.

Where on the Nile River did the first plague occur? Exodus 1:11 says that the Israelites were working at Pithom and Rameses, building store cities for Pharaoh. In chapter 3 I identified ancient Rameses with the capital of Egypt in the time of Ramesses II, located at modern Qantir, and I'll give further details in chapter 11. And where is Qantir? On the Nile Delta (see map 3.1, pg. 30)! Thus the first plague occurred not on the freshwater Nile River, but in the Nile Estuary, exactly where toxic algae are able to live. The time of year, as we've seen earlier, was probably July to September, the hottest part of the Egyptian summer, during the Nile inundation when nutrient-rich soil was brought down the Nile. The most likely time was September, when the Nile flooded and the nutrients would have been at a maximum. So I suggest that at the time of the first plague, toxic red algae were caused to bloom by this combination of very hot weather and the nutrient-rich water. The resulting toxins killed the fish, just as in the estuaries of the U.S. more recently, and the dead fish caused the river to stink, just as described in the book of Exodus. The blood red color of the Nile Estuary was due to a combination of red soil particles and red pigment from harmful algal blooms. Various red toxic algae could have been responsible, for example *Cochlodinium heterolobatum,* which produced red tides on the York River in Chesapeake Bay in the U.S. in the 1990s, killing millions of fish, or *Gymnodinium breve* or species of *Glenodinium,* and so forth. Since it is impossible now to identify the particular species of algae responsible, I propose we use the general scientific term *harmful algal blooms* to refer to these toxic red algae. We therefore have a scientifically verifiable phenomenon for the first plague that is consistent with the description in the book of Exodus.

Finally, an interesting point of detail. How long does it take for fish to die after an outbreak of harmful algal blooms? Studies in the U.S. have shown that typically it takes days or sometimes weeks. Exodus 8:1 says that the second plague started seven days after the first plague—by which time the fish would be dying, rotting, and stinking. Hence we have a consistent scientific story for the first plague.

The Second Plague:
An Invasion of Frogs

This is how the Old Testament describes the second plague:

> The Lord said to Moses, "Go to Pharaoh and say to him, 'Let my people go, so that they may worship me. If you refuse to let them go, I will plague the whole country with frogs. The Nile will teem with frogs. They will come up into your palace and your bedroom and onto your bed, into the houses of your officials and on your people, and into your ovens and kneading troughs. . . .' And the Lord did what Moses said. The frogs died in the houses, in the courtyards and in the fields. They were piled into heaps and the land reeked of them. (Exodus 8:1–14)

What a vivid picture of huge numbers of frogs everywhere, even in the bedroom and on the bed of the king of Egypt! Frogs underfoot, frogs even in the ovens where food was cooked. (What's for dinner? Not toad in the hole again!) Seriously, this plague of frogs must have been truly horrible. Figure 9.1, on the next page, gives an artist's impression of the plague of frogs taken from an early English Bible

The plague of frogs is a natural consequence of the mass death of the fish: the decaying fish would pollute the waters of the Nile Estuary, forcing the frogs ashore, and frogs and toads (the Hebrew word translated "frogs" covers both) are known to travel toward sources of light and heat in search of the insects they feed upon. This fits well the description in the Old Testament of the frogs entering houses, bedrooms, ovens, and kneading troughs.

According to the commentary on the book of Exodus by Houtman, the Nile normally teemed with frogs in September–October, and as we have stated earlier, the rise of the Nile reached its maximum in September, which was the most probable time for harmful algae to produce toxic blooms. Thus a tentative time scale starts to emerge for the plagues. The first plague occurred when the Nile was near its maximum, probably in September. The second plague occurred one week later, in September–October when the number of frogs in the

The Plague of Frogs.   Excod: 8.

ſpake unto Moſes, ſay unto Aron ſtretch forth
: & cauſe Frogs to come upon ẏ lãd of Egypt. v. 1.
ſtretched out his hand over ẏ waters of Egypt,
ame up. and covered ẏ land of Egypt. v. 6.

9.1. Plague of frogs, from a 1680 English Bible.

Nile was naturally at a maximum. This large number of frogs was driven onto the land by the polluted Nile water. When did all the plagues end? The final, tenth, plague occurred at Passover time (Exodus 12:1), corresponding to March–April in our calendar. Thus the ten plagues occupied a total time of about seven months: from September in one year to March–April the following year. This short time scale is consistent with the plagues' being an ecological cascade of events, with one event leading to another.

Hort speculated that the frogs died because they were infected with anthrax. However, I see no need for this hypothesis. When large numbers of frogs left the polluted Nile Estuary and entered houses, the famished frogs were not likely to find enough insects to survive, away from their natural ecosystem of the Nile. So I suggest the frogs suffered a mass death from starvation and dehydration. It was essentially a mass extinction due to lack of food.

The Third and Fourth Plagues:
Swarms of Gnats and Flies

After the plague of frogs came a swarm of gnats:

> Then the Lord said to Moses, "Tell Aaron, 'Stretch out your staff and strike the dust of the ground' and throughout the land of Egypt the dust will become gnats. . . ." And the gnats were upon men and animals. (Exodus 8:16–18)

Following the gnats there was a plague of flies:

> Then the Lord said to Moses, . . . "Say to Pharaoh, 'This is what the Lord says: let my people go so that they may worship me. If you do not let my people go I will send swarms of flies on you and your officials, on your people and into your houses. The houses of the Egyptians will be full of flies.'". . . And the Lord did this. Dense swarms of flies poured into Pharaoh's palace and into the houses of his officials, and throughout Egypt the land was ruined by the flies. (Exodus 8:20–24)

The mass death of the fish, which caused the river Nile to stink, and the rotting bodies of the frogs and toads, piled high into heaps, were followed, not surprisingly, by swarms of gnats and flies. In addition, the gnats and flies were free to breed rapidly because their natural predators, the frogs and toads, had suffered a mass population collapse. But what kind of insects are meant by the Old Testament words translated "gnats" and "flies"?

The Hebrew word translated "gnats" is a broad term that could mean various small flying insects such as mosquitoes, gnats, ticks, mites, midges, and so forth. Marr and Malloy point out that midge larvae feed on microorganisms in decaying animals such as fish and frogs and that the emergence of swarms of midges from "the dust of the ground" might well be how the ancient Hebrews would have described a plague of midges swirling up from the ground like a thick cloud of dust. A number of species of midges live in Egypt, and Marr and Malloy selected the biting midge, *Culicoides canithorax,* as the most likely candidate.

Houtman's commentary on Exodus states that in Egypt there are dense swarms of gnats, particularly in October and November, but he does not define which biological species is meant by "gnats." Hort suggests that the "gnats" were mosquitoes, which could reproduce quickly in the pools and puddles left by the retreating Nile (the Nile is in retreat after September). Without further evidence I believe we cannot be sure whether the gnats were midges or mosquitoes, but the next plague, the death of livestock, provides the key further evidence we need. As we shall see, the evidence strongly suggests that the gnats were *Culicoides* midges and not mosquitoes. Thus we have the Nile Estuary turning to blood (red algae) in September, the plague of frogs in September–October, and the plague of *Culicoides* midges in October–November.

What type of fly was involved in the plague of flies? Figure 9.2, facing page, shows what a fifteenth century A.D. artist thought. There are five main possibilities: the housefly, the blackfly, the horsefly, the tsetse fly, and the stable fly. Swarms of houseflies are unpleasant, but not nearly so unpleasant as some of the other candidates! Since the Exodus account suggests that the plague of flies was particularly unpleasant ("the land of Egypt was ruined by the flies"), we rule out the housefly. We eliminate blackflies because they do not breed very rapidly, and nei-

9.2. Plague of flies, from a woodcut in the 1469 Cologne Bible.

ther do they swarm ("I will send swarms of flies on you"). Horseflies also do not breed rapidly. Tsetse flies live mainly in tropical regions with a high rainfall, and not in the dry, arid conditions of Egypt.

We have therefore eliminated every candidate except one: the stable fly, *Stomoxys calcitrans*. The stable fly has a painful bite that punctures the skin and leaves behind an open wound, exposing the victim to infection. Stable flies also swarm and can breed very rapidly, with a female laying up to five hundred eggs at a time. The stable fly therefore admirably fits the description of the plague of flies given in the book of Exodus, and Hort and Marr and Malloy all argue for the stable fly's being the fourth plague.

The Fifth Plague:
The Death of Livestock

The horrors continued in a fifth plague:

> Then the Lord said to Moses, "Go to Pharaoh and say, . . . 'If you refuse to let my people go, the hand of the Lord will bring a terrible plague on all your livestock in the field—on your horses

and donkeys and camels and on your cattle and sheep and goats.'"... All the livestock of the Egyptians died. (Exodus 9:1–6)

There is an interesting mention of camels in the above quotation from Exodus. Most scholars argue that this is a late addition to the text because, as we have seen, camels were not used for transport at the time of the Exodus (thirteenth to twelfth centuries B.C.). However, we also know from chapter 4 that evidence suggests camels were domesticated for milk in that same period of time.

There are many diseases that can kill livestock. Can we deduce which particular disease might have killed those animals in Egypt three thousand years ago? So far we have seen that the ancient manuscripts of the Old Testament are remarkably accurate in describing the crossing of the river Jordan, so we look to the details of the account of the fifth plague to see if these help in pinning down precisely what might have killed the livestock.

The first detail is that the disease killed a range of animals, but there is no record of humans dying. This rules out bacterial infections such as anthrax, for anthrax would have resulted in substantial human deaths. We can also rule out Rift Valley fever, which is a viral disease spread by mosquitoes, because Rift Valley fever doesn't affect horses, and horses are specifically mentioned as being killed in the Old Testament account.

The second detail in the biblical account is that only certain animals are listed as being killed by the plague, and these are all hoofed mammals: horses, donkeys, camels, cattle, sheep, and goats. Other animals common in Egypt at the time are not mentioned, for example, cats, birds, or pigs. It therefore appears that the disease was specific to certain animals.

Two separate viruses are required to kill all the animals listed, but, importantly, they are spread by the same insect and can therefore be spread at the same time. The first virus is African horse sickness, for which the usual mode of transmission is the *Culicoides* midge, although occasionally mosquitoes can transmit the virus. The second is a related virus called bluetongue, which kills cattle, sheep, goats, and camels.

Culicoides is again the usual mode of transmission of bluetongue, and in this case mosquitoes are not believed to spread the virus. Both viruses cause death of the animals involved within a few days. Since the *Culicoides* midge is the main carrier of both viruses, we can identify this as the most likely cause of the third plague of "gnats," and we can rule out mosquitoes.

Thus the sequence of ecologically connected plagues continues, and we have deduced the probable scientific causes: the first plague of the Nile turning to blood (due to red algae and probably in September) gave rise to the second plague of frogs (in September–October). The third plague of swarms of gnats (*Culicoides* midges) and the fourth plague of swarms of flies (the stable fly), were facilitated by the mass death of the frogs and toads, their natural predator when alive and also the natural food, when dead and decaying, for the midge and fly larvae. The fifth plague of the death of livestock was then due to African horse sickness and bluetongue spread by the *Culicoides* midges of the third plague.

The Sixth Plague: The Plague of Boils

The sixth plague followed:

> Then the Lord said to Moses and Aaron, "Take handfuls of soot from a furnace and have Moses toss it into the air in the presence of Pharaoh. It will become fine dust over the whole land of Egypt, and festering boils will break out on man and animals throughout the land.". . . And festering boils broke out on man and animals. (Exodus 9:8–10).

Unlike the fifth plague, which affected only certain animals, this sixth plague of boils afflicted both animals and humans. There are various possible causes of boils and sores on the skin. Marr and Malloy have analyzed these and suggest that the most likely possibility is a bacterium called *Pseudomonas mallei*, which exists throughout Africa and the Middle East and is popularly known as glanders. Glanders produces festering boils in both animals and humans and was used as a biological warfare agent in the First World War. It is a highly contagious infection that is spread in the air, by direct contact, and by fly bites. Hort suggests that this sixth plague of boils was skin anthrax, which again can be transmitted by fly bites.

I have investigated the cause of this sixth plague of boils, and I have to say that I believe the details given in the Old Testament description of this plague are insufficient for us to identify positively the boils as being due to glanders, skin anthrax, or another disease. The problem is that the Hebrew word translated "boils" is a general term covering a variety of skin sores or inflammations, and indeed in the English language we similarly use the word to refer to a variety of skin sores ranging from small skin cysts to mighty carbuncles! However, various infectious skin diseases can be transmitted by flies, including the stable fly. Although I believe we cannot positively identify the nature of the infectious "boils," can we say anything about the nature of the carrier fly? Unlikely as it seems at first sight, I think we may be able to.

After the Israelites leave Egypt, Deuteronomy 28:27 warns that if they are disobedient to the commands of God, "The Lord will afflict you [the Israelites] with the boils of Egypt." This statement is enlarged in verse 35 of the same chapter: "The Lord will afflict your knees and legs with painful boils that cannot be cured, spreading from the soles of your feet to the top of your head." Hence it appears that "the boils of Egypt" first affected the legs and feet. Now the stable fly of the fourth plague is known to favor biting its victims on the lower part of the body, in particular the legs and feet. Thus whatever the nature of the infectious boils, the details of the Old Testament account are consistent with the stable fly being the carrier.

So the sequence of plagues continues, with the first plague (river of blood) leading to the second (frogs and toads); the second to the third (biting midges) and to the fourth (stable flies); the third (biting midges) to the fifth (death of animals); the fourth (stable flies) to the sixth (boils). This disastrous (for the Egyptians) sequence of biological plagues has now run its course, Pharaoh has still not agreed to let the Israelites go, and the next plague is not a biological one but a physical one from the heavens: hail.

Let's pause for a moment and think about the likely effect of the first six plagues upon the Egyptian people. The first plague struck at the most important natural resource in the land of Egypt: the Nile. The water turned the color of blood, the fish died, and the rotting fish made the water stink so that the water couldn't be drunk. In a sense, this plague caused little discomfort since "the Egyptians dug along the Nile to get drinking water because they could not drink the water of the river" (Exodus 7:24). This may be the earliest recorded example of purifying water by filtration, in this case through the natural sandy banks of the Nile Estuary. The first plague demonstrated the power of Moses and his God over the liquid heart of Egypt: the Nile.

The second plague, of frogs or toads that died and decomposed in the heat of Egypt, brought the plagues into the houses, even into the bedrooms, of the Egyptians, thus escalating the effects of the first plague. The third plague was of biting midges, which bit both animals and humans, another escalation. Then came the fourth plague of stable flies: the bite of this fly is particularly painful, and it leaves open wounds, again in both animals and humans. So the gradual escalation of the plagues continued, but Pharaoh still did not give way, and by now the Egyptian people must have been in considerable discomfort. But the worst was still to come.

The fifth plague, the death of livestock, destroyed the Egyptian horses, donkeys, camels, cattle, sheep, and goats. In ancient times people measured their wealth, as well as their future food supplies, in terms of the number of animals they owned. This plague meant that Egyptian families lost their "life's savings" as well as their future meals and also their means of transport (donkeys). The sixth plague covered both humans and those animals that remained with "festering boils." By this stage the Egyptians must have been absolutely desperate. But still the intransigent pharaoh would not yield.

It is interesting to note that the scientific sequence of the first six plagues, which occurred over three thousand years ago, has been faithfully preserved in the ancient text of the book of Exodus. For example, if plague three, of biting midges, is interchanged with plague five, the death of livestock, then the scientific sequence is lost. Once again we see the remarkable accuracy and coherence of the Old Testament text.

What happened next is described in the following chapter. In particular, we will look at the science underlying the final four plagues, culminating in the death of the firstborn males. We will also ask the intriguing question of whether the death of the firstborn could be a natural consequence of earlier plagues, and the puzzling question of why the Israelites were unaffected by the plagues.

DEATH ON THE NILE

So the Lord rained hail on the land of Egypt; hail fell and lightning flashed back and forth. It was the worst storm in all the land of Egypt since it had become a nation. . . . The Lord made an east wind blow across the land all that day and all that night. By morning the wind had brought the locusts; they invaded all Egypt and settled down in every area of the country in great numbers. . . . They devoured all that was left after the hail, . . . Moses stretched out his hand towards the sky, and total darkness covered all Egypt for three days. . . . At midnight the Lord struck down all the firstborn in Egypt . . . and the firstborn of all the livestock as well.

Exodus 9:23, 24; 10:13, 14, 15, 22; 12:29

Six plagues of ever-increasing severity have come and gone, and Pharaoh still refuses to let the Israelites go. The mighty Pharaoh and his Egyptian gods have withstood all that Moses and his God can throw at them. Pharaoh is immovable, and it looks like a stalemate. However, four more plagues are to come, and this time physical threats alternate with biological ones (hail, locusts, darkness, death of the firstborn).

At first sight, these final four plagues appear to be unconnected events, unlike the sequence of the first six plagues. In addition, although the plagues of hail and locusts clearly are natural events, the terrible tenth plague, in which only the firstborn men and animals die, seems impossible to explain by science. Why should some fatal disease afflict only the firstborn? And why only males?

On the other hand, since the first six plagues form a connected scientific sequence, our expectations are raised that the last four may continue the sequence, but clearly it has to be in a rather different way because we now have physical as well as biological plagues. We must dig more deeply if we are to understand what really happened. We will now look at the last four plagues individually.

The Seventh Plague:
Hail

Exodus 9 gives us a glimpse of the terrible hailstorm:

> When Moses stretched out his staff towards the sky, the Lord sent thunder and hail, and lightning flashed back and forth. It was the worst storm in the land of Egypt since it had become a nation. Throughout Egypt hail struck everything in the fields—both men and animals; it beat down everything growing in the fields and stripped every tree. (Exodus 9:23–25)

In the previous chapter we saw that the first six plagues were all natural events but of an unusually high intensity. The graphic account of the hailstorm in the book of Exodus makes it dramatically clear that this was the case for the seventh plague as well; it was the worst hailstorm in Egyptian history, and it followed the six previous plagues, which had severely weakened the Egyptians and left them covered with painful bites and boils. It must have seemed that the entire wrath of heaven was being poured out on Pharaoh and his people.

In England, severe hailstorms are rare, and hailstones are usually tiny. However, I well remember being at a conference in southern Italy when a severe hailstorm suddenly struck. Everyone ran for cover, and afterward I was amazed to find that the steel bodies of the cars in the street were all covered in small dents from the hailstones. Steve Platt, in *The Ten Plagues of Egypt,* recounts a violent hailstorm in Israel and Jordan in October 1997 that injured sixty people, damaged cars and buildings, and deposited a layer of hail more than three feet thick. The diameter of hailstones can exceed 5 inches, and these solid pieces of ice from the sky can kill both animals and humans. In addition, the hail in Egypt would have caused immense damage to the crops; indeed, the book of Exodus records, "The flax and barley were destroyed since the barley was in the ear, and the flax was in bloom. The wheat and spelt [a grass related to wheat], however, were not destroyed, because they ripen later" (Exodus 9:31–32). As Hoffmeier notes in his book *Israel in Egypt,* the above verses in the book of Exodus show that the writer had an excellent knowledge of the Egyptian agricultural calendar since paintings from the Egyptian tomb of Paheri at el-Kab from the mid–Eighteenth Dynasty (about 1400 B.C.) depict the harvesting of barley and the pulling of flax occurring in adjacent fields, thus demonstrating that barley and flax matured together in ancient Egypt, as stated in the book of Exodus. Once again, we see the remarkable accuracy and attention to detail of the writer. From the description of the flax being in bloom and barley being in ear, but not the wheat and spelt, we can deduce from our knowledge of Egyptian agriculture that the plague of hail occurred in February–March.

The Eighth Plague:
Locusts

Following the hail came a plague of locusts.

> So Moses and Aaron went to Pharaoh and said to him, "This is what the Lord, the God of the Hebrews, says: 'Let my people go so they may worship me. If you refuse to let them go I will bring locusts into your country tomorrow. They will cover the face of the ground so that it cannot be seen. They will devour what little you have left after the hail, including every tree that is growing in your fields. . . .'" So Moses stretched out his staff over Egypt. . . . Never before had there been such a plague of locusts, nor will there ever be again. They devoured all that was left after the hail. (Exodus 10:3–15)

"Locust Army Marches on Its Stomach" is the headline on the front page of the *Times* newspaper of June 19, 2001. The article states:

> Plagues of locusts are devastating crops from Central Asia to the American Mid-West, sending farmers to the book of Exodus for salvation. Not since the Egyptians incurred the wrath of God have so many locusts had their day. A billion-strong army is on

the move, stretching far beyond the more normal swarming grounds of Africa and the Middle East.

This graphic description provides a modern picture of what the eighth plague of Egypt must have been like: truly devastating.

I cannot resist also quoting a later page of the same day's *Times*. Under a heading, "Quack Force Stamps Out Foe," the *Times's* Beijing correspondent reports,

> China's million-strong army of locust-eating ducks are trained to eat at the sound of a whistle. . . . The ducks apparently eat one pound of locusts every day. In the worst affected areas of Xinjiang province up to 10,000 locusts inhabit 10 square feet.

Just think of the locust density: 10,000 in 10 square feet!

Although, as we have seen, the first six plagues form a connected sequence, there appears to be no link between the seventh plague of hail and the eighth of locusts, and no one studying the plagues has suggested a connection. However, I was intrigued to read a letter in the *Times* of June 23, 2001, commenting on the locust articles of several days earlier. B. W. Budd, president of the Indian Civil Service Association, wrote,

> During the Second World War, we were confronted with an invasion of the desert locust in the province of Sind (now Pakistan). We took advantage of the most vulnerable stage in the life cycle of the locust. An invading swarm looks for damp sand in which to lay its eggs and then settles. During the three to four weeks from hatching to growing wings, when they can take to the air and move on, there is a point when all the hoppers in a particular batch move together in one direction like a mighty army. If trenches are dug in their path, they fall in, are unable to get out and can be buried.

Apart from the vivid picture of millions of locusts marching into trenches, the part of the letter that caught my eye was this: "An invading swarm looks for damp sand in which to lay its eggs." Just listen to what the book of Exodus says about the end of the plague of hail: "The thunder and the hail stopped, and the rain no longer poured down on the land" (Exodus 9:33). So the land was very, very wet. It was ideal territory for locusts to lay their eggs in. Immediately following the plague of hail, Moses and Aaron went to Pharaoh and said, "If you refuse to let them [the Israelites] go, I will bring locusts into your country *tomorrow* [my italics]. They will cover the face of the ground so that it cannot be seen" (Exodus 10:4–5). So the locusts came the day after the hail and rain stopped, when the ground was still wet, the locusts being brought in by an east wind (Exodus 10:13) but settling because of the damp sandy soil in which to lay their eggs. Hence the plague of locusts *was* linked to the plague of hail.

The desert locust (Latin name *Schistocerca gregaria*) is part of a large group of insects commonly called grasshoppers. Plagues of locusts occur only when conditions are favorable. For example, no locust plagues were reported anywhere in the world for the years 1970 to 1985. Desert locusts usually fly with the wind, so when the book of Exodus states, "The Lord made an east wind blow across the land all that day and all that night" and adds, "By morning the wind had brought the locusts" (Exodus 10:13), this is consistent with our modern knowledge of locust behavior. For a locust plague to occur, there must be wet soil, which attracts millions of overflying locusts to settle and lay their eggs. The Desert Locust Information Service of the Food and Agriculture Organisation of the United Nations states on its Web pages concerning the 1996–98 upsurge of locusts: "A regional upsurge affected countries along the Red Sea. It developed as a result of a cyclone in June 1996 and heavy rains in November." So, as we have already seen, it is clear that the plague of locusts at the time of the Exodus resulted from the plague of hail, which left the ground very wet.

The life cycle of the desert locust goes from eggs to hoppers to immature adults to mature adults. The eggs hatch to produce hoppers, which do not fly but travel by marching. The hoppers turn into pink immature adults, which have wings, can fly long distances with the wind, and feed voraciously when they land. The immature adults turn into yellow mature adults, which copulate and lay eggs. The female locust digs into the soil with her abdomen to lay her eggs, about four inches below the soil surface, and for the eggs to hatch the soil must be damp to at least this depth. Thus the hail and rain described in the book of Exodus provided the ideal conditions for the locusts to settle. In Egypt, locusts will swarm and breed at any time of the year, including winter, provided the conditions are right. In favorable conditions there can be five generations of locusts per year.

The immature adult locusts consume the most food and eat roughly their own weight in fresh food every day—that is, about 2 grams per day. (Just think of eating your own weight in food every day!) One ton of locusts, which is a very small part of an average swarm, eats the same amount of food in one day as about 10 elephants or 25 camels or 2,500 people. Just imagine the devastation caused by a plague of locusts!

So at the time of the Exodus, the desert locusts arrived just after the plague of hail, in February–March, attracted by the wet soil. The adult locusts devoured what little crops the Egyptians had left after the hail. The plague of locusts was caused by two natural phenomena occurring at the same time: the east wind, which brought the locusts over Egypt, and the very damp soil left from the plague of hail. A delightful fifteenth century A.D. woodcut illustration of the plague of locusts is shown in figure 10.1 on the next page.

The Ninth Plague:
Darkness

But the plagues were not yet over.

> Then the Lord said to Moses, "Stretch out your hand towards the sky so that darkness will spread over Egypt—darkness that can be felt." So Moses stretched out his hand towards the sky, and total darkness covered all Egypt for three days. No one could see anyone else or leave his place for three days. (Exodus 10:21–23)

I was in Kuwait on a scientific visit some years ago and walking along a street close to my hotel. Suddenly a mass of people came run-

10.1. Plague of locusts, from the 1469 Cologne Bible.

ning down the street toward me. I looked up, and behind them I saw a brown cloud stretching from the ground to high into the sky. I watched in amazement until I realized that this cloud, too, was heading toward me! So I, too, turned and ran, straight back to my hotel. I asked the doorman what was happening. "Dust storm," he said. "Hurry, go to your room." So I rushed to my room just in time to see the sun shining brightly through the window, and then, seconds later, totally blotted out by a thick, dark cloud of sand. It was so dark that I had to turn on the bedroom light, and the darkness lasted for several hours until the sandstorm subsided. Afterward I went out in the street again, to find sand piled up against shop doorways like driven snow after a snowstorm.

The sandstorm I had witnessed is called a *khamsin*, which is common in Egypt in the spring. *Khamsins* can last up to two or three days. I believe that the "darkness that can be felt," which lasted for three days, was a *khamsin*, because the description in Exodus fits a *khamsin* perfectly. In addition, we can deduce from the book of Exodus that the plague of darkness occurred in March, because it occurred after the plague of locusts and shortly before the Passover, which was in the first month of the Hebrew calendar (Exodus 12:1, "This month is to be for you the first month"), which corresponds to late March or early April in our calendar.

The first of the *khamsin* storms each year in Egypt normally occurs in March. This first dust storm of the year usually produces a particularly dense and dark dust cloud, because the red earth brought by the Nile from Abyssinia and deposited in Egypt after the retreat of the flooded Nile dries out and is whipped up into the air. Subsequent dust storms are normally less severe because some of the dust is lost in the Nile and in the sea. The ninth plague of darkness was clearly a particularly severe dust storm, which I suggest resulted from a particularly heavy Nile flooding six months earlier in September, depositing unusually large quantities of red earth. Hence the first plague led to the severity of the ninth. Thus we see that the first nine plagues all appear to be natural physical phenomena of unusually high severity, which are linked in a logical sequence. Readers may wonder why the writer of Exodus doesn't say that the three days of darkness were due to a dust storm, if indeed that was the case. There is an interesting parallel in the New Testament, where at the Crucifixion of Jesus, just before the Passover, there were three hours of darkness, starting at noon (Matthew 27:45). A section of the Sibylline Oracles (a collection of books in the Apocrypha in the form of prophesies but believed to be written after the events) describing the Crucifixion, and probably written before A.D. 160, states: "Dust is carried from heaven to earth, and all the brightness of the sun fails at midday from the heavens." This would seem to indicate an early tradition that the darkness at the Crucifixion was due to a dust storm. Similarly I suggest that the three days of darkness recorded in the book of Exodus were due to a dust storm. Indeed the phrase "darkness that can be felt"(Exodus 10:21) fits beautifully the darkness due to a dust storm, which can literally be felt, unlike normal darkness.

The Tenth Plague:
The Death of the Firstborn

The tenth and final plague was particularly shocking. Firstborn male animals and humans would all die. Those biblical scholars who accept that the first nine plagues may have been natural occurrences cannot accept that the terrible tenth plague could possibly have a natural origin. For example, the distinguished Jewish American biblical scholar Nahum Sarna, professor of Judaica at Florida Atlantic University, in his book *Exploring Exodus* writes, "The tenth and final visitation upon the Pharaoh and his people is the one plague for which no rational explanation can be given. It belongs entirely to the category of the supernatural." At first sight this would appear to be obvious, but before agreeing to this we should subject the situation to the scrutiny of science.

I would also like to point out again that, as we have explained in chapter 2, the ancient Israelites regarded natural events as the hand of God. For example, they would have known very well that the plague of hail was a natural event (a hailstorm), but to them it was also a supernatural event in which "the Lord rained hail on the land of Egypt" (Exodus 9:23). The Israelites believed that God worked in, through, and with natural events. We therefore explore the possibility that the death of the firstborn may have a rational explanation, even though at first sight this appears highly unlikely.

First, let us hear the description of the tenth plague in the words of the book of Exodus: "At midnight the Lord struck down all the firstborn in Egypt, from the firstborn of Pharaoh, who sat on the throne, to the firstborn of the prisoner, who was in the dungeon, and the firstborn of all the livestock as well" (Exodus 12:29). This plague was the ultimate disaster for the Egyptians since all the plans and dreams of a family were based upon the firstborn son. Previous plagues had targeted the Egyptians' crops and animals and had inflicted the Egyptian people with painful boils, but this tenth plague struck at the very heart of the Egyptian family and its future.

Viewing this account through the lenses of science, we must ask, Can there possibly be a scientific explanation for a disease that affects only the male firstborn of both humans and animals? We have seen that the first six plagues occurred in a biological sequence in which each plague was a consequence of an earlier one. In addition, the seventh plague, hail, helped to attract the eighth plague, locusts, by providing damp sand for their eggs; and the ninth plague, darkness, was assisted by the large amounts of red dust associated with the first plague. However, the tenth plague, death of the firstborn males, seems to be a separate, unconnected plague. Could it be that the first six plagues, which we have demonstrated to be in a strict ecological sequence in which one plague leads to the next, are like a guiding light, pointing us to the solution that all ten plagues are in fact in a logical sequence culminating in the death of firstborn males?

Marr and Malloy have cleverly suggested a possible scientific chain of events that might explain the death of firstborn males. I don't totally agree with them, so I am going to build upon and modify their theory here. However, let's start with the ideas of Marr and Malloy. The seventh plague of hail would have left whatever of the harvest that survived in a very wet state. The eighth plague of locusts would have consumed most of what was left of the crops and in addition deposited the locusts' feces all over the ground, contaminating the remainder of the harvest. The Egyptians probably would have known from experience that they shouldn't store wet grain, but this was a time of crisis because most of their harvest had been destroyed. Hence I suggest the Egyptians, desperate to save whatever they could of their crops of barley and flax after its near destruction by the hail and the locusts, would have gathered what remained and taken the damp, contaminated harvest to their granary stores.

In fact, locusts' feces are not necessary to make wet grain go moldy; there are always lots of dangerous spores ready to germinate if the conditions are right, which is why so much care has to be taken today in storing grain. However, the locusts' feces would undoubtedly have made the problem much worse. Even with good air circulation, wet grain can start to mold within a few hours in warm weather, but with poor air circulation the situation worsens dramatically. The *khamsin* dust storm would have covered the entrance to the grain stores with sand and dust, preventing air circulation within and keeping the Egyptians indoors for three days (Exodus 10:23), during which time toxic spores and the organisms from the feces of the locusts would have bred and multiplied in the damp and dark conditions.

What organisms could have been in the locusts' feces that would have thrived in the damp storerooms? Marr and Malloy found the answer: mycotoxins. Mycotoxins are poisons that can be deadly that are produced by fungi growing on organic substances such as crops. In

Britain in 1961 over 100,000 turkeys died after being fed moldy peanut meal contaminated by mycotoxins. In the former U.S.S.R. in the Second World War thousands of people and animals died from eating grain contaminated by mycotoxins. Marr and Malloy suggest that the most likely mycotoxin responsible for the deaths of humans and animals in the tenth plague was *macrocylic tricothecenes*, which causes massive internal bleeding leading to rapid and sudden death, just as described in the book of Exodus.

But why did only the firstborn males die? My tentative hypothesis is as follows. In many ancient societies, including Egypt and Israel, the firstborn sons were privileged. For example, they were fed first and often received a double portion. In Egypt, the firstborn son of the king was the crown prince, who was destined to succeed him. In a normal Egyptian family, the firstborn son took over responsibility for the family if the father died. The firstborn son was therefore someone very special. The Egyptians had just suffered six months of devastating plagues, which must have left them extremely short of food. In addition, the severe *khamsin* dust storm would have kept them indoors for three days. As soon as the dust storm stopped, who would have been fed the first meal of mycotoxin-contaminated grain from the almost empty grain store? The firstborn son, of course. And so the firstborn sons died a rapid and sudden death, just as described in the book of Exodus. The quantity of grain in the grain store may have been so low that, in many cases, there was no grain left for the rest of the family. I will return to this point again shortly. I tentatively suggest that this is why the firstborn sons died.

An apparently more difficult problem is why the firstborn male animals died as well as the firstborn sons. Marr and Malloy suggest that the first animals to feed at the feeding troughs full of grain would have been the most dominant ones, typically the eldest. My observation of animals at a feeding trough is that the eldest are often pushed aside by more vigorous younger ones! In addition, grain was precious in ancient civilizations, and I believe it would normally have been reserved for humans, with the livestock left to graze in the fields. So I think we have to look for a different explanation. We should not underestimate the novelty of what we are seeking to understand. For example, Hyatt in his commentary, *Exodus*, states concerning the tenth plague, "Such a plague, striking only the first-born of the Egyptians, sparing those of the Hebrews, and striking also the first-born of the livestock of the Egyptians, would be miraculous in the extreme; no-one has success-fully given a 'natural' explanation of this plague."

We will deal later with why the Hebrews were spared, but how can there be a "natural" explanation of why only the firstborn males of the livestock of the Egyptians died? I suggest that not only firstborn sons but also firstborn male animals were special. This was certainly the case for the ancient Hebrews. While they were still in Egypt the Israelites were instructed as follows: "Consecrate to me [God] every first-born male. The first offspring of every womb among the Is-raelites belongs to me, whether man or animal" (Exodus 13:2). The firstborn male animals were then set apart from the others: "Set apart for the Lord your God every first-born male of your herds and flocks. Do not put the first-born of your oxen to work and do not shear the first-born of your sheep. Each year you and your family are to eat them in the presence of the Lord your God at the place he will choose" (Deuteronomy 15:19–20). Firstborn male animals were set apart from the others and eaten at a religious sacrificial meal. In addi-tion, the meat of the firstborn livestock was given to the Israelite priests to eat, as described in the book of Numbers: "The first-born of an ox, a sheep or a goat: they are holy. . . . Their meat is to be yours [the priests']" (Numbers 18:17–18).

Thus the male firstborn Hebrew livestock were regarded as holy and were set apart for religious sacrifices and for feeding the priests. I have searched ancient Egyptian literature and can find no indication of whether or not firstborn livestock were special to the Egyptians. What is clear is that huge numbers of sheep, goats, and cattle were sacrificed to a variety of gods in Egyptian temples, and it is reasonable to expect that the Egyptian priests later ate those sacrifices. In addition, sacrifices to Egyptian gods were also offered on domestic altars set up in private homes. Cultural customs in ancient civilizations that were situated close to each other were often very similar, and if the ancient Israelites in Egypt regarded their firstborn male animals as special, then it is likely that the ancient Egyptians did as well, particularly since we know that the ancient Egyptians, like the ancient Israelites, regarded firstborn sons as very special. Since the book of Exodus explicitly states that the firstborn Egyptian livestock died, we can deduce from this that firstborn Egyptian livestock must have been identifiable as such, which implies that they were set apart from the other livestock.

Some parts of this book are more tentative than others, and I want to make it clear which parts those are. I believe strongly, for example, that the description in the Old Testament of Mount Sinai is a description of an active volcano and hence that Mount Sinai cannot be in the Sinai Peninsula since there are no volcanoes there that have been active in historical times. On the other hand, my ideas about the death of the firstborn males are very tentative, but I do believe they are plausible. What I suggest may have occurred is outlined below.

By the end of the first nine plagues, the Egyptian people must have been absolutely desperate. Their crops and livestock had been largely destroyed. Only a small amount of grain remained in the grain stores of most Egyptian families. Those animals that had survived the plagues were thin, emaciated, undernourished, and probably close to death. The Egyptian people were faring only slightly better. When the three-day sandstorm (the ninth plague) ended and the Egyptians were able to leave their houses, then how would the head of each family allocate the limited grain in his grain store? None of his family had eaten for three days, and I believe his top priority would have been to feed his firstborn son and heir, to keep him healthy.

I suggest his next priority would have been to feed the firstborn male animals in his flocks and herds, since the powerful Egyptian priests would have been demanding food for themselves and animals for sacrifice to appease their gods and to ward off yet more plagues. In addition, animals were required for sacrifice on domestic altars. If the animals were to be acceptable as sacrifices, then they had to be well fed, yet the locusts had devoured all their food in the fields. Thus I believe the head of the family had no option but to feed his precious grain to some of the animals, the special ones, the firstborn destined for sacrifice and then as food for the priests. I suggest that only after the firstborn males, both human and animal, had been fed were the rest of the family fed, if there was enough grain left.

It may seem curious to us today to think that animals were fed before humans. However, we have to try to think as the ancient Egyptians would have thought. These were real plagues, resulting in massive food shortages, and the Egyptians would have been desperate. I am sure that the top priority of each Egyptian family would have been to feed their firstborn son, on whom the future of the family depended. However, I strongly suggest that the powerful priests of Egypt would have demanded from each family well-fed animals for sacrifices, which the priests would have later eaten. I suggest that the power of the priests, coupled with fear of the Egyptian gods, was so great that after feeding grain to the firstborn sons, the next to be fed would have been the firstborn male animals.

There is an interesting modern parallel of putting animals before humans for religious reasons. In the Western world, when many people see a cow they see a potential hamburger. However, if you are a Hindu in India, then when you look at a cow you see a representation of God: cows are sacred. A Hindu would never kill a cow to feed his family, even though the family might be starving to death. In addition, very poor Hindus in India will spend their precious money buying grass from the caretaker of the sacred cows in order to feed them because this is considered a very holy thing to do. Somewhat similarly, I suggest the ancient Egyptians could have fed their firstborn animals, specially selected for sacrifice to their gods, before feeding their families.

So the firstborn sons and male animals ate the contaminated grain and died a rapid death. If enough grain was left, then other members of the family, of course, would have eaten the grain and perhaps died; the book of Exodus doesn't state that *only* the firstborn died. However, other members of the family may have been less susceptible to poison from the grain because they were older. I would also like to mention that if wet grain is put on top of dry grain in a granary store, the wet grain will contaminate first so that the top layers of grain contain the mycotoxins, and it takes time for these to spread through all the grain. Hence those who eat from the top layers of grain are the most at risk. As I've said earlier, many Egyptian families probably had only a small amount of grain, all of which was damp and toxic, and their firstborn males, both human and livestock, ate this and died. Wealthier Egyptian families probably had more grain in their stores, but as explained above, only the top few inches would have been contaminated and again mainly the firstborn, who ate first, would have died. The Egyptians in the Nile Delta also would have known that the plagues had not affected the nearby region of Egypt in which the Israelites lived. Hence the next day, those Egyptians short of grain could have fed the rest of their family by demanding grain from the Israelites' grain stores. However, the immediate priority following the three days of darkness would have been to feed the firstborn sons and male animals from the Egyptians' own grain stores, which unknown to them were contaminated by a deadly poison.

Thus we have a natural scientific explanation for all ten plagues, which follow a logical, connected sequence. I believe it is noteworthy that the Old Testament book of Exodus records this sequence in an order that we now know is logical and scientific. Let me summarize this chronological order from details I've given earlier. The first plague, the Nile turned to blood, probably happened in September, when the Nile was at a maximum and contained the most nutrients. The second plague, of frogs or toads, was in September–October. The third plague, of biting midges, arrived in October–November. The fifth plague, the death of livestock, would have followed rapidly from the biting midges and so was probably in November–December. The seventh plague, of hail, took place in February–March; the eighth plague, of locusts, in February–March; the ninth plague, of darkness, in March; the tenth plague, of the death of the firstborn, in March–April. The only plagues in which the timing is uncertain are the plagues of flies and of boils. The Old Testament describes the plague of flies as the fourth plague, which would have occurred in about November in our scheme above. This makes sense since the stable flies would have bred in the pools of stagnant water left behind by the retreating Nile, their larvae feeding on rotting vegetation and fish and frogs. The Bible describes the plague of boils as the sixth plague, which would have occurred in December–January in our chronology. Again this makes sense since we have argued that the boils resulted from infections spread by the stable fly and hence would follow rapidly from the fourth plague. We therefore have a logical, coherent chronology for the ten plagues that is highly consistent with the biblical account. The chronology is summarized in the table on the next page.

The Plagues of Egypt

Plague	Cause	Time of Year
1. Nile turned to blood and fish died	Red soil particles plus red harmful algal blooms.	September
2. Frogs/Toads	Polluted Nile forces frogs ashore. Mass death due to starvation and dehydration.	September–October
3. Gnats	The biting midge *Culicoides carnithorix*. Free to breed rapidly due to population collapse of frogs.	October–November
4. Flies	The stable fly *Stomoxys calcitrans*. Free to breed rapidly due to population collapse of frogs.	November
5. Death of livestock	Bluetongue virus and African horse sickness virus, both spread by the biting midge, *Culicoides*.	November–December
6. Boils	Skin infection spread by the stable fly, *Stomoxys*.	December–January
7. Hail	Exceptionally severe hailstorm.	February–March

8. Locusts	The desert locust, attracted by damp sand from hailstorm to settle and lay eggs.	February– March
9. Darkness for three days	First *khamsin* of the year produces particularly dark and dense dust storm.	March
10. Death of the firstborn males	Mycotoxins on grain, possibly *macrocylic tricothecenes*. Due to damp grain from hail contaminated by locusts' feces and stored in a grain store then sealed by sand from the *khamsin* dust storm.	late March– early April

Why Were the Israelites Unaffected by the Plagues?

According to the book of Exodus, there was something extremely curious about the plagues: many of them affected only the Egyptians and not the Israelites. We have seen how science can explain, in a remarkable way, the sequence of the ten plagues recorded in Exodus. Can science now explain the exemption of the Israelites from at least some of these?

The plagues that the book of Exodus explicitly says did not affect the Israelites were swarms of flies, death of livestock, hail, darkness for three days, and the death of firstborn sons and male animals. There may be an implication that at least some of the other plagues did not affect the Israelites because, with the plague of boils, for example, this plague is explicitly stated to have been on "all the Egyptians" (Exodus 9:11), and I think the implication of this is that the Israelites did not have these festering boils. I believe the clue to why they were unaffected by many of the plagues is given in Exodus 8:22: "But on that day I will deal differently with the land of Goshen, where my people live; no swarms of flies will be there." So where was the land of Goshen? It is clear from various references to Goshen in the Old

Testament that Goshen was a region in or close to the east Nile Delta, although the exact boundaries of Goshen are not known. A possible location is shown on an earlier map (3.1, pg. 30). The Israelite slaves lived in their own separate geographical location, the land of Goshen, which almost certainly was not in the prime property market area next to the highly desirable waters of the Nile, which the Egyptians would have kept for themselves. Thus the ancient Israelites were probably living a few miles away from the Nile and its main branches—close enough to where the Egyptians lived to walk into work, but far enough away to be a distinct community.

We have earlier identified the plague of gnats with the midge *Culicoides* and the plague of flies with the stable fly. Both would have been concentrated around the Nile since their larvae would have fed on the decaying fish and frogs that had resulted from the first and second plagues. In addition, both the midge and the stable fly are weak flyers with a range of less than a mile, and I believe this is the reason the cattle of the Israelites, located in the land of Goshen, would not have been bitten by the midges and the Israelites themselves would have escaped the boils due to infection spread by stable fly bites.

Hailstorms and sandstorms are frequently very localized, so it is easy to see that the geographically separate region of Goshen could have been spared both the hailstorms and then the sandstorms causing the three days of darkness. The crops of the Israelites therefore would not have been stored damp in sand-covered stores and thus would not have developed mycotoxins, and the Israelites and their livestock would not have been poisoned by them. We therefore have a coherent scientific story of why the Israelites escaped the plagues, the key clue coming from the Old Testament records that the Israelites lived in a different location from the Egyptians. Somewhat similarly, until recently the plague of BSE in cows and the consequent outbreak of vCJD in humans have been localized geographically to the U.K. Many scientists believe that it is only because the U.K. sold infected animal feed to the rest of the world that other countries are now at risk; otherwise these plagues might have been geographically restricted to the U.K.

The Response of Pharaoh

Just as we have to try to get inside the mind of Moses to understand how he led his people out of Egypt, so we need to learn about the personality of Pharaoh, the man who opposed him. We have already said that the pharaohs of ancient Egypt had immense power—far more than today's president of the United States or the prime minister of England, because Egypt was no democracy. As we saw in chapter 3, the pharaoh Moses negotiated with was probably Ramesses II, the greatest pharaoh of them all. Picture the scene: Moses, the leader of the Israelite slaves, pitted against the most powerful man in the world. As Moses said, "Since I speak with faltering lips, why would Pharaoh listen to me?" (Exodus 6:30) Why indeed? Pharaoh could have swatted Moses like an irritating fly. As we saw in chapter 7, "The Exodus Strategy," the only reason Pharaoh listened to Moses was because of the devastating plagues. Let's take a closer look at the negotiations between Moses and Pharaoh.

Before the first plague, Moses said to Pharaoh, "The Lord, the God of the Hebrews, has sent me to say to you: Let my people go so that they may worship me in the desert" (Exodus 7:16). But Pharaoh didn't listen, so the water of the Nile was turned blood red and all the fish died. Before the second plague, Moses repeated his request: "This is what the Lord says: Let my people go so that they may worship me" (Exodus 8:1). Pharaoh refused, so the second plague, of frogs, occurred. Now Pharaoh started to weaken. He summoned Moses and Aaron and said, "Pray to the Lord to take the frogs away from me and my people, and I will let your people go to offer sacrifices to the Lord" (Exodus 8:8). But when the frogs died, and Pharaoh saw that the plague had ended, he broke his word: "But when Pharaoh saw that there was relief, he hardened his heart and would not listen to Moses and Aaron" (Exodus 8:15). How typical of human nature today!

So the conflict continued. And the third plague, of gnats, occurred, but Pharaoh still would not listen. So it was followed by the fourth plague, of flies. Then Pharaoh started to listen, and, skillful negotiator that he was, he offered a compromise: "Then Pharaoh summoned Moses and Aaron and said, 'Go, sacrifice to your God here in the land'" (Exodus 8:25). Pharaoh was offering to give the Israelites time off from their slave labors provided they stayed in Egypt to perform their sacrifices. By doing so he would lose their services for only about a day. But Moses stood his ground and rejected this offer. He cleverly said, "That would not be right. The sacrifices we offer the Lord our God would be detestable to the Egyptians. And if we offer sacrifices that are detestable in their eyes, will they not stone us? We must take a three-day journey into the desert to offer sacrifices to the Lord our God, as He commands us" (Exodus 8:26–27). Pharaoh accepts the argument of Moses that the Israelites cannot stay in Egypt and offer sacrifices to their God. So Pharaoh gives way and says, "I will let you go to offer sacrifices to the Lord your God in the desert, but you must not go very far" (Exodus 8:28). Moses appears to accept this and prays to God to call off the flies, but as soon as this happens, Pharaoh changes his mind once again and refuses to let the Israelites go to offer their sacrifices in the desert.

So the deadly plagues continue, and Pharaoh refuses to let the Israelites go even after the fifth plague, on the livestock, and the sixth plague, of boils. How like negotiations today! If an agreement between opposing parties is reached and then breaks down, it is often far harder to obtain an agreement again because both sides go back to their starting positions and dig in firmly. So it was with Pharaoh and Moses. But after the seventh plague, of hail, the mighty Pharaoh had had enough and comprehensively gave in. Just listen to the conciliatory words the humbled Pharaoh said to Moses and Aaron: "This time I have sinned. The Lord is in the right and I and my people are in the wrong. Pray to the Lord, for we have had enough thunder and hail. I will let you go; you don't have to stay any longer" (Exodus 9:27–28). What a contrite confession from the most powerful man on earth! But it was superficial and wasn't really genuine: as soon as the hail had stopped and the sun started to shine again, Pharaoh refused to let the Israelites go.

So the contest of wills continued. Moses warned Pharaoh that unless he let the Israelites go into the desert to worship their God, then God would send a plague of locusts. Pharaoh responded with an unacceptable compromise: "Let only the men go" (Exodus 10:11). Moses rejected this, so the locusts came and devastated all the crops that were left after the plague of hail. Next came the plague of darkness, after which Pharaoh compromised further: "Go, worship the Lord. Even your women and children may go with you; only leave your flocks and herds behind" (Exodus 10:24). Again this compromise was unacceptable to Moses: the Israelites would need their flocks and herds of animals as food for survival in the desert when they left Egypt and as carriers for water bags. So the final plague was sent: the death of the firstborn males. Only after this terrible tenth plague did Pharaoh truly give way and say in desperation to Moses and Aaron, "Up! Leave my people, you and the Israelites! Go, worship the Lord as you have requested. Take your flocks and herds as you have said, and go" (Exodus 12:31–32).

So Pharaoh finally agreed to let the Israelites leave Egypt and go on a three-day journey into the desert to worship their God, taking with them their men, women, and children and their flocks and herds of animals. Moses and his God had triumphed over Pharaoh and the gods of the Egyptians. Moses was about to achieve the first objective he had been given at the burning bush in Midian: "Bring my people the Israelites out of Egypt" (Exodus 3:10), by using the first strategy he had been given for achieving this objective: striking the Egyptians with a crescendo of plagues until the desperate Pharaoh finally gave in.

So Moses had won, but would Pharaoh change his mind again, true to form? And if he did, how could Moses and his band of Israelite slaves defeat Pharaoh and his mighty army? The extraordinary story of the Exodus has begun, and we will now try to reconstruct what really happened when the Israelites left Egypt and crossed the Red Sea. It is an even more remarkable story than that of the ten plagues.

In the next chapter we demonstrate how modern archaeology has found the starting point, Rameses, of the Exodus. We also investigate what the mysterious pillars of cloud and of fire could have been that guided the Israelites to Mount Sinai, and we show that these have a spectacular natural cause.

PART FOUR

THE ROAD
TO THE RED SEA

ELEVEN

THE JOURNEY STARTS: THE PILLAR OF CLOUD AND THE PILLAR OF FIRE

By day the Lord went ahead of them in a pillar of cloud to guide them on their way and by night in a pillar of fire to give them light, so that they could travel by day or night. Neither the pillar of cloud by day nor the pillar of fire by night left its place in front of the people.

Exodus 13:21–22

We have reached what many people believe to be one of the greatest events in world history: the Exodus of the Israelites from Egypt. Picture the dramatic scenes. Midnight strikes, and the firstborn males of the Egyptians die. Midnight strikes, and the long night of mourning begins for the Egyptians. Midnight strikes, and the historic day of the Exodus dawns for the Israelites. What an amazing start to the Exodus journey! But can we reconstruct what happened next? A mighty building needs massive foundations to support it. In previous chapters we provided the foundations we need to understand what really happened when the Israelites left Egypt. In addition, we saw just how accurate the Old Testament writings about the Exodus are, but we also suggested that these writings have been misunderstood and misinterpreted. So what really happened when the Israelites left Egypt and traveled to Mount Sinai? For example, what was the pillar of cloud that guided them by day and the pillar of fire by night? As I have said before, try to imagine you were there, and try to think as Moses would have thought.

Rameses—the Start of the Journey

The ancient writings of the Old Testament tell us precisely the starting point and the start day of the Exodus from Egypt. The fourth book of the Old Testament, Numbers, states,

> Here are the stages in the journey of the Israelites when they came out of Egypt by divisions under the leadership of Moses and Aaron. At the Lord's command Moses recorded the stages in their journey. This is their journey by stages: The Israelites set out from Rameses on the fifteenth day of the first month. (Numbers 33:1–3)

The book of Exodus confirms this. Thus, on the fifteenth day of the first month (later called the month of Nisan) of the Jewish lunar calendar, the Israelites set out from Rameses in Egypt. As we saw in chapter 9, the fifteenth day of the first month of the Jewish lunar calendar corresponds to late March or early April in our solar calendar. It is my preferred time of year to visit Egypt and Israel: pleasantly warm but not too hot. It is an ideal time for walking in the desert, so the Israelites set out at the best time of the year for traveling. But where was Rameses, the starting point of the Exodus, and can we locate it after three thousand years?

Rameses was the place where the Israelite slaves had been working, as is clear from the opening chapter of the book of Exodus: "And they built Pithom and Rameses as store cities for Pharaoh" (Exodus 1:11). What is meant by the Hebrew term *store cities*? We know from Egyptian archaeology that palaces and temples in what is called the New Kingdom period (c.1540–1069 B.C.), which covers the time of Moses and the Exodus, were surrounded by large numbers of storage rooms. For example, the mortuary temple of Ramesses II, called the Ramesseum, in Thebes, now called Luxor, was surrounded by more than 160 storage chambers, all made of mud brick. I saw this magnificent temple and the surrounding storage rooms myself on a visit to Egypt in 1996.

If the temple where Ramesses II was buried is in ancient Thebes, modern Luxor, then where was the main palace in which he lived?

Archaeology reveals (see, for example, *Israel in Egypt* by Hoffmeier) that the Nineteenth and Twentieth Dynasty pharaohs of Egypt (c.1295–1069 B.C.) lived in the Nile Delta in a place the Egyptians called "House of Ramesses Beloved of Amun, Great of Victories," which was built by Ramesses II in the early years of his reign (by the Israelite slaves if our chronology is correct; see chapter 3). The short Egyptian name of this site was Pi-Ramesses, which means "the house of Ramesses," which was the delta capital of Egypt. There can be little doubt that the Rameses in Exodus 1:11, where the Israelite slaves worked, is the same place as the Rameses in Exodus 12:37 and Numbers 33:3, the starting point of the Exodus journey, since clearly the Israelites started their Exodus journey from where they were living. There can also be little doubt that the Hebrew Rameses is the same place as the Egyptian Pi-Ramesses. So where was the Egyptian Pi-Ramesses, where Pharaoh Ramesses II lived?

Two possible sites have been identified in the Nile Delta for Pi-Ramesses. Originally archaeologists favored modern Tanis, which is still identified with Rameses on some modern maps (see map 1.3, pg. 10), but now they are almost unanimous that modern Qantir is ancient Pi-Ramesses.

At Qantir, near the town of Fakus, we can find the archaeological remains of the foundations of a royal palace and inscriptions that actually say on them "Pi-Ramesses." Hence we can be virtually certain that after three thousand years we can pinpoint the starting place of the Exodus, Rameses, as modern Qantir. Archaeological excavations at Qantir reveal that it "was probably the vastest and most costly royal residence ever erected by the hand of man. As can now be seen its known palace and official center covered an area of at least four square miles, and its temples were in scale with this, a colossal assembly forming perhaps the largest collection of chapels built in the preclassical world by a single ruler at one time" (Eric Uphill, *Temples of Per-Ramesses*, 1). Archaeology reveals that whereas ancient Nineveh and Babylon covered areas of 1,800 and 2,250 acres respectively, Pi-Ramesses covered 2,500 acres.

In the spring 2001 edition of *Egyptian Archaeology: The Bulletin of the Egyptian Exploration Society,* it is reported that a well is being excavated near Qantir. Inscribed on the inner face are two lines of the protocol of Ramesses II, and the well contains 2.5 million shards of Ramesses-period pottery. What a huge number! All from a single well in Qantir.

If the pharaoh of the Exodus was indeed Ramesses II (see chapter 3), we can now see why he was so reluctant to give the Israelite slaves one week off from their labors so they could take a three-day journey into the desert. Ramesses II was obsessed with building! He constructed Pi-Ramesses to be the greatest site in the preclassical world. At this magnificent site at Pi-Ramesses, modern Qantir, the Israelites worked. At this superb site Moses dueled verbally with the mighty Pharaoh. At this breathtaking site, the apparently all-powerful Pharaoh was humbled by the ten plagues. What an incredible setting for the start of the Exodus journey! Think of the most luxuriant, exotic, and overwhelming film setting you have ever seen, and then multiply this in your mind one thousand times. This spectacular site was the starting point for the Exodus: an extraordinary journey on a truly epic scale.

The Next Step: Rameses to Succoth

The Old Testament books of Exodus and Numbers agree that Succoth was the next stage in the Exodus journey after Rameses. Exodus 12:37 simply states, "The Israelites journeyed from Rameses to Succoth," and Numbers 33:5 says, "The Israelites left Rameses and camped at Succoth." The brevity, simplicity, and directness of these two statements suggest that the journey from Rameses to Succoth was relatively uneventful. So where was Succoth?

Modern scholars are virtually unanimous that Succoth was a region on the eastern frontier of ancient Egypt near the border between Egypt and the Sinai Peninsula, around Tell el-Maskhuta, close to modern Ismailiya (see map 3.1, pg. 30).

An analysis of ancient Middle Eastern languages shows that the Hebrew word for Succoth corresponds to the Egyptian consonants *tkw*, which is the ancient Egyptian region of Tjeku, and the Arabic word *Maskhuta* preserves this ancient name. (The initial two letters of Maskhuta, *Ma*, mean "place" in Arabic. Taking these away leaves the root *s-kh-t*, which is similar to the root of Succoth. For further information see, for example, the book by Hoffmeier, *Israel in Egypt*.)

So what do we know about ancient Tjeku, which the Old Testament calls Succoth? Egyptian texts quoted by Hoffmeier in *Israel in Egypt* suggest that Tjeku was both a region and a specific place within that region, in the same way that New York is both a state and specific place within that state. Egyptian texts describe Tjeku as being fortified and containing horses and chariots in the time of Ramesses. In other words, Tjeku (Succoth) was an Egyptian military fortified zone on the eastern Egyptian frontier with Sinai, which contained troops and chariots for the defense of Egypt.

However, although I agree with Hoffmeier's description of Tjeku and its identification with Succoth, I do not agree with his statement on page 181 of *Israel in Egypt:* "They [the Israelites] surely would not have camped beside one of the fortresses in Tjeku." Why not, since the Israelites had been given specific permission by Pharaoh to leave Egypt? Indeed, Moses probably had some kind of tangible permission from Pharaoh that he would have shown to the troop commander in Tjeku. There is no way the Israelites would have been let out of Egypt without the permission of Pharaoh, but this permission would surely have entitled them to camp at Tjeku/Succoth on the Egyptian border with Sinai, just as described in the Old Testament. I therefore believe we can identify with some certainty both the starting point and the first stage of the Israelites' journey. They started from Rameses, modern Qantir, and traveled to Succoth, modern Tell el-Maskhuta, near Ismailiya on the Egypt–Sinai frontier.

The Journey Time from Rameses to Succoth

The distance between Rameses (modern Qantir) and Succoth (modern Tell el-Maskhuta) is twenty-five miles, which corresponds to a typical day's journey, or distance between night encampments, as discussed in chapter 4. Indeed, there is an Egyptian papyrus from the Nineteenth Dynasty (1295–1186 B.C.), Papyrus Anastasi V, which states that an Egyptian official, pursuing two runaway slaves, left the courts of the Royal Palace (at Rameses) one day and arrived at the enclosure wall of Tjeku on the following day. Moses and the Israelites probably took the same route from Rameses to Succoth. Can we estimate how long the journey took the Israelites?

As we saw in chapter 4, a day's journey of twenty-five miles is based on walking at about three miles per hour for eight hours. Could the Israelites, burdened with their flocks and children, have traveled at this pace? The speed at which we travel is partly governed by our motivation and the forces acting on us. So what forces were acting on the Israelites? First, imagine you were one of the Egyptian people: you had just suffered ten truly terrible plagues because your stubborn Pharaoh had refused to let the Israelites leave Egypt on a three-day journey. Wouldn't you want to drive out the Israelites as rapidly as possible? This is precisely what Exodus 12:33 records: "The Egyptians urged the people to hurry and leave the country. 'For otherwise,' they said, 'we will all die!'" Exodus 12:39 emphasizes this: "They [the Israelites] had been driven out of Egypt."

Now imagine you were Moses. He knew that Pharaoh had agreed to let the Israelites leave Egypt during the second plague, of frogs, during the fourth plague, of flies, during the seventh plague, of hail, and during the eighth plague, of locusts, but as soon as each plague had ended, Pharaoh had changed his mind. Pharaoh had finally given in after the deaths of the firstborn males, but Moses knew from experience that Pharaoh was not to be trusted and could break his word again at any time. So Moses knew that time was not on his side. He had to get the Israelites out of Egypt, and out of Egyptian-controlled territory, as rapidly as possible. So the forces on the Israelites, both from their leader Moses and from the Egyptian people, acted to drive them out of Egypt at maximum speed. And this is just what the Old Testament documents describe. Deuteronomy 16:3 records, "You left Egypt in haste," and Exodus 13:21 states that the Israelites marched by both day and night.

I suggest that the Israelites, with their animals and children, might have found walking at three miles per hour difficult, but two or two and a half miles per hour would certainly have been possible. Hence the twenty-five miles from Rameses to Succoth could have been covered in a long day of walking, eight to twelve hours, and I suggest this was the objective of Moses. We cannot be certain how long the journey took, but I think it probable that the Israelites left Rameses early in the morning and arrived at Succoth later that same day to camp there for the night. Such an early start is consistent with the haste described in the biblical texts. For example, Exodus 12:37 states, "During the night Pharaoh summoned Moses and Aaron and said, 'Up! Leave my people, you and the Israelites! Go, worship the Lord as you have requested.'" This suggests that the Israelites might well have left while it was still night. In any case, if they had left Rameses at daybreak, about 6 A.M. in spring in Egypt, then they would have arrived at Succoth before 6 P.M.

One of the things I have learned while poring over the ancient writings of the book of Exodus is that there are very few wasted words. Every statement would have been significant to the original readers, and if we are to reconstruct the extraordinary Exodus journey, we have to understand the original meaning of the book of Exodus. So what is the significance of our being told, "The Israelites set out from Rameses on the *fifteenth day* of the first month" (Numbers 33:3)? I suggest there are two reasons for specifying the precise day, as well as the actual place. First, it means that the author intended to root the Exodus account firmly in the ground of history. Where did the Exodus start? From Rameses. When did the Exodus start? On the fifteenth day of the first month. Thus the author anchored the origin of the Exodus not only in space but also in time.

However, I believe there is a second reason we are told it was the fifteenth day of the month. As we saw earlier, the Jewish calendar was a lunar calendar in which the first day of the lunar month was determined by the first observation of the crescent of the new moon, so the new light from the new moon signified a new month. On average, a lunar month lasts for 29.5 days, so some months are 29 days long and some 30. Thus the fifteenth day of the month is full-moon time. In our modern world, the full moon does not look very bright because of street lights and car lights. However, out in the desert, away from light pollution, the full moon looks dazzlingly bright. It would have looked even brighter three thousand years ago when atmospheric pollution was a lot less than it is now.

I have walked in a desert at midnight in the light of the full moon. It is easy to see your way. It is even possible to walk in a desert at night in the light of the half-moon. So when the writer of the book of Exodus tells us that the Exodus started on the fifteenth day of the month, the original readers, who were familiar with the lunar calendar, would have known this was full-moon time and that the ancient Israelites would have seen their way easily to walk through the desert at night. In addition, as we saw earlier, the "first month" of the Jewish lunar calendar corresponds to our March–April, and this time of year has the ideal climate for long walks through the desert. Thus the writer of Exodus is implying that the timing was perfect for long marches through the desert both by day and by night. Perfect timing once again!

The Route from Egypt

Curiously, the book of Exodus first tells us the route the Israelites *didn't* take when they left Egypt: "When Pharaoh let the people go, God did not lead them on the road through the Philistine country" (Exodus 13:17). Why are we first told the route the Israelites avoided? To understand this, let's go back to the instructions God gave Moses by the burning bush. The first instruction was "to bring my people the Israelites out of Egypt" (Exodus 3:10). Moses was now on the verge of achieving this. He had led the Israelites to Succoth, on the Egypt-Sinai border, and he had permission from Pharaoh to cross the border and leave Egypt for a three-day journey into the desert. But which way was he to go when he left Succoth?

God had given Moses two further instructions at the burning bush: "Bring them up out of that land [Egypt] into a good and spacious land, a land flowing with milk and honey, the home of the Canaanites . . ." (Exodus 3:8) and: "When you have brought the people out of Egypt you will worship God on this mountain [Mount Sinai]" (Exodus 3:12). However, which of these two instructions was meant to come first? Was God saying, Lead the Israelites first to the promised land of Canaan and afterward take them to Mount Sinai? Or was Moses first meant to take the Israelites to Mount Sinai and then to Canaan? My impression from Exodus 3 is that Moses was first to take the Israelites to Mount Sinai and after this to Canaan, but the intended order of these events is not totally clear. In addition, given the choice of milk and honey in Canaan or of inedible black volcanic lava at Mount Sinai, I think Moses and the Israelites would have gone first for the milk and honey! I suggest that going first to Sinai formed no part of Moses' original plans. His purpose was to take the Israelites directly to the promised land. But it was not to be. And that is why I think we first have the negative instruction "when Pharaoh let the people go, God did not lead them on the road through the Philistine country" (Exodus 13:17), which was the road to Canaan.

What was "the road through the Philistine country"? Scholars are agreed that it was an ancient military route that led northeast along the shore of the Mediterranean Sea into the southwest corner of Canaan. This ancient route was called by the Egyptians the Way of Horus, and it was the nearest route from Succoth to Canaan (see map 1.3, pg. 10).

Excavations have shown the route to have been heavily fortified. The famous Egyptologist Sir Alan Gardiner writes of this route, "There can be little or no doubt but that the road . . . has witnessed the marches of nine-tenths of the armies that have sought to invade Palestine from Egypt, or Egypt from Palestine, along the land route" (A. H. Gardiner, "The Ancient Military Road Between Egypt and Palestine"). So the Israelites did not travel up this heavily fortified road to Canaan. This would have been asking for trouble if Pharaoh had changed his mind about their leaving Egypt.

Since Canaan was not the first objective after leaving Egypt, it is clear that Moses knew he had to lead the Israelites to Mount Sinai, and the book of Exodus gives the route he took: "by the desert road towards the Red Sea" (Exodus 13:18). What was this desert road toward the Red Sea? Understanding this is so important that I devote the next two chapters to it. As we will see, I believe biblical scholars have misunderstood what was meant, and they have Moses traveling on the wrong road. First, however, let's try to construct a very approximate Exodus route from Egypt to Mount Sinai.

The Route to Mount Sinai—As the Crow Flies

My summer holiday in 2001 was a long weekend in a small seaside town called Southwold on the east coast of England. There is no direct road between Cambridge, where I live, and Southwold, so I had to think about the best route for getting there. I checked a road map, located Cambridge and Southwold on the map, and then drew in my mind an imaginary straight line between Cambridge and Southwold. This line represented the shortest distance between these two places, and in England we call this the distance "as the crow flies" because crows usually fly in a straight line between two places. Having found the route between Cambridge and Southwold as the crow flies, I then looked on the map for convenient major roads lying close to this route in order to choose the actual roads I would drive along. The route as the crow flies is a useful approximate guide to the actual route to be traveled.

I suggest that Moses may well have planned his Exodus route from Rameses to Mount Sinai in a similar way. He knew where Mount Sinai was because he had visited it before, when he was in Midian. In his mind or on a piece of papyrus or on a stone tablet, he may have sketched out the route the Israelites would take. Perhaps he started by marking in Rameses and Mount Sinai on his sketch and then drawing a straight line between them—the route as the falcon flies, as Moses might have said. Moses would then have looked for convenient trade routes lying close to this crow-flies route in order to choose the actual route the Israelites would take.

I am now going to try to reconstruct the route between Rameses and Mount Sinai as the crow flies. This will be an approximate guide to the real route, and we will attempt to fill in the real route in later chapters. Earlier in this chapter we identified ancient Rameses with modern Qantir. But where was Mount Sinai? I'm going to consider two possibilities: first that Mount Sinai is at its traditional site in the Sinai Peninsula, and second that it is a volcano in Midian. The traditional site for Mount Sinai, as we have seen in earlier chapters, is at Jebel Musa, the Mountain of Moses, in the south of the Sinai Peninsula.

On the map I have drawn a straight line between Rameses (Qantir) and Jebel Musa. This is the route as the crow flies to the traditional location of Mount Sinai (but, as we have seen, it is a late tradition).

We do not yet know where the real Mount Sinai is (this will be revealed in the last chapter of this book), but I have suggested that it should be located in a volcanic region in Midian. It is useful to summarize the arguments we have used so far that suggest Mount Sinai is in Midian.

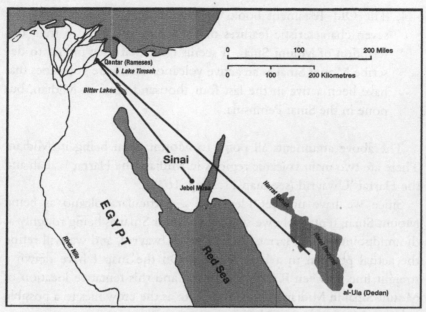

11.1. The route "as the crow flies" from Rameses to Jebel Musa, the traditional Mount Sinai, and to the volcanic regions of Midian.

1. After Moses had killed an Egyptian slave master he fled to Midian and led the flock of Jethro to Mount Sinai (Exodus 3:1). Since the book of Exodus does not record that Moses left Midian in order to go to Mount Sinai, the natural interpretation of this account is that Mount Sinai is in Midian.

2. There is documentary evidence that every spring Midianite shepherds have traditionally taken their sheep eastward from the hot coastal plains of Midian to higher and cooler volcanic regions in Midian. When Moses led the flock of Jethro, the Midianite priest, to the far side of the desert he was probably following this traditional practice. If so, then Mount Sinai is in Midian. There is no tradition of Midianite shepherds leading their flocks to the Sinai Peninsula.

3. Two possible natural mechanisms kept the burning bush burning—either a shallow deposit of natural gas in the ground below or a volcanic vent. There are natural gas deposits and volcanic vents in Midian but not in the Sinai Peninsula.

4. The Old Testament books of Exodus and Deuteronomy give seven characteristic features of a volcanic eruption in their description of Mount Sinai. It seems clear that they intend to describe Mount Sinai as an active volcano. There are volcanoes that have been active in the last four thousand years in Midian, but none in the Sinai Peninsula.

The above arguments all point to Mount Sinai being in Midian. There are two main volcanic regions in Midian, the Harrat Rahah and the Harrat 'Uwayrid (see map 11.1, pg. 163).

Since we have not yet identified a particular volcano as being Mount Sinai, tentatively we will take Mount Sinai as being roughly at the midpoint of the Harrats Rahah and 'Uwayrid, and we will refine the actual position in a later chapter. On the map I have drawn a straight line between Rameses (Qantir) and this tentative location of Mount Sinai in Midian. This is the route as the crow flies to a possible volcanic Mount Sinai in Midian.

So we are now thinking about two possible locations for Mount Sinai, either Jebel Musa in the Sinai Peninsula or a volcanic mountain in Midian, and we have an approximate route as the crow flies from the starting point of the Exodus journey, Rameses, to each of them. We now turn to what must have been one of the most spectacular sights of the Exodus journey: a pillar of cloud by day and a pillar of fire by night to guide the Israelites along the route to Mount Sinai. What were these puzzling pillars? And along which route did they guide: the one to Jebel Musa or the one to a mountain in Midian? As we will see, I believe these pillars themselves provide a key clue to the location of Mount Sinai and to which of the two crow-flies routes drawn on our map is correct.

The Pillar of Fire and the Pillar of Cloud

When I'm driving along a major road at night and I want to relax, I sometimes settle in behind a car going at a suitable speed and let the rear red lights of the car ahead act as my guide along the road. Somewhat similarly, when Moses and the Israelites traveled to Mount Sinai, during the day a pillar of cloud was in front of them to guide them in the right direction, and by night (when cloud is hard to see), a pillar of fire was their guide. Let's look again at how the book of Exodus describes these remarkable pillars:

> After leaving Succoth they camped at Etham on the edge of the desert. By day the Lord went ahead of them in a pillar of cloud to guide them on their way and by night in a pillar of fire to give them light, so that they could travel by day or night. Neither the pillar of cloud by day nor the pillar of fire by night left its place in front of the people. (Exodus 13:20–22)

The traditional interpretation of the pillars of cloud and of fire is that these pillars were just in front of the Israelites and that they moved with the Israelites as they marched, rather like a tour group leader holding up a rolled umbrella and walking at the head of the group. But the book of Exodus does not imply that the pillars of cloud and of fire were just in front of the Israelites, and neither does it state that they were moving pillars; they could have been a considerable distance ahead and fixed, like a beacon on a hill giving a guiding light.

Let's look at this account through the lenses of science. We already saw how the miracles of crossing the Jordan, the burning bush, the plagues of Egypt, and the mountain of fire may all have scientific explanations that fit the descriptions in the Old Testament with remarkable accuracy. Could the pillar of cloud and the pillar of fire also have a scientific explanation?

There is in fact a natural event that fits perfectly the description "pillar of cloud by day and pillar of fire by night": a volcanic eruption. This is how Pliny the Younger described the eruption of Vesuvius in A.D. 79, which he saw when he was eighteen, in a letter he later wrote to the Roman Historian Tacitus in A.D. 104.

> On the 24th August [A.D. 79], about one in the afternoon, my mother desired him [Pliny the Younger's uncle, not surprisingly called Pliny the Elder] to observe a cloud of very unusual size and appearance. . . . It was not at that distance discernible from what mountain this cloud issued, but it was found afterwards to be Vesuvius. I cannot give you a more exact description of its

11.2. A pillar of cloud by day from an erupting volcano.

figure than by resembling it to that of a pine-tree, for it shot up a
great height in the form of a trunk. . . .

Notice that Pliny says it was daytime (about one in the afternoon) and that what he saw was a vertical cloud of great height in
the form of a trunk of a pine tree. Pine trees are renowned for
being tall and straight, like pillars. We make telephone poles out of
the trunks of pine trees because they are very tall and straight. In
other words, Pliny was describing a pillar of cloud! Notice also that
Pliny says that from a distance the source of the cloud (Vesuvius)
was not discernible. In other words, what Pliny saw was a vertical
pillar of cloud apparently hanging there in the sky. The photograph
11.2, shown above, shows a typical pillar of cloud from an erupting volcano.

So we have a possible explanation of the pillar of cloud by day. But
what about the pillar of fire by night? Let us continue with the same
letter from Pliny the Younger to Tacitus: his uncle had sailed his ship
closer to Mount Vesuvius, and it was now night. Pliny the Younger
writes, "Mount Vesuvius was blazing in several places with spreading

11.3. A pillar of fire by night, from a volcano in Hawaii.

and towering flames whose refulgent brightness the darkness of the night set in high relief." So Pliny tells us it was night, and instead of seeing a pillar of cloud he saw "towering flames": in other words, a pillar of fire by night (photograph 11.3, above)!

In a large volcanic eruption huge towering flames leap out of a volcano surrounded by thick clouds of vapor. By day often only the surrounding cloud is visible, reflecting the light of the sun. But by night the cloud is invisible (just as clouds in the sky are visible in the daytime but not at night), and the volcanic fire becomes visible. Think of a smoky bonfire seen from a distance: by day you mainly see the smoke, and by night you mainly see the flames.

Madame Louise Vigée-Lebrun, who had painted Queen Marie Antoinette's portrait, emigrated to Italy at the start of the French Revolution. In a letter she wrote, "Now I must tell you of my various expeditions up Vesuvius. . . . Then night came on, and the smoke was transformed into flames, the most beautiful sight imaginable." Notice what she says: the smoke by day was transformed into flames by night, just as described in the ancient book of Exodus for the pillars of cloud and of fire.

The descriptions of Pliny and others of the cloud by day and fire by night from a volcanic eruption match so closely the biblical pillar of cloud by day and pillar of fire by night (and see the striking photos) that I believe we can have little doubt that when the book of Exodus describes the pillars of cloud by day and fire by night, these pillars must have been due to a volcanic eruption.

Relating the pillars of cloud and of fire to a volcanic eruption is not my original idea. Listen to the words of the brilliant American author Mark Twain, in a letter he wrote from Hawaii in 1872 describing the eruption of Kilauea in Hawaii:

> A colossal column of cloud towered to a great height in the air immediately above the crater. . . . I thought it just possible that its like had not been seen since the children of Israel wandered in their long march through the desert so many centuries ago over a path illuminated by the mysterious "pillar of fire." And I was sure that I now had a vivid conception of what the majestic "pillar of fire" was like, which almost amounted to a revelation.

But is there a volcano that could have been responsible for the pillar of cloud and fire at the time of the Exodus? There are no volcanoes in Egypt (which in any case would be behind the Israelites and not in front of them and therefore could not act as a guide). There are no volcanoes in the Sinai Peninsula. There is a famous volcano in the Mediterranean called Santorini, but, as we've seen, the most probable date for its eruption is 1628 B.C. (from tree-ring dating), hundreds of years before the Exodus, and in any case it is in the wrong direction. But there *are* active volcanoes in Midian in Arabia, as we have seen earlier.

In addition, clearly it makes sense for the erupting volcano that produced the pillars of cloud and of fire to guide the Israelites to be none other than Mount Sinai itself, since the purpose of the pillars was to guide the Israelites to Mount Sinai. Thus a consistent story is starting to emerge. The pillars of cloud and of fire that guided the Israelites to Mount Sinai were themselves due to a volcanic eruption on Mount Sinai in Midian. Mount Sinai was therefore not only the mountain of God, it was also the guiding light drawing the Israelites to itself, like a mountain with a fiery beacon on its summit.

Could the Israelites have seen the cloud and fire from a volcano located far away in Midian when they were in the Sinai Peninsula? We do not yet know which particular volcano in Midian was Mount Sinai, but the volcanic regions in Midian are shown on the map (see map 11.1, pg. 163). The direct distance, as the crow flies, from the Sinai Peninsula to these volcanic regions in Midian is between 220 and 375 miles, depending on which volcano is involved and where in the Sinai Peninsula the Israelites were when they first saw the pillars of cloud and fire. These are huge distances: surely the pillars of cloud and of fire from a volcanic eruption cannot be seen over such distances? Well, they can! Musil, in *The Northern Hegaz,* describes the view he had from the volcanic regions of Midian as follows: "To the west we could see the Sinai Peninsula, not only the mountains of the southern part of the peninsula, but also the plain extending to the north of these mountains. . . . We were traveling at a height of about 1460 meters [4,788 feet]." These words of Musil give some idea of the very large distances that can be seen in the clear skies in these regions from the high lava fields in Midian, which are about one mile above sea level. So if Musil could see the high el Tih plain, 2,500 feet above sea level, on the Sinai Peninsula from the volcanic regions of Midian, then Moses and the Israelites could have seen from the el Tih plain on the Sinai Peninsula a colossal pillar of cloud and of fire, rising miles into the sky, emitted by a volcano in Midian.

Three modern authors, Ambraseys, Melville, and Adams, have collected together historical accounts of earthquakes and volcanoes in their book *The Seismicity of Egypt, Arabia and the Red Sea: A Historical Review.* This is their description of a documented volcanic eruption on June 30, 1256, which occurred near Medina in Arabia:

> The eruption began on 30 June, east of Medina. The exact location of the crater is not known. Huge clouds of smoke and fire were emitted for a number of days, visible at Mecca, Yanbu and as far as Taima. It is alleged that at night the glow of the eruption could be seen from as far as Bosra in Syria, more than 900 kilometers [500 miles] to the north.

Thus the pillars of cloud and of fire from a volcanic eruption in Midian could have been visible from the Sinai Peninsula, which is

11.4. The pillar of cloud from the eruption of Mount St. Helens in 1980.

much closer to Midian than is Bosra in Syria. The reason volcanic eruptions can be seen from far away is that the pillars of cloud and of fire can reach high into the sky. For example, before its eruption in 1980, Mount St. Helens in Washington State was 9,677 feet high, but the "pillar of cloud" from the volcanic eruption rose more than 50,000 feet into the air. This huge pillar of cloud was visible from great distances (photograph 11.4, above).

In addition, as the Israelites marched across the Sinai Peninsula, if they were indeed traveling toward Midian then they were for most of their journey on the high plateau mentioned above called the Plateau of el Tih (see map 3.1, pg. 30). From this high plateau they would have had an excellent unobstructed view of the pillars of cloud and of fire. They would not, of course, have been able to see the source of the pillars, the volcano itself, just the pillars of cloud and of fire, which would have appeared to be suspended in the sky. Thus the pillars of cloud and of fire were indeed directly ahead of the Israelites as they crossed the Sinai Peninsula, guiding them on their way, particularly at night, like an enormous finger pointing down to the real Mount Sinai. What a spectacular story!

Let's read again the words of Exodus 13:21–22: "By day the Lord went ahead of them in a pillar of cloud to guide them on their way and by night in a pillar of fire to give them light, so that they could travel by day or night. Neither the pillar of cloud by day nor the pillar of fire by night left its place in front of the people." What a brilliantly accurate portrayal of the cloud and fire from a volcano toward which one is walking! I believe that Mark Twain would have been fascinated to be alive today and see his "revelation" given more substance. Indeed, by the end of this book we will know precisely which volcano three thousand years ago guided the Israelites across the Sinai Peninsula by emitting its towering pillars of smoke and of fire: we will have found the true Mount Sinai.

So far we have tracked the Israelites from their starting point, Rameses, to Succoth, on the Egypt-Sinai border, and we have shown how the pillars of fire and of cloud guided them across the Sinai Peninsula. But what detailed route did they take? The book of Exodus says they took the road to the Red Sea, but what was this road to the Red Sea? Indeed, what body of water was meant by the Red Sea? The biblical translation "Red Sea" has been called the most famous mistranslation in history. Whether the Israelites crossed the Red Sea or an inland Sea of Reeds has been debated for many years. This is the next key problem we have to solve, and it is a fascinating detective story, with a surprising result. All will be revealed in the next chapter.

TWELVE

WHERE WAS THE
BIBLICAL RED SEA?

So God led the people around by the desert road towards the Red Sea.
Exodus 13:18

When I was at school, many years ago, I was taught a subject called religious education by Major Evans, a Welsh-
man who had taken early retirement from the army. I
remember only one thing from those lessons: Major Evans drummed
into us that "Red Sea" was the biggest mistranslation in the Bible.
"Always remember," he thundered in a commanding voice, "the correct translation is 'Reed Sea,' not 'Red Sea.' Moses and the Israelites
didn't cross the Red Sea, they crossed an inland reedy lake called the
Reed Sea."

Major Evans was in good company: nearly all modern biblical
scholars believe that the Hebrew Old Testament words translated
"Red Sea" should be translated "Sea of Reeds." For example, the
leading biblical scholars I have referred to previously in this book,
Hyatt, Hoffmeier, and Houtman, all believe this, and they therefore
believe that Moses and the Israelites crossed an inland Sea of Reeds
and not the Red Sea (by "Red Sea" we mean the Gulf of Suez, the
Gulf of Aqaba, and the main body of the Red Sea: they are all called
the Red Sea because they are the same body of water; see maps 1.3,
pg. 10 and 11.1, pg. 163).

When I stood on the summit of the traditional Mount Sinai in the spring of 1995 and began my quest for the real Mount Sinai and the true route of the Exodus, I resolved to have no preconceptions. I would scrutinize every detail of the Exodus story afresh. So my long-standing belief, held ever since the lucid lesson of Major Evans, that the Red Sea was really the Reed Sea, had to be torn up and I had to discover the truth for myself. What I found was an exquisite puzzle, with twists and turns every bit as fascinating as a top-notch detective story. One week I believed the Red Sea was the Reed Sea, the next week it was back to the Red Sea, and so on. In the end, solving the puzzle involved visiting the Sinai Peninsula and discovering something that no one else has recognized as being important. More of that later. For now I would like you to read this chapter as if you were reading a detective story.

Before we start, let us remind ourselves of the importance of knowing where the biblical Red Sea is. The crossing of the Red Sea is probably the most memorable miracle in the whole of the Old Testament. When I tell people that I am writing a book about some of the miracles in the Old Testament, their first question always is, "What happened at the crossing of the Red Sea?" If we don't know which body of water Moses and the Israelites crossed, then we cannot really understand what happened at this remarkable event. Identifying the biblical Red Sea is so important that I am going to devote two whole chapters to it.

The Evidence for the Sea of Reeds

Why do virtually all modern scholars believe that the biblical Red Sea is really the Sea of Reeds? Their arguments are very strong. The Hebrew words in the Old Testament traditionally translated "Red Sea" are *yam suph*. What do these words really mean? Well, *yam* is the Hebrew word for "sea," although it can also mean a large lake or river. Similarly, today we sometimes use the word *sea* to refer to inland freshwater lakes like the Sea of Galilee as well as to saltwater seas like the Caribbean Sea or the North Sea. *Suph* means "reeds" or "marshes": for example, when Moses as a baby was placed in a basket in reeds or rushes on the banks of the River Nile, *suph* is the word used for the reeds in Exodus 2:3, 5. The Hebrew word *suph* is probably related to an Egyptian word meaning papyrus reeds. Hence *yam suph* literally means a sea, lake, or river of reeds or rushes.

When I was a teenager I was a keen botanist. Thinking back to my teenage years, I remembered that reeds grow only in freshwater rivers and lakes and not in saltwater seas, but to be sure I went to a library and checked this out. I found that, although salt-tolerant reeds and rushes exist that grow in slightly salty water, they cannot grow in very salty water like seawater. I believe this is a key piece of scientific information. It would seem that the name *yam suph,* meaning Sea of Reeds, cannot refer to a salty sea, like the Red Sea, because no reeds can grow there. *Yam suph* must therefore refer to an inland freshwater reedy lake in which reeds grow: hence the name "Sea of Reeds."

So are there such freshwater lakes in the Sinai Peninsula? This is where we must look for the Sea of Reeds, because in the previous chapter we left Moses and the Israelites camped at Succoth, about to cross the border from Egypt into the Sinai Peninsula. The answer is yes, and possible locations of these lakes are shown on an earlier map (map 3.1, pg. 30). They include Lake Menzaleh, a lake bordering the Mediterranean, or the marshy lagoon just south of it; Lake Sirbonis (modern Lake Bardawil); Lake Ballah; Lake Timsah; and the Bitter Lakes. All of these lakes contain reeds. Scholars believe that each of these lakes is a possible candidate for being *yam suph,* and they also believe that the term *yam suph* possibly applied collectively to all of them, similar to the way the modern name "Great Lakes" applies to Lakes Erie, Huron, Michigan, Ontario, and Superior.

Having looked at the evidence that *yam suph* means "Sea of Reeds," I must say that I find it very convincing. How can it mean anything else?

The Evidence for the Red Sea

I believe there can be no doubt that *yam suph* literally means "Sea of Reeds," so why traditionally has *yam suph* been translated as "Red Sea"? It is a fascinating story.

The oldest complete version of the Old Testament that we possess today is the Septuagint, older complete versions having been lost or destroyed. As we saw in chapter 3, the Septuagint version of the Pentateuch (the first five books of the Bible) dates back to the third century B.C. and is a translation from the Hebrew into Greek by Jewish scholars living in Alexandria in Egypt. Alexandria is on the coast of Egypt, on the western side of the Nile Delta, whereas Rameses, where the Israelites started their Exodus journey, is on the eastern side of the delta (map 3.1, pg. 30).

The name Septuagint, which means seventy, comes from a legend that seventy (-two) Jewish interpreters, six from each of the twelve tribes of the Jews, did the translating in seventy (-two) days. The Hebrew Masoretic Text, from which modern Bibles in English are translated, although later than the Septuagint, is known to be based on Hebrew manuscripts that are earlier than the Septuagint.

Modern translations of the Old Testament usually try to give a reasonably literal translation of the ancient Hebrew Masoretic Text, although we have seen in earlier chapters how occasionally the preconceptions and prejudices of the translators creep in. The Greek Septuagint version of the Hebrew Old Testament is rather less literal. Although the Jewish translators presumably wished to make an accurate translation, inevitably they interpreted passages as they themselves understood them.

What is really interesting is that when these Jewish scholars in Egypt in the third century B.C. translated into Greek the Hebrew words *yam suph,* literally meaning "Sea of Reeds," they did not give the Greek words for "Sea of Reeds" but they "translated" *yam suph* as *eruthra thalassa,* which is Greek for "Red Sea." Why did they do this? These Jewish scholars would have known very well that *yam suph* literally meant "Sea of Reeds," but instead of giving this literal translation they preferred to tell their readers where they believed *yam suph* really was: it was the Red Sea. From their traditions they knew that Moses and the Israelites had crossed the Red Sea and not some reedy inland lake. The third century B.C. Septuagint is the earliest known reference to where the *yam suph* crossing occurred: at the Red Sea. The Septuagint was written in Alexandria, a major center for scholars and only 140 miles away from inland reedy lakes like the Bitter Lakes, and therefore we must give the evidence from the Septuagint significant weight.

When the writers of the New Testament referred to the Red Sea crossing (in Acts 7:36 and Hebrews 11:29), the Greek words they used were *eruthra thalassa*, meaning "Red Sea," and not the Greek words for "Sea of Reeds." When Latin scholars translated the Old Testament into Latin (the Vulgate version of the Old Testament), they rendered *yam suph* as *mare rubrum*, again meaning "Red Sea," and when the Hebrew Old Testament was translated into English in the famous King James Version of the Bible in A.D. 1611, *yam suph* was again rendered as "Red Sea." Essentially all these translations followed the lead given by the Septuagint. Thus both Jewish tradition from at least the third century B.C. onward and Christian tradition from the first century A.D. onward have consistently interpreted *yam suph* as "Red Sea" and not as "Sea of Reeds."

I hope you can now see why I kept oscillating in understanding what *yam suph* really means. To start with, I was convinced that *yam suph* means "Sea of Reeds," and that is indeed the literal meaning. However, according to two New Testament writers, the crossing of *yam suph* by Moses and the Israelites occurred not at an inland reedy lake but at the Red Sea, and the evidence we have suggests that if we could go back to the first century A.D. and ask any Jew or Christian walking in the street—or any scholarly rabbi or apostles like Peter and Paul—which body of water Moses and the Israelites crossed, they would all have said, without hesitation, "the Red Sea."

So I now believed that although *yam suph* literally meant "Sea of Reeds," it really referred to the "Red Sea." However, there is another possibility. Could *yam suph* mean *both* "Red Sea" and "Sea of Reeds"?

The Sea of Reeds and the Red Sea

Before coming to the University of Cambridge in 1990, I had been head of the department of materials engineering at the University of Liverpool for five years. Liverpool University has a small but world-famous Department of Archaeology and Oriental Studies, and I got to know two world-class experts on ancient Egypt and Israel in that department, Professors Kenneth Kitchen and Alan Millard.

In 1997 I was asked to give a science talk late on a Friday afternoon back in my old Department of Materials Engineering. I arranged to stay in Liverpool overnight and then to meet Ken Kitchen and Alan Millard the next morning. So on Saturday morning I went to Alan Millard's office, which I was interested to see had a terra-cotta pot containing a thriving Egyptian papyrus plant, from which the word *suph* is derived. So my first question to Alan and Ken had to be about *yam suph!*

I explained to them my belief that although *yam suph* literally meant "Sea of Reeds," it must really refer to the Red Sea because of the interpretation given in the Septuagint. They disagreed. They explained that the Septuagint is a secondary source written a thousand years after the events described and that the primary source is the Hebrew text of the Old Testament. Since this has *yam suph* meaning "Sea of Reeds," then "Sea of Reeds" has to be what was meant. However, they added that the term *yam suph* was a broad term that covered not only the inland reedy lakes in the Sinai Peninsula, but also the Gulfs of Suez and Aqaba and possibly the main body of the Red Sea as well.

Hyatt in his commentary *Exodus* says something similar: "The Old Testament uses *yam suph* with more than one meaning. . . . *Yam suph* could have been the name of several different bodies of water." Kenneth Kitchen, in his article entitled "Red Sea" in the *New Bible Dictionary*, is explicit: "In the Old Testament the term *yam suph*, 'Sea of Reeds,' is used to cover: (a) the Bitter Lakes region . . . and (b) the Gulfs of Suez and Aqaba and possibly the Red Sea proper beyond these."

So modern scholars are saying that *yam suph* is almost a catch-all term referring to any body of water in the Sinai Peninsula. The more I thought about this, the more unlikely it seemed, for two reasons. First, why should the reed-free Gulfs of Suez and Aqaba be included in the catch-all term Sea of Reeds? This appears to make no sense. Second, we started this chapter with a quotation from the book of Exodus stating that the Israelites traveled "by the desert road towards the Red Sea (*yam suph*)." To my mind, this quotation is referring to a particular road leading to a definite place. If there are a number of places called *yam suph*, then this quotation makes no sense. Let me give a modern example. If I tell someone that I traveled from Cambridge by the highway to London, this statement implies that there is a well-known, and probably unique place called London. The statement makes no sense if there are six different places around Cambridge all called London. Similarly, the statement that the Israelites left Succoth and traveled by the desert road to the Red Sea implies that there was a well-known, and probably unique, desert road from Succoth to a place called the Red Sea (*yam suph*). I suggest this statement would not have been made if there were six different places around Succoth all called *yam suph,* or if there were, then the desert road to *yam suph* must refer to the particular *yam suph* that is reached by traveling across the desert.

A few years ago I was lecturing to a class of students, and in the front row a student wore a T-shirt emblazoned with the letters MAIK. I asked him what it meant and he said, "Man, Am I Confused." (Okay, he couldn't spell, either!) I must say that at this stage of my Exodus investigations I felt confused. After a lot of thought and reading I still had no answer to the question of where the biblical Red Sea was situated except that scholars thought *yam suph* was a catch-all term for any lake or sea in and around the Sinai Peninsula.

It is interesting to note that some scholars have suggested that *yam suph* doesn't mean Sea of Reeds but instead should read as *yam soph,* which means "the furthest sea." However, not many scholars take this seriously because it seems that *soph* is an Aramaic word that was introduced into Hebrew at a later date. So this suggestion doesn't work.

It then occurred to me to ask a question I should have asked before. Does the Old Testament identify *yam suph* with a particular body, or bodies, of water?

King Solomon's Ships

In the Old Testament there are two books called Kings (they are called, not surprisingly, 1 Kings and 2 Kings), which describe the history of the ancient kings of Israel. The first king of Israel, King Solomon, famed for his wisdom, wealth, and wives, lived in about 1000 B.C. Here is how the Old Testament describes one of his shipyards: "King Solomon also built ships at Ezion Geber, which is near Elath, in Edom, on the shore of the Red Sea [Hebrew *yam suph*]" (1 Kings 9:26). Once again, notice the care with which the Bible spells out the geography of the situation. The writer pinpoints precisely where Solomon built his ships: at Ezion Geber, near Elath in Edom, on the shore of the Red Sea.

We know from both the Old Testament and other ancient texts that Edom was the country immediately to the north of Midian, and the southern boundary of Edom ran through the northern head of Gulf of Aqaba at modern Aqaba (see map 4.1, pg. 46).

The precise locations of ancient Elath and Ezion Geber are uncertain, although many scholars believe that Elath was in, or close to, modern Aqaba in Jordan (see map 4.1, pg. 46), on the northeast side of the head of the Gulf of Aqaba.

It should be noted that Elath is not believed to be modern Eilat in Israel, on the northwest side of the head of the Gulf of Aqaba. Some scholars believe that Ezion Geber was close to modern Aqaba. Others believe it was slightly farther away, on a small island with an ancient harbor, called Jazirat Faraun, or Pharaoh's Island, in the Gulf of Aqaba (see map 4.1, pg. 46). I have visited Pharaoh's Island (photograph 12.1, below) with its secluded harbor (photograph 12.2, on the next page) and can confirm that this would have been an excellent place for Solomon to have built his ships.

12.1. Pharoah's Island, near the head of the Gulf of Aqaba.

12.2. Sheltered harbor at Pharoah's Island.

Since 1 Kings 9:26 states that Solomon built his ships at Ezion Geber, near Elath in Edom, on the shore of the Red Sea, and since we can identify ancient Edom as a country adjacent to the Gulf of Aqaba, we can say with reasonable certainty that the biblical Red Sea is the Gulf of Aqaba. It may be other places as well, but what is beyond reasonable doubt is that the biblical Red Sea includes the Gulf of Aqaba. Hence the translation of *yam suph* as "Red Sea" in the Septuagint, the New Testament, and the KJV must be at least partially correct.

At last I felt I was making a little progress, but I had some unanswered questions. Why was the reed-free Gulf of Aqaba called *yam suph,* Sea of Reeds? Was the Gulf of Aqaba really free of reeds? Why was the Red Sea so called? In all of my travels I have never seen a red sea! So I decided to travel to the Gulf of Aqaba and see if I could find answers. It was one of the best decisions I ever made.

Are There Reeds in the Gulf of Aqaba?

So it was that I booked a holiday to Taba for one week at Easter time 1999 for my wife, Sarah, and me. Taba is in Egypt, on the west shore

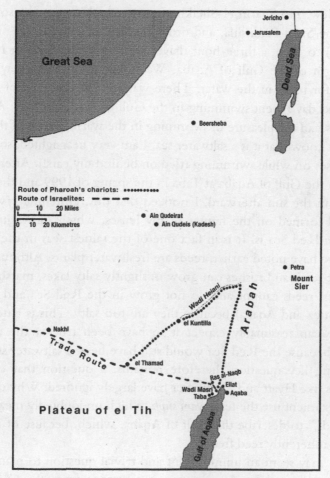

12.3. Map of region around head of the Gulf of Aqaba.

of the Gulf of Aqaba, and very close to the modern border with Israel (see map 12.3).

We stayed at the Taba Hilton because this is the hotel nearest to the border, and from the hotel it is only a few minutes' walk to the border crossing, which is called the Taba border crossing. I knew that we would want to cross over into Israel a lot during our stay, and the Taba Hilton has a special arrangement with the border crossing staff so that residents of the Taba Hilton have a fast-track route through the crossing. I mention all this in case any readers want to follow up anything in this book.

We flew into Sharm el-Sheikh airport, which is near the southern tip of the Sinai Peninsula, and drove up the coastal road (as much as possible) to Taba, a three-hour drive. We therefore drove for most of the length of the Gulf of Aqaba. We stopped along the way, and I looked for reeds in the water. There wasn't even the trace of a reed! The next day I went swimming in the Gulf of Aqaba at Taba. Anyone who has had the pleasure of swimming in the warm waters of the Red Sea will know that it is a saltwater sea. I am very nearsighted, so I keep my glasses on while swimming (tied on behind my ears!). After swimming in the Gulf of Aqaba at Taba in the spring of 1999 and then drying off in the sun afterward, I noticed that tiny, glistening crystals of salt had formed on the frames of my lenses, which shows just how salty the Red Sea is. It is in fact one of the saltiest seas in the world.

As we have noted earlier, reeds are freshwater plants. Although salt-tolerant reeds and rushes can grow in slightly salty lakes, marshes, and estuaries, reeds cannot and do not grow in the Red Sea and its two gulfs (Suez and Aqaba) because they are too salty. This is true today, and we can reasonably expect it to have been true at the time of Moses because the Red Sea would still have been a saltwater sea. The following key question therefore remains, a question that eminent scholars like Hyatt and Hoffmeier have largely ignored: Why does the Old Testament use the term *yam suph,* which undoubtedly means "Sea of Reeds," to describe the Gulf of Aqaba, which, because of its salti-ness, is inherently reed free?

This may seem an unimportant and trivial question to many read-ers, but we saw in earlier chapters just how accurate the Old Testa-ment writers are in describing geographical locations. Why then should they write apparent nonsense in this case? I had a hunch that if I could solve this problem it might help to answer the question of where the Israelites crossed the Red Sea, which we will come to in a later chapter.

Why Is the Red Sea Called the Red Sea?

As I stood on the shore of the Gulf of Aqaba at Taba and looked out over the deep blue sea, lapping the shingle shore, I couldn't imagine why anyone would call this the Red Sea. This water was deep blue from one side of the gulf to the other, and I also knew it was deep blue all along its length, since I had traveled from one end of the Gulf of Aqaba to the other.

Are there other bodies of water in the world called Red Sea that may give us a clue to the origin of this curious name? As far as I am aware, on a modern map of the world it is only the Gulfs of Suez and Aqaba plus the main body of the Red Sea that are called the Red Sea. However, in ancient times it is well documented that the Greek term *eruthra thalassa* and the Latin *mare rubrum* (both meaning "Red Sea") were used to describe not only the present-day Red Sea and its two gulfs, but also the Persian Gulf and the Indian Ocean. Hence, for some reason, all these bodies of water were called "Red Sea." However, and I believe this is important, I can find no record of "Red Sea" ever being used to describe an inland reedy lake.

As we have seen a number of times in this book, place-names often have a geographical or physical significance. Let me give another example of this. I am writing part of this chapter sitting on a Virgin Atlantic Boeing 747 plane flying from Heathrow to Los Angeles to speak at a scientific conference in Long Beach, California. When I arrive in Long Beach I will be disappointed if I don't see a long beach! Similarly, the name Red Sea raises our expectations that this sea can look red. I was convinced that I should look for a physical explanation of the name, but what could it be?

I had taken with me to Taba a suitcase containing some of the key books on the Exodus, so I looked up what they said about the origin of the name Red Sea. Unfortunately, they were not very helpful. The authoritative three-volume commentary on the book of Exodus by Houtman states, "The origin of the name 'Red Sea' is unknown," and Hoffmeier writes in *Israel in Egypt*, "There is still no convincing explanation for the origin of the name 'Red Sea.'"

I was sitting in our bedroom on the sixth floor of our hotel in Taba and had just finished reading this passage. My wife was lying on the beach below, reading a book. I stood up to go and join her and glanced out of our hotel room window. The normally deep blue Red Sea was covered with large red patches of color, as if someone had sprayed red paint on it. The effect was very clear and striking and could be seen from some distance away. I was amazed by this spectacular sight. I blinked several times because I thought there must be something wrong with my eyes! But there were no red patches on the white walls of our hotel room. Could the same red color be seen close up, and what caused it? I rushed excitedly from the room, ran down six flights of stairs, not waiting for the elevator, and strode rapidly out of the hotel, past the swimming pool, and on to the pebbly shore. The large red blotches of color on the water of the Gulf of Aqaba were still there! Some were very close to the shore. I turned to my wife and said, "Look at the water. Do you notice anything?" "Yes," she said, "it's red." I took off my sandals and ran into the warm waters to investigate what was causing the red regions of color. The mystery was revealed. It was low tide, and red coral lay only a few inches below the surface. The coral grows in large patches, and I walked on the seabed between these patches in order not to damage the coral. The red blotches of color on the water were due to the red coral just below the water surface.

There I was, standing on the seabed close to the shore, with water up to my thighs, by the edge of a coral reef with the most amazing brightly colored fish swimming around my legs. It was a wonderful experience, and the red color of the coral was reflected up through the water. Out farther from the shore the seabed slopes steeply downward, but the coral rises up through the water and at low tide the top of the coral is again just below the water surface. Thus large patches of red color can be seen at low tide on account of the red coral just below the surface, and at Taba these red patches both lie close to the shoreline and extend out from the shore.

After about thirty minutes, the striking red patches of color on the water had totally disappeared, since the tide had risen enough for the coral to be more deeply covered with water.

I saw this effect at low tide several times when I visited Taba in 1999 but not when I visited again in 2001. I believe the reason is that in 1999 I visited at full moon, and in 2001 it was half-moon time. At both new and full moons the gravitational forces of the moon and the sun on the water act in concert to produce a particularly high tide followed by a particularly low tide. These are called spring tides, although they have nothing to do with the seasons. Hence when I visited Taba at full moon, the low tide was very low and the red light reflected from the coral shone strongly through the thin covering of water.

Having witnessed this remarkable and beautiful phenomenon of red patches of color on a deep blue sea, I suggest that this is the reason for the name Red Sea. Coral is widespread all down the Gulfs of Aqaba and Suez and in the main body of the Red Sea, and I believe it is clear why the Red Sea is so called. Interestingly, coral also grows in the Persian Gulf and in the Indian Ocean, and I suggest this explains why in ancient times these bodies of water were also called the Red Sea. The fact that all three bodies of water were called the Red Sea and that coral grows in all these places is, I suggest, strong evidence for the name Red Sea.

While visiting Taba I observed another reason for the Red Sea appearing red. Running along the eastern shore of the Gulf of Aqaba, in modern Jordan and Saudi Arabia, there are mountain ranges that in many places come down to the sea. These mountains are largely composed of red granite and red sandstone, and they reflect and scatter sunlight onto the water of the Gulf of Aqaba. However, instead of casting sharp reflections that outline the shapes of the mountains, they scatter large, broad bands of red color onto the water. This red coloration was visible when I stayed at Taba in the springs of both 1999 and 2001, and it typically lasts between ten minutes and one hour. It can be particularly marked at sunset, when the reflections from the red mountains of the red setting sun can make the Red Sea a really deep red color. However, not every sunset turns the water of the Gulf of Aqaba red. The red coloration of the water appears to depend on the position of the sun in the sky and also on the form of the wave ripples on the surface of the water, since the red bands of color move with the water waves. This red coloration was visible most days at irregular times when I visited Taba, and the effect is different and distinct from the red coloration due to the red coral at low tide. Presumably this mechanism for turning the Gulf of Aqaba red does not apply to the Persian Gulf or the Indian Ocean since, as far as I am aware, there are no suitable red mountains present there.

Thus the Red Sea is so called because it really does have large red patches of color on it at certain times of the day. Ancient travelers were not stupid, and the name Red Sea exists for these very good reasons. Conversely, it would seem highly unlikely that a reedy inland lake would be called the Red Sea, or *eruthra thalassa* in Greek, since coral cannot grow in freshwater lakes. In addition, as far as I am aware, there are no red mountains on the shore of any of the inland lakes in the Sinai Peninsula.

The Most Famous Mistranslation in History?

Now that we understand the scientific reasons for the Red Sea's appearing red, we can say beyond reasonable doubt that when the Jews of Alexandria in Egypt in the third century B.C. rendered the Hebrew *yam suph* as the Greek *eruthra thalassa*, they clearly intended to refer to the Red Sea and not to an inland reedy lake. The tradition handed down to them of where the momentous miracle of the Re(e)d Sea crossing occurred must therefore have been that it was at the Red Sea and not at an inland Sea of Reeds. Similarly, the tradition handed down to the New Testament writers of the books of Acts and Hebrews must have been that the crossing was at *eruthra thalassa*, Red Sea, and not at an inland Sea of Reeds.

Now that we have performed a more detailed analysis of the Red Sea/Reed Sea question, various problems remain. In particular, why does the Hebrew Old Testament call the Gulf of Aqaba, where Solomon had his shipyard, *yam suph*, meaning Sea of Reeds, when the Gulf of Aqaba is reed free? Why does the Hebrew Old Testament have Moses and the Israelites crossing *yam suph*, Sea of Reeds, whereas the Greek Septuagint and the New Testament locate the crossing at the Red Sea, which name, as we have seen, cannot include an inland Sea of Reeds? Either ancient writers were extremely confused about the location of one of the most important events in the history of Israel or else we are missing a key piece of the jigsaw puzzle. Most modern scholars believe the former: they believe the Septuagint and the New Testament are wrong here and that the Israelites crossed an inland reedy lake.

The current belief about the location of the biblical Red Sea is well summarized in a book written in 2001 by Bruce Feiler, *Walking the Bible: A Journey by Land Through the Five Books of Moses.* Feiler is an award-winning American author who traveled the Exodus route to

Mount Sinai (the traditional route in the Sinai Peninsula) with Avner Goren, who was the chief archaeologist and preserver of antiquities of the Sinai Peninsula for the fifteen years that Israel controlled this region, from 1967 to 1982. Feiler states,

> Inevitably, efforts to decipher where this event [the Re(e)d Sea crossing] took place have preoccupied biblical readers for centuries. . . . It was the Greek Septuagint, translated by the Jews in Alexandria in the third century B.C.E., that introduced the most famous mistranslation in history, *"Eruthra Thalassa,"* Red Sea, for what should have been Sea of Reeds. This mistake was picked up by the Latin Vulgate and embedded into English with the King James Bible in 1611. . . . There are five main candidates for the Sea of Reeds: (1) the Mediterranean; (2) the marshy region just south of the Mediterranean; (3) Lake Timsah; (4) the Bitter Lakes; (5) the Red Sea itself, specifically the Gulf of Suez. . . . Papyrus grows only in fresh water, which would seem to rule out the Mediterranean and the Red Sea.

Feiler then chooses Lake Timsah (see map 3.1, pg. 30) for the site of the Reed Sea crossing, mainly because it is "relatively shallow, often no more than three feet deep." He adds, "It's tempting to imagine the Israelites, on a windy day, wading across this body of water, while the Egyptians mindlessly followed and got their chariots stuck in the mud."

As we will see in a later chapter, our reconstructed Re(e)d Sea crossing is much more dramatic than this, and I believe very much more in line with the epic nature of the biblical account. However, what was the sea the Israelites crossed? Is the Septuagint translation of *yam suph* as *eruthra thalassa* really the most famous mistranslation in history? Could this interpretation be correct? Could the New Testament be correct in describing the crossing at *eruthra thalassa,* Red Sea? Are modern scholars wrong about this? Can we know after three thousand years? Could the Old Testament, the Septuagint, and the New Testament *all* be right about the location of the Red Sea crossing? The next chapter tries to answer all these questions, based on observations of the Gulf of Aqaba never before reported.

THIRTEEN

THE RED SEA REVEALED

I will establish your borders from the Red Sea to the Sea of the Philistines and from the desert to the River.

Exodus 23:31

The visit my wife, Sarah, and I made to Taba in Egypt in the spring of 1999 had already proved useful. I believed I had discovered how the Red Sea got its name. I had also found out that the Red Sea is extremely salty and had observed no traces of reeds or rushes growing there. However, a key puzzle remained that no biblical scholar has solved; indeed, none of the many commentaries on the book of Exodus that I've read even comments on it as a problem. The puzzle is this: Why does the Hebrew Old Testament call the Gulf of Aqaba *yam suph,* meaning Sea of Reeds, when reeds do not and cannot grow there because it is too salty?

I believe that most biblical scholars don't recognize this as a problem because they do not believe the Old Testament text to be very accurate. They therefore gloss over problems like this as simple mistakes. But we have seen earlier in this book just how accurate the geography is in the Old Testament account of the crossing of the river Jordan and how the correct order of the ten plagues has been faithfully preserved over three thousand years. Because of this I was totally mystified that the ancient Hebrews would have called the reed-free Gulf of Aqaba the Sea of Reeds. Either this was a glaring error or else I was missing a key piece of the puzzle.

With these thoughts in my mind, Sarah and I decided to visit the town of Aqaba in Jordan. I was keen to visit Aqaba because that was the place, or near to it, where King Solomon had his shipyard, on the shore of *yam suph,* which in this case, as I've shown in the previous chapter, is the Gulf of Aqaba. Perhaps a visit to Aqaba would throw light on why the Hebrew Old Testament calls the Gulf of Aqaba the Sea of Reeds when it is, in fact, free of reeds.

Visiting Aqaba from Taba is an interesting experience. First we went through the Taba border crossing. We then took a taxi from the Israeli side of the Taba border crossing and drove through Eilat to the Arava (the Hebrew pronunciation of what we call the Arabah) border crossing between Israel and Jordan.

Then we took another taxi from the Jordanian side of the Arava border crossing into Aqaba, which is on the northeast tip of the Gulf of Aqaba (see map 12.3, pg. 181) and walked around the town and part of the sea.

As expected, there was no trace of reeds in the waters of the gulf. The town of Aqaba is rich in history, being at the junction of several important trade routes (see map 4.2, pg. 52): the route north, from Aqaba to Damascus in modern Syria, is known as the King's Highway; the route south leads to southern Arabia (modern Yemen) and is called the Incense Route; the route west leads to Egypt, and as we have seen in chapter 4, I believe it is the route Moses took when traveling from Egypt to Midian and then back to Egypt.

While in Aqaba we walked to the remains of the ancient Roman city of Aila (map 4.1, pg. 46), which was a port city that flourished between the first century B.C. and the seventh century A.D. Aila is located within modern Aqaba, and it is largely covered by sand dunes. Excavations have revealed various structures at Aila, including a fourth-century Christian church, one of the oldest Christian churches in the world. There is also a wadi (riverbed) that runs through Aila, which was dried up when we visited. The wadi runs from the Arabah, through Aila, and down to the Gulf of Aqaba.

And then I saw them. Reeds! Great clumps of tall reeds, four to six feet high on the far bank of the wadi running through the archaeological site of Aila. I couldn't believe what I was seeing! I had been thinking about reeds (in fact, I had been thinking about the absence of reeds) many times since our arrival in Egypt three days before, and here they were! How very curious. The archaeological remains of Aila are about 200 yards north of the present northern sea line of the Gulf of Aqaba. Since ancient Roman literature describes Aila as a harbor on the seacoast, we can deduce that in Roman times, two thousand years ago, the waters of the Gulf of Aqaba must have extended 200 yards farther to the north. This is consistent with the Gulf of Aqaba's being part of the Great Rift Valley, a huge, four-thousand-mile long fissure in the earth's crust, in which the ground on both sides is slowly moving apart so that the water level falls slowly as time advances. In addition, the northern shore of the Gulf of Aqaba here is very flat, so only a small vertical drop in sea level is required for the sea to retreat horizontally for 200 yards. So two thousand years ago, in Roman times, it is likely that the waters of the Gulf of Aqaba extended up to Aila and freshwater reeds were growing close to the water's edge.

Apart from the land around Aila, which has been left untouched, most of the shoreline at Aqaba has been built up with hotels and other buildings, and so any other reeds that might have grown there are now below concrete. However, one thing is clear, and it has gone totally unnoticed in biblical commentaries: there are large patches of reeds at the northern head of the Gulf of Aqaba, and the site of these reeds would probably have been adjacent to the sea at the time of Moses.

As my wife and I left Aqaba and returned to Taba, I resolved to search for reeds around the northwestern head of the Gulf of Aqaba, at Eilat in modern Israel. Each day we left our hotel in Taba and passed through the Taba border crossing, getting our passports stamped with Egyptian and then Israeli stamps. Each day the Israeli security staff at the border crossing asked us why we were entering Israel. I like to tell the truth, but I suspected it was not wise to say we were looking for reeds! So I said we were going shopping, which was also true, since we bought books in Eilat, and we then passed through the border control rapidly. However, after five consecutive days of crossing the border for "shopping" and amassing pages full of stamps in our passports, we were confronted on the sixth day by a young female security officer who fired questions at us while fixing her eyes on mine. I returned the eye contact and smiled at her. "I'm going to win this and get through here quickly," I thought. Well, I didn't. She took away both of our passports and kept us waiting for about an hour before returning them and letting us through.

On the previous few days we had walked around the head of the Gulf of Aqaba at Eilat, soaking up the atmosphere and looking out for anything of historical interest. However, much land has been reclaimed in recent years; millions of tons of soil must have been deposited here and many hotels built. It is impossible to say where the shoreline might have been three thousand years ago, and any reeds that were here would now be below concrete.

On the final day of our holiday, I had an idea. Looking at a modern map of the head of the Gulf of Aqaba, on the west there is Eilat in Israel and on the east is Aqaba in Jordan. Between the two is the Israel-Jordan border. A street map of Eilat showed that Israel had not yet built hotels right up to the Israel-Jordan border, and I wondered if the land in this area had been filled in yet. So Sarah and I walked east along a road near the coast leading out of Eilat and to the high wire fence of the border with Jordan. Above the fence was barbed wire, and above the wire were sentry boxes on towers. There was no public entrance here (the Arava crossing is to the north).

We walked past the last hotel in Eilat, rather curiously called Herod's Hotel. There was now bare earth on either side of the road. We passed no one as we headed toward the high wire fence. There were no cars, no people, and no noise. The silence was eerie after the bustling noise of downtown Eilat. The armed guards in their sentry boxes must have wondered what we were playing at: two people walking through uninhabited territory toward a high wire border fence at a sensitive time politically. We came to a bridge over a small stream running south toward the Gulf of Aqaba. On the east of the stream, toward the border fence, the soil level was about four to six feet lower than on the west. The ground on the west, toward Eilat, had been filled in with huge volumes of soil, but the ground on the east of the stream had not yet been altered.

And there they were again! Reeds! A huge bed of reeds on the unaltered ground! This time the reeds were of a different type from those in Aqaba and were about three feet high. My wife and I clambered down beside the bridge, and I took a photograph (see photograph 13.1, on the next page).

13.1. Reeds growing on unreclaimed groud in Eilat, near the head of the Gulf of Aqaba. Herod's Hotel is in the background.

Then I noticed the soil the reeds were growing in. Thick clay (photograph 13.2, on the next page). How unexpected to find thick clay in an undeveloped part of desert close to the sandy shore of the Gulf of Aqaba. The clay was so clinging that imprints of the soles of my sneakers were left behind in it (see photograph 13.3, on the next page).

I couldn't help thinking that chariot wheels wouldn't get far in clay like this. Suddenly my thoughts were disturbed by the noise from a large military truck driving past on the road we had just left. It had clearly come from the Israel-Jordan border and was full of soldiers. It drove past very slowly, and all the soldiers looked at us. However, the truck did not stop but went farther up the road, turned around, and drove slowly past us for a second time, the soldiers again looking at us intensely. Sarah looked at me nervously: "I think we should leave," she said, so we did.

We returned to Taba in the spring of 2001 to do some more exploring. While walking along the ancient Wadi Masri, now called the Wadi Shlomo (also called Wadi Solomon: Shlomo is the original Hebrew form of the name Solomon), which runs into the Gulf of Aqaba from the west, at a point between Taba and Eilat (see map 12.3,

13.2. Large area of thick clay soil, with reeds, near head of the Gulf of Aqaba, Eilat.

13.3. Imprints of my sneakers in the thick clay soil near the head of the Gulf of Aqaba, Eilat.

13.4. Reeds growing in Wadi Masri close to the head of the Gulf of Aqaba.

pg. 181), I noticed some more reeds near the entrance to the wadi close to a modern building called the Texas Ranch.

This time it was a small clump of reeds about four feet high (see photograph 13.4, above) of a type that looked similar to those I had seen in Aila.

Thus I observed patches of reeds growing in three separate places around the head of the Gulf of Aqaba and close to the water. It is reasonable to infer that before the massive development that has occurred around the head of the Gulf of Aqaba there were probably many more areas covered with reeds. But why should freshwater reeds grow at the end of the saltwater Gulf of Aqaba? In all my travels, I couldn't recall seeing reeds growing adjacent to a saltwater sea anywhere else in the world. Is there something special about the geography of the Gulf of Aqaba?

The Physical Geography of the Gulf of Aqaba

The Gulf of Aqaba, as we saw above, forms part of what is called the Great Rift Valley, the greatest geological rupture on the earth's surface. The Great Rift Valley runs south from Syria and Lebanon, through the Jordan Valley, which contains the Jordan River (where slippage along the fault gave rise to the earthquake that enabled the crossing of the river Jordan as described in chapter 2), through the Dead Sea, the Arabah, the Gulf of Aqaba, and the main body of the Red Sea. It then continues across Ethiopia and ends in Mozambique.

The Arabah mentioned above is a long sandy valley running between the Dead Sea and the head of the Gulf of Aqaba (see map 12.3, pg. 181), and it is bordered on the east and the west by high mountain ranges.

We can partially reconstruct the situation prior to all the filling in of land that has occurred in recent years from descriptions given in earlier literature. The geography is well described by John Lloyd Stephens, who gave up a lucrative career as a lawyer to become an archaeologist and who in 1837 wrote a travel book called *Incidents of Travel in Egypt, Arabia Petraea, and the Holy Land*. In this book Stephens writes,

> Standing on the shore of the northern extremity of the Red Sea [that is the Gulf of Aqaba], I saw before me an immense sandy valley [the Arabah]. The valley varied from four to eight miles in breadth and on each side were high, dark and barren mountains, bordering it like a wall. On the left were the mountains of Judea and on the right those of Seir.

The Czech explorer Musil, in *The Northern Hegaz*, written in 1926, describes an extremely unusual feature of the northern seashore at the head of the Gulf of Aqaba: it contains *fresh* water. Normally, if you dig down into the sand on a seashore you get saltwater, from the saltwater of the sea, but the situation at the head of the Gulf of Aqaba is very different. Here is how Musil describes the ancient Roman site of Aila, which as we have seen is situated at the head of the Gulf of Aqaba in modern Aqaba in Jordan: "At low tide the rocky shore [at Aila] was laid bare for a distance of about two hundred meters, uncovering numerous springs which gushed forth with great strength." The excellent quality of this freshwater is then emphasized by Musil: "But the animals [camels] did not wish to drink from the fresh water from the well [at Aila], preferring to go to the sea shore where they very readily drank from the many springs which flowed there." The clear inference of this passage from Musil is that the surface water on the seashore from the springs at the head of the Gulf of Aqaba was superior in freshness even to the water from a freshwater well.

Where did the water in these freshwater springs on the seashore come from? It seems clear that it was from rain falling on the mountains bordering the Arabah, and from springs in these mountains. This water is then funneled along and under the sand of the Arabah down toward the Gulf of Aqaba. The soil at the head of the Gulf of Aqaba has a high clay content, and so the freshwater funneled down the Arabah remains close to the surface, with impervious clay underneath, to break out on the seashore as freshwater springs. Although the rainfall per square foot in this desert region is very low, the Arabah and its bordering mountains act like a giant funnel, collecting the rain over a very large area and then funneling it down to a much smaller area at the head of the Gulf of Aqaba. There is therefore a plentiful supply of freshwater at the head of the Gulf of Aqaba.

The head of the Gulf of Aqaba thus has an extremely unusual physical geography. The seashore is a boundary between the saltwaters of the gulf to the south and the freshwater coming down to the seashore from the north. In addition, it appears that there used to be a large marsh where Eilat in Israel now stands. Edward Robinson was the professor of biblical literature at Union Theological Seminary in New York when he visited the Sinai Peninsula in 1838. He published his findings in 1841 in *Biblical Researches in Palestine*. In it he states, "We reached the N.W. corner of the Gulf of Aqaba and entered the great Haj road, which comes down the western mountains and passes along the shore at the northern end of the sea. . . . On the north of the path, towards the western side, a large track [of land] has the appearance of moist marshy ground. . . ." Now the northwest corner of the Gulf of Aqaba is modern Eilat, which did not exist of course when Robinson wrote his book. Thus it appears that there used to be a marsh where Eilat is today, and this undoubtedly would have been a freshwater marsh fed by freshwater funneled down the Arabah.

A somewhat more recent explorer confirms this. Major C. S. Jarvis was the governor of Sinai when this territory was ruled by Britain, and in 1931 he wrote a marvelous book called *Yesterday and Today in Sinai*. In this book he describes the road at the head of the Gulf of Aqaba: "The road then runs close to the sea across a clay pan, but if there has been rain recently this is impassable and one must go north through very bad and rough sand country, or, if the tide is low, it is possible to get on to the sea shore and run on the damp sand." Thus not only did freshwater used to come down the Arabah and right onto the seashore, but also adjacent to the seashore was a large tract of freshwater marshy land with clay soil, providing ideal conditions for the growth of reeds.

In my travels to Taba, as described above, I found that even today reeds grow in at least three places around the head of the Gulf of Aqaba. Books written before the housing and hotel developments around the head of the Gulf of Aqaba show that there was a large marshy tract of land apparently where Eilat now is. I suggest we can reasonably deduce that at the time of Moses, when the waters of the Gulf of Aqaba came higher up the shore than they do now, the Gulf of Aqaba terminated in reedy marshland.

As I have written before, people living three thousand years ago were not stupid, but the content of their knowledge was different: we know much more science and technology, but they would have known more about surviving in a desert. We obtain water, almost un-thinkingly, by turning on a tap. They would have obtained water by laboriously carrying it from a well or a river. They would have known that the water of rivers was fresh to drink and that seawater was too salty to drink. They would have been well aware that certain plants, like reeds, grow in freshwater and not in saltwater. Just as a knowl-edgeable modern gardener can instantly tell whether soil is acid or al-kaline by observing the types of plants growing there, so people three thousand years ago would have known whether a sea, lake, or river was salty or freshwater simply by observing the types of plants growing in and around it. I believe they would have been amazed to find reeds growing at the head of the saltwater Gulf of Aqaba because it was so totally unexpected. So I suggest the ancient Hebrews called the Gulf of Aqaba *yam suph*, Sea of Reeds. I suggest that other travelers were equally amazed by the striking red patches of color that appeared on the waters of the Gulf of Aqaba, and Greek-speaking travelers called this Gulf *eruthra thalassa*, Red Sea, and in time this name replaced *yam suph*. So in Old Testament times, *yam suph* and *eruthra thalassa* de-scribed the same place: the Gulf of Aqaba. The Jewish writers of the Greek Septuagint deliberately chose to use the more modern Greek name, *eruthra thalassa*, Red Sea, to describe the Gulf of Aqaba, instead of translating into Greek the ancient Hebrew name for the same place, *yam suph*.

So I believe we have answered, for the first time in many centuries, one of the questions we posed at the start of this chapter: Why does the Old Testament describe the Gulf of Aqaba as *yam suph*, Sea of Reeds, when there are no reeds in this saltwater sea? The answer is because this gulf terminated in a freshwater marsh of reeds on account of the extremely unusual physical geography of the region.

Some readers may well be thinking this is pure speculation. Have we any evidence that in the ancient world people would have thought it unusual to find freshwater springs adjacent to a saltwater sea? Let me tell you a fascinating story. Several months after I wrote the first draft of this chapter, my wife, Sarah, and I went on a vacation to the island of Sicily, off the southern coast of Italy. We stayed at a place called Taormina, from where, on a clear day, Mount Etna is visible. Mount Etna is one of the most active volcanoes in the world, and this is why I had gone, in the spring of 2002, to Sicily: to experience something of what an active volcano was really like. More of this in the final chapter of this book.

Two and a half thousand years ago, Sicily was a major junction on the sea routes across the Mediterranean. It is the largest island in the Mediterranean and has a remarkable history, having been fought over and occupied by ancient Phoenicians, Greeks, Africans, Spaniards, and Romans.

In April 2002 Sarah and I boarded a coach at the bus stop adjacent to some Byzantine tombs in Taormina and set off for a day trip to Syracuse, on the eastern coast of Sicily. Syracuse once rivaled Athens as the largest and most beautiful city of the Greek world. The apostle Paul stayed here (Acts 28:12), Archimedes was born and lived here (c.287–212 B.C.), and Plato visited here (c.397 B.C.).

Imagine my surprise when our guide told us that he was going to show us a famous freshwater spring adjacent to the saltwater sea in the harbor at Syracuse! This spring is called the Occhio della Zillica, and it feeds the Fountain of Arethusa next to the harbor. Our guide said, "This fountain was one of the most famous fountains in the ancient Greek world, and it was written about by various writers, including

Virgil. The ancient Greeks thought it so unusual to find a freshwater spring beside a saltwater sea that a famous Greek legend arose to explain it. The legend is that when the beautiful nymph Arethusa was bathing in the river Alpheus near Olympia in Greece, the river god fell in love with her. To escape from him she jumped into the Ionian Sea and swam all the way to Syracuse in Sicily. When she emerged from the sea, the Greek goddess Artemis transformed her into a spring, and that's how the ancient Greeks explained a freshwater spring being next to the saltwater sea."

We can see from this that in the ancient world it really was recognized as being highly unusual to have a freshwater spring beside a saltwater sea. The spring now flows into a pond, built in 1843, that is inhabited by ducks. As I stood looking at the pond, I couldn't help but notice a huge clump of reeds growing on an island in the center of the pond, so I asked our guide about them and then listened in amazement to what he told me. "These are genuine papyrus reeds," he said. "Syracuse is the only place in the whole of Europe where papyrus reeds grow. The ancient Greeks were so amazed to find a freshwater spring beside the saltwater sea that they wanted to make it really obvious to everyone that it was a freshwater spring."

"How did they do that?" I asked.

"Well," he said, "they brought over papyrus from Egypt and planted it by the spring of Arethusa so that everyone would know it was a freshwater spring, because in the ancient world everyone knew that papyrus grows only by freshwater."

"When was it brought over from Egypt?" I asked.

"Traditionally it is said to have been a gift of Ptolemy Philadelphus, but it was probably brought over by Hieron II in about 240 B.C.," he said. He added that the papyrus had thrived so well that it was then planted in various places in Syracuse, paper was made in Syracuse from this papyrus, and there is today a papyrus museum in Syracuse! I then photographed the reeds in the pond. Immediately behind the pond is a walkway and then the saltwater sea (photograph 13.5, on the next page).

I therefore suggest that when ancient travelers found freshwater springs and reeds at the head of the saltwater Gulf of Aqaba, they would have recognized this juxtaposition as extremely unusual.

13.5. *Reeds growing in a freshwater pond adjacent to the saltwater sea at Syracuse, Sicily.*

In fact, it was so unusual that they called the place *yam suph,* the Sea of Reeds.

What Bodies of Water Were Called *Yam Suph?*

We have seen why the Gulf of Aqaba was called *yam suph* in Hebrew and *eruthra thalassa* in Greek: it could be described both as the Sea of Reeds and the Red Sea. But were there other bodies of water that could also be described in this way?

I haven't visited the head of the Gulf of Suez and looked for reeds there, but it is worth noting that the slightly salty Bitter Lakes, in which reeds grow, are today only eleven miles north of the Gulf of Suez. Hoffmaier, in *Israel in Egypt,* gives various pieces of evidence that suggest that three thousand years ago, at the time of Moses, the Gulf of Suez stretched farther north than it does today and that the Bitter Lakes stretched farther south, to the point where they may have connected. Let me quote directly the conclusion of Hoffmaier: "Geological, oceanographic, and archaeological evidence suggests that the Gulf of Suez stretched further north than it does today and that the southern Bitter Lake extended further south to the point where the two could have actually been connected during the second millennium [B.C.]. This linking may have stood behind the Hebrews naming the lake *yam suph* as well as the Red Sea to which it was connected."

The biblical geographer J. Simons, in his book *The Geographical and Topographical Texts of the Old Testament,* argues that the Bitter Lakes and the Gulf of Suez were at least seasonally connected. My view is that the evidence suggests that the Gulf of Suez and the Bitter Lakes could well have been sufficiently close that there was a marshy area between them in which reeds grew. If this was the case, then *both* the Gulf of Aqaba and the Gulf of Suez terminated with reed-filled marshes three thousand years ago, which I suggest is a particularly compelling argument for calling both gulfs the Sea of Reeds. In addition, since the Gulf of Suez, like the Gulf of Aqaba, contains coral, it would also have been called, in Greek, *eruthra thalassa,* Red Sea. Since both gulfs connect to the main body of the Red Sea in a continuous stretch of water, I suggest that it may have been logical for all of them to have been called *yam suph* in Hebrew and later *eruthra thalassa* in Greek.

I suggest that the above arguments solve the long-standing problem of why both the Septuagint and the New Testament "translate" *yam suph* (Sea of Reeds) as *eruthra thalassa* (Red Sea). Both are correct, provided they described the Red Sea and its two gulfs, Aqaba and Suez. On the other hand, inland lakes such as Lake Timsah, the Bitter Lakes, and so forth cannot be described as *eruthra thalassa,* and I have found no evidence that they were ever called *yam suph* either, and hence the majority of modern biblical scholars who interpret the Re(e)d Sea as an inland lake and place the Re(e)d Sea crossing there are, I believe, incorrect.

Biblical References to *Yam Suph*

Are there any direct clues in the Bible about the location of *yam suph?* If I have counted correctly, the Hebrew term *yam suph* is used twenty-four times in the Old Testament. I have analyzed all of these and found that only on a few occasions is it clear what body of water is being referred to. In each of these cases, I believe the body of water is the Gulf of Aqaba. We have already discussed the reference to King Solomon's ships and shown that *yam suph* in that passage refers to the Gulf of Aqaba. Here are three other references. Numbers 21:4 states, "They [the Israelites] traveled from Mount Hor along the route to *yam suph* to go round Edom." Since Edom is adjacent to the Gulf of Aqaba but far from the Gulf of Suez and also far from inland lakes, *yam suph* here must refer to the Gulf of Aqaba. Another reference comes in Deuteronomy 2:1: "Then we turned back and set out towards the desert along the route to *yam suph,* as the Lord had directed me. For a long time we made our way around the hill country of Seir." *Yam suph* again clearly means the Gulf of Aqaba because the hill country of Seir is known to be an alternative name for the country of Edom, which is adjacent to the Gulf of Aqaba.

Another reference to *yam suph* is in Exodus 23:31, in which the future boundaries of the nation of Israel are given: "I will establish your borders from the Red Sea [*yam suph*] to the Sea of the Philistines and from the desert to the River." We know from the Old Testament and from other ancient literature that the Sea of the Philistines was the Mediterranean Sea, along whose eastern coast Philistine cities were located, and this marks the western border of the future nation of Israel. The River is the Euphrates, and this marks the northeastern border. The desert is the Sinai Desert, and this marks the southern border. *Yam suph* here is clearly not an inland lake but a major body of water acting as a boundary marker. The only body of water that makes sense is the Gulf of Aqaba, which then marks the southeastern border. These boundaries are consistent with the land promised to the descendants of Abraham in Genesis 15:18 and with the land later ruled over by King Solomon in about 1000 B.C., which is spelled out in 1 Kings 4:21–24. We know that King Solomon's territory extended to the Gulf of Aqaba since he had a shipyard there. As far as I can see, there are no references to *yam suph* in the whole of the Old Testament that indicate that it is an inland lake or the Gulf of Suez; the few references that enable us to pinpoint *yam suph* all have it as the Gulf of Aqaba. Thus although *yam suph* literally means "Sea of Reeds," I can find no evidence that the inland lakes in the Sinai Peninsula were actually called *yam suph*.

However, we should also consider that after the plague of locusts, Exodus 10:19 states "a very strong west wind caught up the locusts and carried them into *yam suph*." The ancient Hebrews used only the four cardinal points, north, south, east, and west, and did not use intermediate terms such as northeast. Hence a west wind can mean any wind direction ranging from northwest to southwest. Since, as we have seen, the plague of locusts occurred in a region of Egypt around Rameses, in the eastern Nile Delta, a west wind in principle could have carried the locusts into one of the reedy inland marshes to the east of Rameses or into the Gulf of Suez or into the Gulf of Aqaba (see map 3.1, pg. 30). We cannot say for certain which body of water the author intended, but the Gulf of Aqaba is possibly too far away. An inland lake is probably too small to have blown into it millions and millions of locusts. My feeling is that a large body of water is indicated here, and the most likely candidate is the Gulf of Suez, but the Gulf of Aqaba cannot be ruled out.

Finally, I will mention a reference to *yam suph* that has long puzzled biblical scholars. Numbers 33 lists the encampment sites of the Israelites on their Exodus journey. It gives *yam suph,* the Red Sea, as a campsite at least five days' journey after the crossing of *yam suph,* the Red Sea. How strange! We will consider the meaning of this in detail in chapter 17; at present we will simply note that if *yam suph* means an inland reedy lake, then we are either seeking two inland lakes on the Exodus route at least five days' journey apart, or there was a return to the inland lake already crossed, which is extremely unlikely. The map of the area (map 3.1, pg. 30) shows that the inland lakes in the Sinai Peninsula are all closer than five days' journey apart. On the other hand, if *yam suph* means the Gulfs of Suez and Aqaba and the main body of the Red Sea, then the problem is solvable geographically because it is easy to find many places that are five days' journey apart on these large bodies of water.

Let me end this chapter by briefly summarizing my main findings about the Re(e)d Sea. An analysis of all the evidence suggests that the term *yam suph* definitely refers to the Gulf of Aqaba and probably also refers to the Gulf of Suez and to the main body of the Red Sea. There is no support for *yam suph* referring to an inland lake. The Greek Septuagint interpretation of *yam suph* as *eruthra thalassa* is not therefore "the most famous mistranslation in history," but on this occasion I believe it is absolutely correct.

Thus, if my arguments are accepted, the Hebrew Old Testament, the Greek Septuagint, and the New Testament all agree that the crossing of Moses and the Israelites occurred at the Hebrew *yam suph,* meaning Sea of Reeds, which was later called in Greek *eruthra thalassa,* meaning Red Sea, both terms referring to the Gulf of Aqaba and probably also to the Gulf of Suez and the main body of the Red Sea. We have come to the end of a complex series of arguments and have reached a simple conclusion, one that disagrees, however, with that of the overwhelming majority of modern scholars.

There are very few areas in modern life in which amateurs can compete with professionals. Rather curiously, astronomy is one of them. The majority of new comets found in the last thirty years have been discovered by amateur astronomers with telescopes in their gardens and bedrooms. Professional astronomers, with their huge expensive telescopes, have missed them. Why is this? Because the professional astronomers have not pointed their telescopes in the right direction to see the new comets. Many thousands of amateur astronomers all over the world can cover a much larger area of the night sky with their telescopes than can a smaller number of professionals.

I believe the situation is somewhat similar with my discoveries of the red coloration of the Red Sea and of the reeds growing adjacent to the head of the Gulf of Aqaba. Why haven't biblical scholars discovered these? I believe the answer is that they haven't looked. If they had, then they would have seen them. I find it refreshing that amateurs in biblical scholarship can discover new things. However, when an amateur astronomer discovers a new comet, it adds to existing knowledge about the universe; it does not overturn that knowledge. What I find really exciting is that if my findings and conclusions are correct (and I believe the evidence is very strong), then we will be overturning many of the beliefs of modern biblical scholars about the Exodus.

The next chapter is another detective story, but of a different type. We are going to try to find a biblical site that has been lost for centuries. It is the key third site on the Exodus route: a place called Etham. How do you find an ancient site for which no archaeological remains have yet been found? Come with me into the next chapter to find out.

FOURTEEN

THE LOST SITE OF ETHAM

After leaving Succoth they camped at Etham on the edge of the desert.

Exodus 13:20

When I was a child I used to dream of being an archae-ologist unearthing a mysterious mummy in a tomb or discovering an ancient city lost in the mists of time. Just think of the thrill the archaeologist Howard Carter must have had when in 1922 one of his laborers stumbled upon a stone step in the desert in Egypt and Carter dug down to find a stone staircase lead-ing to a walled-up door. Behind the door was a second sealed door, and behind that was the finest royal tomb ever found in Egypt: the fabulous gilded tomb of Tutankhamen. Or think of the tingle in the spine the Swiss explorer Burckhardt must have experienced when, in 1812, he discovered the rose red rock-hewn temples of the won-derful lost city of Petra.

Discovering Tutankhamen's tomb and the city of Petra was difficult enough, but I think that discovering lost sites on the Exodus route is even more difficult, because in most cases there is probably nothing left to see: no gilded tombs, no temples. Of course, there are archaeo-logical remains at some sites mentioned in the book of Exodus, such as Rameses, the starting point of the Exodus journey, and we can use these to identify ancient Rameses with modern Qantir, but how do we identify sites that have left no archaeological clues behind (as far as we know)? That is a really challenging problem.

Some years ago the British heavyweight boxing champion, Frank Bruno, fought the then-unbeaten world champion, Mike Tyson. Frank Bruno was interviewed before the fight by the TV commentator Harry Carpenter. Harry said, "Frank, people are saying that Mike Tyson is invincible. Does this worry you?" Frank thought for a moment, scratched his head, and said, "Well, Harry, that's a real problem, because if you can't see him, you can't hit him."

So how do you discover an ancient historical site that is no longer visible? In this chapter we are going to try to do just that: we are going to try to discover the lost site of Etham, the third mentioned place on the Exodus route—not by using archaeology but by looking at the clues provided in the Old Testament and by using science. Is it really possible to do this after three thousand years?

The Importance of Etham

Etham is the third place on the Exodus route as given in the books of Exodus and Numbers. For example, Numbers 33:5–6 states, "The Israelites left Rameses and camped at Succoth. They left Succoth and camped at Etham, on the edge of the desert." We have already identified Rameses and Succoth: Rameses is modern Qantir in Egypt, and Succoth is near modern Ismailiya, on the border of Egypt and the Sinai Peninsula. But where was Etham? The standard commentary by Hyatt on the book of Exodus simply states, "Etham cannot be identified." The book by Hoffmeier, *Israel in Egypt,* says, "Unfortunately, with the knowledge presently available, the location and nature of this encampment, as well as the meaning of Etham, will have to remain uncertain." In fact, all the major biblical scholars regard the location of Etham as unknown. What a challenge to find it!

Why is locating Etham so important? Etham is important because it is the first named stage of the Exodus journey after the Israelites left Succoth, on the Egypt-Sinai border. Knowing where Etham is therefore defines the direction the Israelites took when they left Egypt. Conversely, if we do not know where Etham is, then we cannot be sure what route the Israelites took when they left Egypt. Etham is therefore an absolutely key place, yet the leading scholars in the world do not know where it is. Because Etham is so important, we are going to devote one chapter of this book to finding it.

Finding Etham

Let me explain why I think scholars have not located Etham. They have been looking in the wrong place. Because, as we have shown, Succoth is a day's journey from Rameses (see map 3.1, pg. 30), most biblical scholars have assumed that Etham must be roughly one day's journey from Succoth, so that is where they have been looking intensely on ancient maps, but to no avail. However, neither Exodus nor Numbers implies that Etham is one day's journey from Succoth: Etham is simply the third listed stage on the route and in principle could be quite a long way from Succoth.

Let me give you a modern example of what I mean. A few weeks ago an American tourist pulled up his rented car beside me in Cambridge, wound down his window, and said, "Please can you help me? How do I get to London from here?"

"What part of London do you want?" I replied. "London is a big city, and it covers a very large area."

"Well," he said, "I want a place called Southgate."

"I know Southgate because some friends of mine live there," I said. "There is a major road we call the M11 motorway that runs from just outside Cambridge to London. To get onto the M11 motorway, drive out of Cambridge along the Trumpington Road, which you are now on, to a small village called Trumpington, about two miles from Cambridge, where you will see the sign for the M11 motorway to London. You then drive forty miles south along the M11, and this takes you to the edge of London." I then explained how he should get from the edge of London to Southgate. As he left me, I summarized the route for the first part of his journey: "The route is Cambridge to Trumpington, use the M11 motorway, go from Trumpington to London."

Let's compare my route with that given in the book of Numbers for the first part of the Exodus journey: Rameses to Succoth, then Succoth to Etham. In my route, Trumpington is two miles from Cambridge, while London is forty miles from Trumpington; so Cambridge, Trumpington, and London are far from being equidistant. Similarly we should not assume that Rameses, Succoth, and Etham are equidistant places, because the list of place-names for the Exodus route in the books of Exodus and Numbers does not imply this at all. Let's now do some detective work on the Exodus route given in the books of Exodus and Numbers to try to find out as much as we can from the Bible about the location of Etham. Since we will be looking at two different Old Testament books, it is possible that they may give us different information about Etham.

When detectives interview two witnesses, their stories often appear to differ in points of detail, and the detectives will work away at these differences until a coherent story emerges. That is precisely the approach I am now going to take to the two accounts of the Exodus route given in the Old Testament books of Exodus and Numbers. We will restrict ourselves in this chapter to comparing the names of the first ten places on the Exodus route. The account of this part of the route in the book of Exodus is considerably longer than that in Numbers because Exodus includes a description of what happens in most of the places visited, whereas Numbers simply presents a list of the camping places on the route. Thus the account of this part of the route in the book of Exodus spans four chapters, whereas in Numbers it occupies only seven verses. I am, therefore, compressing the text in the book of Exodus to give only place-names, but I am giving these in the exact order they occur in Exodus, and similarly in Numbers. Placing these two lists side by side gives the following sequence of places on the route:

EXODUS (12:37–15:27)	NUMBERS (33:3–9)
Rameses	Rameses
Succoth	Succoth
Etham	Etham
Pi-hahiroth	Pi-hahiroth
Migdol	Migdol
Baal-Zephon	Baal-Zephon
Crossed the Red Sea	Crossed the Red Sea
Desert of Shur	Desert of Etham
Marah	Marah
Elim	Elim

The first striking point about these two lists is the great similarity between them. Police detectives would be surprised and delighted if two witnesses agreed so well. This suggests to me that the lists have a common source, and I see no reason why the source doesn't go back to Moses himself. In fact, Numbers 33:2 explicitly states, "At the Lord's command Moses recorded the stages in their journey." However, there is an obvious difference between the lists: the desert the Israelites entered after crossing the Red Sea is called the Desert of Shur in Exodus and the Desert of Etham in Numbers. Are these two deserts the same or different? Exodus 15:22 states, "Then Moses led Israel from the Red Sea and they went into the Desert of Shur. For three days they traveled in the desert without finding water. When they came to Marah . . ." Numbers 33:8 states, "They passed through the sea into the desert, and when they had traveled for three days in the Desert of Etham they camped at Marah." Comparing these two passages—the references to the Red Sea crossing, three days in the desert, and then camping at Marah—makes it absolutely clear that the Desert of Shur and the Desert of Etham must be the same place. Hence Shur and Etham must be different names for the same place. We will see the reason for this shortly.

As we have seen many times in this book, place-names often have meanings. Let me give two more examples: Monument Valley in Arizona is a valley of fantastic spires of rock rising up from the desert like monuments. The Lake District in the U.K. is a region full of lakes. If we understand the meaning of a place-name this can help us to locate it. So does the Desert of Shur have a meaning? The answer is intriguing: *shur* is a Hebrew word meaning "wall," and it is used in this way several times in the Old Testament. For example, Psalm 18:29 states, "With your help I can advance against a troop; with my God I can scale a wall." The Hebrew word translated "wall" here is *shur,* and clearly it means a high wall that the psalmist can climb with the help of God, not a low wall he can easily step over. Just as the Lake District in England is a district of lakes, could it be that the Desert of Shur is a desert of walls? How extremely unlikely this sounds for a desert! Yet could this be a cryptic clue that will help us locate the Desert of Shur?

What about the meaning of the Desert of Etham? Unlike *Shur, Etham* is not a Hebrew word and hence does not have a Hebrew meaning. The New International Version Study Bible has a footnote to Exodus 15:22 concerning the Desert of Shur that says, "In Numbers 33:8 the 'Desert of Shur' is called the 'Desert of Etham.' Shur and Etham both mean 'fortress wall' (Shur in Hebrew, Etham in Egyptian)." In fact, scholars are divided as to whether or not Etham is related to the Egyptian *htm*, which means "fort," although everyone agrees that *Shur* is the Hebrew for "wall." We will come back to this later.

There is another curious feature in the list of the Exodus route place-names we quoted above. Take a look at the lists and see if you can spot it. In both the books of Exodus and Numbers the Israelites reach Etham before they cross the Red Sea, and in the book of Numbers the Israelites enter the Desert of Etham after crossing the Red Sea. How can Etham be both before and after the Red Sea? This puzzled me for some time until one day, as I was going to a meeting in London and walking beside the river Thames, the obvious solution struck me. I was in London on one side of the Thames, but if I crossed a bridge to the other side, I would still be in London. London was on both sides of the river Thames. Of course! Thus if Etham was both before and after the Red Sea crossing site, Etham must be a district on both sides of the Red Sea, possibly covering a large area like London. As if to ram this point home, Numbers 33:8 says, "When they had traveled for three days in the Desert of Etham . . ." In other words, the Desert of Etham covered a significant area, just like London.

But where was Etham, which we have deduced was also called Shur in Hebrew, which means "wall"? We just showed that Etham was a region both before and after the site of the Red Sea crossing. In the previous chapter we showed that the Red Sea (*yam suph*) was definitely the Gulf of Aqaba, and possibly also the Gulf of Suez and the main body of the Red Sea. However, we found no evidence that it was an inland reedy lake. Both the Gulfs of Aqaba and of Suez are deep except at their head (see chapter 16). This suggests that the site of the Red Sea crossing is probably at the head of the Gulf of Aqaba or of Suez. Hence, if all our deductions are correct, Etham must have been around the head of the Gulf of Aqaba or the Gulf of Suez. Could the name Etham still be found on old maps?

I went to my collection of secondhand copies of books about the Sinai Peninsula and Midian written by travelers and explorers. These books often contained old maps that folded out from within their pages. So I took out the most relevant books, and opened the maps on our dining room table. I looked at one map while my wife, Sarah, with her sharper eyesight, looked at another. Before long Sarah said excitedly, "I've found Etham."

"Where is it?" I asked.

"It's here," she said, "almost touching the head of the Gulf of Aqaba." And so it was.

The map on which we had found Etham is at the end of the second volume of Richard Burton's *The Land of Midian,* published in 1879. On the map is printed "Map of the Land of Midian, constructed from reconnaissances and surveys, made by Officers of the Egyptian General Staff under the command of Captain R. F. Burton. 1878." At the head of the Gulf of Aqaba, by a mountain peak, is printed "El Yitm Peak" and in brackets underneath "(Lithm, Etham)." I have reproduced part of this map in this book (see map 14.1, which is magnified in map 14.2, pg. 214). Clearly, Lithm and Etham are alternative names for Yitm (Lithm is probably from el-Ithm). Interestingly, this is the only place on the whole map where alternative names are given. Burton, in *The Land of Midian,* also states, "This Yitm, which Burckhardt first wrote El Ithem." Burckhardt is the famous Swiss explorer who discovered the fabulous rose red city of Petra in 1812 and who then visited Midian in 1814 before Burton's later expedition.

Hence we have now identified Etham on a map. On a modern map of Aqaba the mountain peak Etham is usually spelled Ithm, Itm, or Yitm (it is sometimes called Bagir, after a local Arab), and it is the highest peak of the range of mountains on the east of the Arabah (or Arava) coming down to the Gulf of Aqaba. Interestingly, T. E. Lawrence, in his book *The Seven Pillars of Wisdom* (first printed privately in 1926), has Ithm on his maps in the book but spells the same place as Itm everywhere in the text. Thus ancient Etham is the same as modern Ithm (also spelled Itm, Yitm, Lithm, and Ithem). Note again the fluidity in the transliteration of Arabian words and the importance of the consonants. The key point is that Etham is to be found on a map in precisely the place I had deduced it should be found: at the head of the Gulf of Aqaba. Modern maps show that at the foot of the Ithm mountain peak there is the Wadi Ithm, a major

14.1. *Section of map from* The Land of Midian, *by Richard Burton, published in 1879. "Etham" is at the top of the map.*

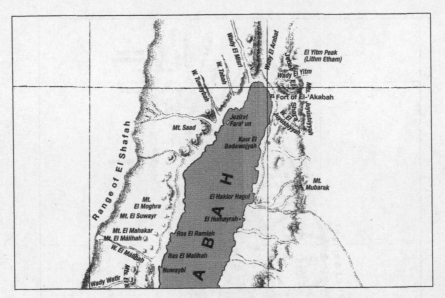

14.2. *Magnified section of map 14.1 showing "Etham" more clearly.*

wadi (riverbed that can dry up in summer), which runs into the head
of the Gulf of Aqaba and which channels rainwater falling on the
mountain to the head of the Gulf of Aqaba. Thus even in the present
day, the name Ithm (ancient Etham) describes a region: both a tall
mountain and a wadi. I have spent hours poring over ancient maps of
the Sinai Peninsula, and I have found no other place in the peninsula
with a name resembling Etham—not around the Gulf of Suez nor
around inland lakes nor anywhere else in the peninsula. Let me add a
word of caution when looking at old maps of the Sinai Peninsula.
Some mapmakers have been so convinced that Mount Sinai is Jebel
Musa on the Sinai Peninsula that they have invented locations for
places on the Exodus route like Etham and written them on their
maps so that they form a route to the traditional Mount Sinai! The
more honest mapmakers who have done this have followed the name
with a question mark. On such maps there is often a line of exodus
route names, for example, "Pi-hahiroth?" "Migdol?" and so forth (see
map 1.3, pg. 10). Do not be fooled by such maps.

Sometimes a whole region is called after the mountain it contains.
For example, the Greek island of Santorini is so called after the volcano named Santorini that erupted and created it and that is located in

the middle of the gulf of the island. The highest mountain in England and Wales is Snowdon (height 3,560 feet), which gives its name to over 800 square miles of land surrounding it called Snowdonia. It is therefore easy to see that the highest mountain on either the east or the west of the Arabah, Ithm (ancient Etham) could give its name to the district surrounding it. So I suggest that Etham was both the tallest mountain peak around the head of the Gulf of Aqaba and also the name of the region surrounding it.

Let us now return to our earlier detective work, that in the time of Moses Etham must have been the same place as Shur, which means "wall." How can a mountain be described as a wall? Just listen to the description of Burton in *The Land of Midian:* "Jebel [meaning mountain] el-Yitm [Etham] . . . is certainly the highest visible peak of the grand wall that forms the right bank of the Wadi Yitm [Etham]." The grand wall! So Etham, which is the same place as Shur, which means "wall," is named after a natural phenomenon: a wall of mountains rather than a manmade wall, such as a fortress wall, which many scholars have supposed.

Let us continue our detective work. So far we have identified a wall of mountains on the east of the Gulf of Aqaba and associated this with Shur or Etham. But earlier we deduced that Shur/Etham was an extended geographical region that existed on the west of the Gulf of Aqaba as well as on the east. Is there any evidence for this? Let me repeat a quotation I gave earlier from one of the great explorers, J. L. Stevens, in his *Incidents of Travel in Egypt, Arabia Petraea and the Holy Land,* published in 1837:

> Standing near the shore of this northern extremity of the Red Sea [that is, the Gulf of Aqaba], I saw before me [looking north] an immense sandy valley [the Arabah, or the Arava]. The valley ranged from 4 to 8 miles in breadth, and on each side were high, dark and barren mountains, bounding it like a wall. On the left were the mountains of Judea, and on the right those of Seir.

So Stevens is saying that both on the east and on the west of the Arabah and the Gulf of Aqaba there is a range of mountains, like a wall on both sides. On my own visits to the Gulf of Aqaba in 1999 and 2001 I observed this myself. The word *wall* describes beautifully the mountain range both east and west of the head of the Gulf of Aqaba: the mountains do indeed rise up like high towering walls, and I suggest it is the region containing these majestic wall-like mountains on both sides of the Gulf of Aqaba that the Bible calls Etham or, in Hebrew, Shur, meaning "wall."

So we have a consistent story. Etham, also called Shur, refers to the region on both sides of the head of the Gulf of Aqaba, with *Shur* being the Hebrew word and *Etham* the local Midianite word to describe the same region. (I write "local Midianite word" rather than "Arabic word" because the Arabic language had not yet been developed. We are in pre-Arabic language times.) *Shur* means "wall," and this term aptly describes the wall of mountains on each side of the head of the Gulf of Aqaba; indeed, the word *wall* was used by explorers over one hundred years ago to describe this range of mountains, which form natural walls. I believe that we have therefore located Etham, otherwise known as Shur, the third named place on the Exodus route.

Can We Be Sure About Shur?

In the second chapter of this book we described how by using the lenses of science we could be sure, beyond reasonable doubt, about how the crossing of the river Jordan occurred and where it occurred. We have since used modern science to throw light upon the burning bush and the ten plagues of Egypt. Can we use science to be really certain, beyond reasonable doubt, about the location of Shur? Although it may seem highly unlikely, I think we can.

As we saw, *Shur* is Hebrew for "wall." In principle this wall could be either manmade or a natural feature, and we strongly suggested above that the Shur of the Exodus is so called after the mountain walls on each side of the Arabah and the head of the Gulf of Aqaba.

This set me thinking. As a scientist, I have been privileged to travel all over the world. I have seen many, many mountains, but I would not normally describe them as walls because mountains do not usually look like walls. The magnificent Grand Canyon may have particular features that look like a wall, but I would never describe the Grand Canyon itself as a mountain wall. The north face of the Eiger in Switzerland is sometimes called the north wall of the Eiger, but no one would look at the Eiger mountain and call it a wall. Yet the mountains on each side of the Gulf of Aqaba, which run up each side of the Arabah, do look like walls, and the well-traveled explorers Burton and Stephens describe them as such. Why? Is there a scientific reason that some mountains and not others should look like walls?

I wondered whether I could recall anywhere else in the world, apart from the Gulf of Aqaba, where mountains looked like walls, and then it struck me. Iceland! I had been invited to Iceland in 1999 as a member of a small international science committee, and my host had taken our group to visit a place called Thingvallir, which is the site of the oldest parliament in the world, dating back to A.D. 930. At Thingvallir in Iceland I stood in a narrow valley, and on each side of me were mountains that rose up like steep walls. I remember shouting and hearing multiple echoes of my voice as the sound reflected off the mountain walls on each side.

Thingvallir and the Red Sea have an important geological feature in common. A rift valley, where two tectonic plates are diverging, runs through both of them. As the plates pull apart, the region in between subsides, forming the rift valley. The rift valley is bounded on each side by rift walls, which are the sides of steep mountains. Geologists actually use the words *rift walls* to refer to these bounding mountains, because they look just like walls.

As we already saw, the Red Sea forms part of what is called the Great Rift Valley, which is a huge, four-thousand-mile fissure in the earth's crust beginning in Syria and Lebanon and ending in Mozambique.

Here is how Colin Willock begins his Time-Life book *Africa's Rift Valley:*

> I first saw the Great Rift Valley during a journey north from Nairobi, the capital of Kenya. Thirty miles from the city, I came suddenly, without any warning, to the lip of a gigantic chasm. The scrub-covered slope fell away almost vertically in front of me. Spread out 2,000 feet below was an immense yellow plain,

stretching into the distance. Thirty miles away, blue in the haze, I could see another almost vertical wall, very similar to the one on which I stood, rising to the same height.

Notice how Willock calls these sides of the rift valley "walls."

Now for the really important point. Mountains on each side of a rift valley are naturally called walls because they look like walls. Other mountains are not usually called walls because they don't look like walls. If we now look at the geography of the Exodus and at the various sites scholars have mentioned for the Red Sea crossing, we note that the Gulf of Suez is not part of a rift valley, and therefore any mountains around the Gulf of Suez would not look like walls. So Shur, if the name means a natural mountain wall, cannot be located there. We also note that the various inland lakes proposed for the Red Sea crossing (the Bitter Lake, and so forth) do not lie on a rift valley, so any nearby mountains would not look like walls, and Shur therefore is not located there.

On the other hand, the Arabah and the Gulf of Aqaba are both part of the Great Rift Valley, and the mountains on each side, for geological reasons, will be steep and look like walls. Thus, using the insights of science, in particular geology, we can say that the third mentioned place on the Exodus route, Shur, if the name means a natural wall, is probably located on a rift valley, and since the books of Exodus and Numbers place Shur/Etham around the Red Sea crossing site, Shur must be at the head of the Gulf of Aqaba. It cannot be at the head of the Gulf of Suez or within the Sinai Peninsula since these places are not on a rift valley.

I therefore believe that science has helped us identify the previously unknown place of Shur/Etham, and this identification fits perfectly the Old Testament account. Shur and Etham are the ancient Hebrew and pre-Arabic names, respectively, for the region of land surrounding the head of the Gulf of Aqaba, including the walls of mountains on each side. This identification of Shur/Etham also provides independent evidence that the site of the Red Sea crossing was indeed the head of the Gulf of Aqaba.

Is There More than One Place Called Shur?

I would like to mention a possible complication. Place-names are often not unique. For example, if I tell you that I live in Cambridge, you wouldn't know if I lived in Cambridge, England, or in Cambridge, Massachusetts, or Cambridge, Ontario (except that you would probably guess from my accent!). The situation can be more confusing if there are two places with the same name in the same country. For example, the Old Testament mentions two places called Bethlehem in Israel: one is the city of David, six miles south of Jerusalem, in the region called Judea; the other is seven miles northwest of Nazareth and is referred to in Joshua 19:15. Matthew's Gospel deliberately specifies that Jesus was born "in Bethlehem in Judea" (Matthew 2:1), that is, in the city of David, in order to avoid confusion.

In the Old Testament, Etham is mentioned only in the books of Exodus and Numbers, on each occasion in connection with the Exodus from Egypt, and, as we have seen, I believe Etham was a region around the head of the Gulf of Aqaba. Shur, on the other hand, is mentioned six times in the Old Testament, in various contexts in the books of Genesis, Exodus, and 1 Samuel. Most biblical scholars believe that they know where Shur was, and they place it in a very different location from my site at the head of the Gulf of Aqaba. Let me quote directly from the eminent professor Kenneth Kitchen, writing in the *New Bible Dictionary:* "Shur. A wilderness-region in the N.W. part of the Sinai isthmus. . . . Shur lay on the direct route to Egypt from S. Palestine." This is a very clear and definite statement. This position of the wilderness of Shur is shown on map 1.3, pg. 10, based on a standard biblical map.

Since, as we have seen, Shur means "wall," scholars have suggested that the name Shur refers to a wall built by the Egyptians as a defense against invasion.

We therefore have two possibilities for the location of Shur. First, there is my suggestion that Shur was a region around the head of the Gulf of Aqaba. The name Shur then refers to the natural walls of mountains on each side of the Gulf of Aqaba. Second, there is the belief of most biblical scholars that Shur was a wilderness region in the northwest of the Sinai Peninsula. The name Shur then refers to walls built by the Egyptians. It is also possible that, like Bethlehem, there were two Shurs and hence both of the above locations are correct. I would like to look briefly at one of the references to Shur in the Old Testament and see if this helps us decide which location of Shur is more likely to be correct or if both locations may be correct.

The reference to Shur I have chosen is in Genesis 25:18: "His [Ishmael's] descendants settled in the area from Havilah to Shur, near the border of Egypt, as you go towards Asshur." Now Ishmael is traditionally the ancestor of the Arabs, and Ishmael's descendants settled in Arabia (including Midian, which was northwest Arabia). According to Genesis 10:26, Havilah was one of the sons of Joktan, and Joktan (known in Arabic as Qahtan) is the predecessor of South Arabian kingdoms, so the place Havilah is almost certainly a region in South Arabia, sometimes identified with Khawlan in the Yemen. "The border of Egypt" is in fact ambiguous since, as we have seen, although the Sinai Peninsula was never formally part of Egypt, it was under Egyptian control during the rule of many pharaohs, with Egypt's owning and exploiting copper and turquoise mines there and Ramesses II's building a temple there. Thus although the formal eastern border of Egypt was the boundary between Egypt and the Sinai Peninsula, Egyptian territory effectively included the Sinai Peninsula: it was part of "greater Egypt."

If Shur is a region around the head of the Gulf of Aqaba, as I suggest, then "from Havilah to Shur" is the territory from south Arabia to north Midian, precisely the area known to have been occupied by the descendants of Ishmael. Shur is also near the border of land controlled by Egypt. "From Havilah to Shur . . . as you go towards Asshur" may then have brought to mind the long sweep of the ancient trade route going from southern Arabia up the eastern coast of the Red Sea, up the eastern coast of the Gulf of Aqaba, continuing north up to Damascus and then to Assyria. (Asshur in the Old Testament sometimes refers to the city of Asshur in Assyria [see map 4.2, pg. 52], and it sometimes refers to the whole country of Assyria.)

However, Assyria is a long way from Arabia, so is there another place called Asshur closer to Arabia to which Genesis 25:18 may be referring? Intriguingly, there is. Genesis 25:3 states, "The descendants of Dedan were the Asshurites, the Letushites and the Leummites."

Now important people sometimes gave their name to the place in which they lived. So the place Dedan (modern al-Ula; see map 4.1, pg. 46) is named after the person Dedan. Since the Asshurites were the descendants of Dedan, I would expect them to have lived close to Dedan, so we can tentatively deduce that Asshur must have been near to Dedan, in northwest Arabia.

James Montgomery, in *Arabia and the Bible,* says that "Asshur" appears in a south Arabic text, where it refers to a district in northwest Arabia. Putting this Arabic text together with the Hebrew text of Genesis 25:3, we can therefore deduce with some confidence that Asshur was a region close to Dedan.

Let's return to Genesis 25:18. What is meant by "His [Ishmael's] descendants settled in the area from Havilah to Shur, near the border of Egypt, as you go towards Asshur"? I suggest the meaning is now clear. This text is defining where the pre-Arabian tribes that descended from Ishmael settled. The southern boundary was Havilah in south Arabia; the northern boundary was Shur, at the head of the Gulf of Aqaba; the eastern boundary was Asshur, near to Dedan; the western boundary didn't need to be stated—it was the Red Sea. So Genesis 25:18 is defining the geographical boundaries of ancient Arabia, and it makes total sense. Genesis 25:18 has never been interpreted in this way before because scholars haven't recognized that Shur is a district around the head of the Gulf of Aqaba.

My location of Shur at the head of the Gulf of Aqaba is consistent with, and makes sense of, Genesis 25:18. The traditional location of Shur, in the northwest of the Sinai Peninsula, is not consistent with Genesis 25:18 because going from Havilah to *this* Shur is not on the way to Asshur near Dedan, nor is it on the way to Asshur in Assyria, and the Arab descendants of Ishmael didn't settle in the Sinai Peninsula.

This book is not the place for a detailed analysis of the other references to Shur in the Old Testament, except to say that I have performed such an analysis myself and I believe my location of Shur at the head of the Gulf of Aqaba is consistent with all of them. It is also worth adding that not all scholars are as definite as my friend Kenneth Kitchen about where Shur is. For example, Hoffmeier, in *Israel in Egypt,* writes, "Thus while a number of plausible identifications for

Shur in north-eastern and north-central Sinai have been suggested, a consensus has not developed around any one of these." I think this is academic language for "We don't really know where Shur is"! My view is clear: Shur is around the head of the Gulf of Aqaba. It is of course possible that there is another Shur in north Sinai, but I see no biblical evidence for this. Incidentally, so convinced are many biblical scholars that Shur is in north Sinai that most maps of the Sinai Peninsula in biblical times locate the Wilderness of Shur in north Sinai with no question mark following, as if it is an accepted fact. For example, this is the case with the maps in the widely used New International Version (NIV) of the Bible, on which map 1.3, pg. 10, is based.

This example of the location of Shur shows that if the arguments in this book are correct, then history books and biblical commentaries about the Exodus will have to be rewritten. The conclusions of this book will also affect the interpretation of some other parts of the Old Testament because we are relocating a number of accepted geographical sites, like Shur, that are referred to in various other places in the Old Testament.

The Route to the Red Sea

Let us now go back to the route I gave to the American tourist: "Cambridge to Trumpington, use the M11 motorway, Trumpington to London," and compare this with the route given in the book of Exodus: "Rameses to Succoth (Exodus 12:37), desert road toward the Red Sea (Exodus 13:18), Succoth to Etham on the edge of the desert (Exodus 13:20)." In my route to London, Trumpington is where you get on the M11 motorway, and London is where you leave the motorway. Similarly in the Exodus route, Succoth is where the Israelites started on the "desert road toward the Red Sea," and Etham is where this route finished and they left it. Succoth and Etham therefore mark the start and finish of the "desert road toward the Red Sea," which I believe is none other than the ancient trade route from Succoth to the head of the Gulf of Aqaba (see map 3.1, pg. 30).

I will look at this route in more detail in the next chapter. When Exodus 13:20 states "Etham on the edge of the desert," I therefore believe it means Etham on the far edge of the desert, with Succoth being on the near edge, the desert between them being the desert across the Sinai Peninsula. So everything fits together and makes sense. I will discuss this further in the next chapter.

In this chapter we have found the lost region of Etham, and we have also fixed the route of the Exodus between Egypt and the Red Sea crossing, at the head of the Gulf of Aqaba. In the next chapter we will reconstruct how twenty thousand Israelites and their flocks could have crossed the barren Sinai Peninsula, why they turned back, and then how Pharaoh trapped them by the Red Sea. This entrapment must rank as one of the most perfect military strategies ever: a brilliant checkmate from which there was no escape. Or was there?

FIFTEEN

TRAPPED BY PHARAOH

The Egyptians—all Pharaoh's horses and chariots, horsemen and troops—pursued the Israelites and overtook them as they camped by the sea near Pi Hahiroth opposite Baal Zephon.

Exodus 14:9

As I started to think about the best-known miracle in the Old Testament, the crossing of the Red Sea, I began to wonder why it happened at all. When Moses fled from Egypt to Midian after killing the Egyptian slave master, he didn't cross the Red Sea. He presumably walked around it. So why didn't Moses and the Israelites simply walk around the water? The Exodus account suggests that Moses and the Israelites were so well and truly trapped that they had no option but to cross the Red Sea. But if this was the case, then how had Pharaoh and his army managed to cut off all their escape routes? Trying to find out just how Pharaoh had trapped the Israelites was the main reason I returned to Taba in the Sinai Peninsula in 2001 after my earlier visit in 1999. I also wanted to walk part of the Exodus route myself to experience something of what it was like. It turned out that this walking of the route was critical to understanding how Pharaoh trapped the Israelites in a brilliant military maneuver.

Why Did the Israelites Cross the Red Sea?

The question of why the Israelites crossed the Red Sea has puzzled biblical scholars for centuries. For example, Hyatt, in his commentary,

Exodus, states, "The fact is that it was not absolutely necessary for the Israelites to cross a body of water in order to travel from Egypt into the Sinai Peninsula." Hyatt believes the Red Sea crossing occurred at a reedy inland lake situated between Egypt and the Sinai Peninsula but, nevertheless, the point he makes is a good one. For the Israelites to go from Egypt into the Sinai Peninsula, it would have been easy for them to walk between two lakes, and it is difficult to see how the Egyptians could have so trapped them that they were forced to cross the Red Sea. I agree with Hyatt here, but I believe the crossing was not at an inland sea of reeds. However, if the crossing was at the Gulf of Aqaba or the Gulf of Suez, then how did Pharaoh trap the Israelites? That is the problem we will address later in this chapter.

Hyatt continues, "We can only conjecture the reason why the Israelites found themselves faced with the necessity of crossing water. Perhaps they did not know their way and found themselves accidentally trapped." I find this very hard to believe. Moses had previously visited Mount Sinai from Egypt, as we have seen in earlier chapters, and he also returned to Egypt from Mount Sinai. He knew well the way to Mount Sinai. In addition, the Israelites had the pillars of fire and of cloud to guide them, like a fixed beacon at the end of the route. I therefore believe we can rule out that the Israelites lost their way.

Hyatt then gives another reason the Israelites crossed the water: "They may have pursued such a course intentionally in order to trap the Egyptians with their heavy chariots." I cannot agree with this either. The book of Exodus records that the pursuing Egyptians had horsemen and troops as well as chariots. For the Israelites to have deliberately taken on the heavily armed Egyptians would have been to invite massive defeat. The book of Exodus says that the Israelites were terrified by the Egyptians marching after them, and that is what I would expect.

Hyatt then says, "As a third possibility, they [the Israelites] may have been pushed into a trap by the Egyptian army." Yes, I strongly agree with this. Clearly the Israelites were trapped by Pharaoh and his army and had no option but to cross the Red Sea. But how did Pharaoh achieve this? Can we reconstruct this epic trap after three thousand years? If so, it will be necessary for us to understand as much as possible about the actual Exodus route the Israelites followed.

The Route to the Red Sea

Can we deduce the route the Israelites took to the Red Sea? We saw earlier how the term *yam suph* certainly refers to the Gulf of Aqaba and possibly also refers to the Gulf of Suez and the main body of the Red Sea. We also located Etham, which according to the book of Exodus was near the Red Sea crossing site, as being a region around the head of the Gulf of Aqaba. This strongly suggests that the Red Sea crossing site was the head of the Gulf of Aqaba.

So what route did Moses and the Israelites take from Succoth to the head of the Gulf of Aqaba? I knew where to look, and I picked out of my bookcase a delightful small book, less than a hundred pages long, that I have referred to before. The book, *The Route of the Exodus of the Israelites from Egypt*, was written in 1938 by Mr. A. Lucas, the director of the Government Chemical Department, Egypt, and the honorary chemist of the Egyptian Department of Antiquities. Lucas lived for forty years in Egypt and had a huge knowledge both of Egyptian archaeology and of the Sinai Peninsula. Written inside the front cover of my copy of the book is: "To Padre Champion. With the author's compliments, Cairo, 1943," and it is then signed by the author.

Lucas's book is useful because it lists and describes the principal routes in ancient times out of the Egyptian delta on the eastern side. There were six of them, but only two of these went through ancient Succoth (modern Tell el-Maskhuta). One of these ancient routes went from Succoth to Hebron, about twenty-five miles south of Jerusalem; the other went from Succoth to Aqaba, at the head of the Gulf of Aqaba (see map 3.1, pg. 30). Lucas calls this route "the ancient trade route from Arabia," as indeed it was. Lucas writes, "This road still exists . . . and is in fairly good condition. It answers well to the Biblical 'way of the wilderness by the Red Sea' (Exodus 13:18) and seems a most likely road for Moses to have taken both on his way to Midian (Exodus 2:15) and on his return journey to Egypt (Exodus 4:20)." I strongly agree with this and the route is sketched out on map 3.1, pg. 30.

I believe this ancient trade route was indeed the "desert road to the Red Sea" as Exodus 13:18 describes it. Moses would have been familiar with it because of his previous journeys from Egypt to Midian and back. It was the obvious route for him to have taken across the desert of the Sinai Peninsula to the Gulf of Aqaba when he fled Egypt after killing the slave master. But could thousands of Israelites and their flocks have survived this desert crossing? How would they have managed to eat and drink?

Food and Water for the Journey

After the terrible tenth plague, when the Egyptian firstborn males had died at midnight, Pharaoh finally gave permission for the Israelites to leave Egypt and go on a three-day journey into the desert to offer sacrifices to their God. Since they were going on a three-day journey, Pharaoh's suspicions would not have been aroused by the Israelites' taking with them food and water for about seven days (three days out, one day for the sacrifices, and three days back, as we suggested earlier). The Israelites did indeed take out food, leaving in great haste in case Pharaoh changed his mind: "So the people took their dough before it was leavened, having their kneading bowls bound up in their clothes on their shoulders" (Exodus 12:34), but it is not recorded that they took out water. Isn't this strange since water was so vital?

I am reminded of my student days. I was an undergraduate at Imperial College in London, where I studied physics. For my first year at college, astonishingly, I had gourmet meals every evening. I lived with two other students at a house in Chiswick, London, and we shared the house with the elderly owners, who were a Greek chef and his French wife. The Greek chef worked at a very high-class club in London, and each day he brought home surplus uncooked food, which his wife then cooked for the three students. Before the evening meal was served she would announce, in French, "Tonight we have roast duck with orange sauce, baby carrots, and green beans," or, "Today, we have Dover sole with white wine sauce and garden peas." We must have been the best-fed students in London! However, when announcing the meal, the French wife never mentioned water, although a jug of water was always on the table. She assumed, as we assumed, too, that water would always be there. She didn't need to mention the water. So I believe it was with the Israelites at the Exodus from Egypt. When going into the desert, then as now, you always take water. Water is an absolute necessity in the desert: it is much more important than food. The need for water is so obvious that you don't need to waste words mentioning it. Also, the more water you can carry, either yourself or on animals, or both, the less time you have to spend searching for it, and so the farther you can walk each day.

How did the ancient Israelites carry their water? Modern Bedouin use water skins slung across camels or donkeys, and we can expect that the ancient Israelites did something similar. Earlier we noted that when Moses left Jethro in Midian to return to Egypt and confront Pharaoh, he took with him his wife and two sons, and the book of Exodus records that they traveled on donkeys (Exodus 4:20). I think we can be virtually certain that the donkeys also carried water for Moses and his family traveling from Midian to Egypt, in water bags slung across their backs.

When the Israelites left Egypt at the Exodus, the livestock they took with them included donkeys because they are specifically mentioned in the Exodus story. For example, Exodus 13:13 says, "Redeem with a lamb every firstborn donkey," and in Numbers 16:15 Moses says, "I have not taken so much as a donkey from them [the Israelites]." I therefore suggest that the Israelites left Egypt with about a week's supply of water carried on donkeys.

How Did the Israelites Travel Across the Desert?

In this book I have often written, "Imagine you were there." So how are we to picture the Israelites crossing the Sinai Peninsula on the high desert plateau of el Tih? Did they go in single file like Indian warriors? Or did they travel many abreast like Chinese on the streets of Beijing? We have just thought about the supply of drinking water for the Israelites, but where did their livestock find drinking water in the Sinai desert? Is this part of the Exodus story really plausible? Can we know after three thousand years have elapsed? These questions filled my mind as I thought more about the practical realities of twenty thousand Israelites, and their livestock, surviving in the Sinai desert as they marched across to the Gulf of Aqaba.

I felt drawn to revisit the Sinai Peninsula to try to answer these questions. So it was that in the spring of 2001 my wife and I returned to Taba in the Sinai Peninsula to walk some of the Exodus route ourselves to see what it was really like and to get some feel of the realities of surviving in the desert. It would have been foolish for us to take off alone into the desert, particularly at a time of high tension in the Middle East, so we sought local help.

We left our hotel in Taba, walked over into Israel at the Taba border crossing, and took a taxi to the Tourist Information Centre in Eilat. "I'm looking for a local guide who is knowledgeable about archaeology and history and who could drive us where we want to go and spend a day with us," I said to the woman behind the desk of the Tourist Information Centre. Without hesitation she said, "You want Alfonso," and she gave me his telephone number.

So it was that we set off with Alfonso in his four-wheel-drive jeep with "Alfonso Desert Tours" painted across the sides. Alfonso is a marvelous man with a huge knowledge about, and love for, the desert. He has also been involved in various archaeological excavations in the Middle East and has made a number of important discoveries himself. He told me a lot of useful information, for example, that the annual rainfall in Eilat is only 25 millimeters (one inch) and that Eilat is officially called an extreme arid area. However, the annual rainfall in nearby Aqaba is 50 millimeters (two inches) because of the higher mountains around Aqaba (particularly Mount Etham, I thought). Alfonso then said, "When there is water runoff, for example into wadis, the 25-millimeter (one inch) annual rainfall around Eilat becomes effectively at least 75 millimeters (three inches) annual rainfall; hence there is a great increase in the number and variety of plants in wadis." Alfonso added, "There is always a danger of flash floods in wadis. In fact, more people die of drowning than of thirst in the deserts around Eilat because of the water that can rush down wadis, even in this extreme arid area." William Facey also tells me that drowning due to flash floods in wadis in Arabia is commonplace, and shortly before I visited Petra in Jordan in 1995, about twenty tourists drowned in the Siq there from a flash flood.

I asked Alfonso how ancient traders traveling along the trade route between the head of the Gulf of Aqaba and Egypt had managed to survive on the journey. Alfonso replied, "Caravans of camels would be loaded up with water in Aqaba, and they and the traders could get to Egypt without any additional water supply. If there were only a few traders and a few camels then they could stop and get water along the way, but large numbers of travelers would take all the water they needed with them from Aqaba. When they returned from Egypt they would take all the water they needed for the journey from Egypt." Just like the Exodus, I thought!

Alfonso then added, "Donkeys were domesticated before camels. Both were used to carry water. A donkey can survive for one week without water in the desert, and a camel can last for twenty-one days without water." I asked Alfonso how long it would take to travel on foot from Egypt to the Gulf of Aqaba along the ancient trade route. He said, "Typically a camel with a walker does 40 kilometers [25 miles] per day. A person also does 40 kilometers [25 miles] a day if some animal is carrying the water. If you are really in a hurry then you can do more than this."

I then asked Alfonso how the ancient trade caravans used to travel along trade routes: in single file, or did they spread out sideways? "Oh," Alfonso replied, "they used to spread out to maximize the supply of food and water for the animals and also to minimize the danger from attack. It was much safer to travel in a bunch than to be stretched out in a long line. The modern Bedouin do the same when they travel." Later that day, as we were walking along a dried-up wadi in the desert, Alfonso suddenly stopped and said, "Look, a caravan of Bedouin has been here." Alfonso pointed out that beside the wadi there were eleven parallel tracks in the ground that the Bedouin had traveled along to maximize the food supply and water for their animals. The tracks were faint but clearly visible, and I photographed them (see photograph 15.1, on the next page).

Alfonso then showed Sarah and me how certain desert plants were "indicator plants," which told experienced travelers not only where water was but also its depth. So a traveler could dig around these plants and know how deep to dig before finding water. Alfonso said that the leaves and roots of many desert plants stored water, and so by eating these plants animals received not only food but also precious water. Humans could also obtain water from plants. "If you heat up a single desert broom plant," said Alfonso, "you will get one liter [about

15.1. *Very faint parallel tracks left by Bedouin traveling in the desert.*
Sarah and Alfonso in the picture.

a quart] of water." However, in their march across the Sinai Peninsula, being pursued by the Egyptian army, the Israelites would not have wanted to stop to do this; to move fast they needed to take their own water with them.

This trip with Alfonso was proving to be invaluable. I was now beginning to understand how twenty thousand Israelites, plus their animals, could have survived in their march across the Sinai Peninsula. When I returned to England, I looked up some books about this. E. H. Palmer, a former professor of Arabic at my university, Cambridge, spent eleven months walking in the Sinai Peninsula and recorded his findings in a book I've referred to before, *The Desert of the Exodus,* published in 1872. He writes,

The desert of el-Tih is a limestone plateau of irregular surface. . . . The surface is an arid, featureless waste. . . . In spite of the utterly arid nature of the soil, a quantity of brown parched herbage is scattered over the surface . . . which bursts into sudden life with the spring and winter rains.

So Palmer is saying that on the el Tih plateau, despite its being an arid wasteland, flocks of animals can survive, provided it is springtime when the plants come to life.

I am reminded of trips to Arizona, where I have gone to visit the physicist and lover of classic sports cars Professor John Spence a number of times. The Arizona desert appears to be a barren wilderness devoid of all vegetation except cacti. But when the spring rain comes, the desert bursts into life with yellow desert poppies and dwarf blue lupines carpeting the ground. It is a most remarkable transformation, and the yellow and blue color combination is stunning. This lush vegetation lasts for a few weeks, and then it is gone until the following spring. According to Palmer, the el Tih plateau was similar: totally barren except in the spring.

And when did the Exodus start? In the Jewish month of Nisan, corresponding to March–April in our calendar. It was springtime! So crossing the el Tih plateau of the Sinai Peninsula was indeed possible not only for the Israelites but also for their flocks. Hence, this part of the Exodus story is certainly plausible. But is it plausible for as many as twenty thousand Israelites with their flocks?

The great Czech explorer Musil, in *The Northern Hegaz,* addresses this point from his considerable experience. Although Musil believes (I think wrongly) that the Red Sea crossing was at an inland sea of reeds, he then has the Israelites crossing the Sinai Peninsula to the Gulf of Aqaba, as I do, because, like me, he doesn't believe Mount Sinai is in the Sinai Peninsula. He writes, "The quickest and most convenient way for them [the Israelites] to get away from the sphere of Egyptian authority was upon the transport route leading from Egypt to the northern extremity of the Gulf of Aqaba." So, like me, Musil has the Israelites traveling along the ancient trade route from Egypt to Aqaba.

Musil continues, "Upon this route the leader proceeded with his retinue, while the remainder of the Israelites marched with their flocks to the right and left of the route and parallel to it." So Musil is saying exactly the same thing as Alfonso had told me; and this traditional practice of traveling in a group has continued up to modern times with the Bedouin traveling in the same way, as a group marching in parallel lines.

Musil adds, "If today a tribe numbering five thousand families migrates with its flocks, it forms a column at least twenty kilometers [twelve miles] wide and five kilometers [three miles] deep. The wider the line is, the more pasture the flocks will find." How interesting that Musil refers to a tribe numbering five thousand families; this is not so very different from the twenty thousand people I believe were involved in the Exodus from Egypt. So, if Musil is correct here, and I believe he is, we have to think of the Israelites marching across the Sinai Peninsula as a massive human wall about twelve miles wide and three miles deep. What an impressive sight!

Now imagine you were there! The atmosphere would be intoxicating: a heady mix of elation at leaving Egypt and fear at the possibility of being pursued and caught by Pharaoh's army. The adrenaline would be pumping through your veins as you encouraged others on. Unbelievably, you now had freedom at last from years of slavery. Not only that, you were going to have your own land. A land flowing with milk and honey. A land to call your own. A promised land and a land of promise. At last Israel would be a notable nation instead of subservient slaves. At last Israel would be free to worship its own God. The atmosphere would be electric and victorious. You would have that rare feeling of knowing that history was being made and that you were part of it.

What does Musil say about the Israelites and their flocks surviving as they crossed the Sinai Peninsula? He writes, "If the Israelites migrated from Egypt in the month of March and if there had been an abundance of rain on the peninsula of Sinai that year they would have found rain pools of various sizes in all the cavities and in all the hollows of the various riverbeds, and they could comfortably have replenished their water bags and watered their flocks." So, according to Musil, who was a great expert on the Middle East, there would have been no problem in the Israelites and their flocks crossing the Sinai Peninsula if it were March, as indeed it was (or at least March–April: in some years the month of Nisan falls mainly in March and in some it is mainly in April).

I am once again struck by the remarkable timing of the events of the Exodus. This journey across the Sinai Peninsula was possible for the Israelites' flocks, which were vital for their food supply, only if the journey was in the spring. The journey started in the spring because the ten plagues ended in the spring. The ten plagues ended in the spring because of a natural sequence of events, in each of which the timing was critical for the sequence to continue to its climax. Similarly, the crossing of the Jordan was possible because at the precise time the Israelites were gathered on its banks, an earthquake caused a mud slide upstream at Adam, which stopped the flow of the Jordan.

How Long Did the Journey Take?

I would like to estimate the journey time from Succoth to the head of the Gulf of Aqaba because this is relevant to the amount of water the Israelites needed to carry for the journey. From Succoth to the head of the Gulf of Aqaba is over 180 miles, depending on the exact route taken. By comparison, the route from the head of the Gulf of Suez to the head of the Gulf of Aqaba is over 150 miles. We have earlier estimated the length of "a day's journey," but let us return to this. Musil, in *The Northern Hegaz,* states that, for traveling along the ancient coast road from Aila (modern Aqaba) at the head of the Gulf of Aqaba to Mecca in Arabia (see map 4.2, pg. 52), the daily marches of the Muslim pilgrims were 28 to 30 miles. For the pilgrims' route from Damascus in Syria to Medina in Arabia, Musil writes, "A day's march on the Pilgrims' Route always amounts to about 60 km [37 miles]." Houtman, in *Exodus,* writes, "Pilgrims covered about 50 km [31 miles] per day." So it seems that "a day's journey" along a trade route was between 28 and 37 miles, depending on the difficulty of the route.

On the other hand, Lucas, in *The Route of the Exodus,* states, "It is impossible to suppose that even when hastening from their enemies, the Israelites, with women, children, and flocks can have gone more than about 10 miles in a day's march." Lucas is supported by a number of other scholars. So how far did the Israelites travel in a day across the Sinai desert? Imagine you were there: an Israelite fleeing Egypt three thousand years ago. You knew that Pharaoh had given you permission to leave on a three-day journey into the desert, but your plan, inspired by your leader, Moses, was to keep going and escape. You knew that Pharaoh would be furious when he found out and that he would probably give chase. You knew that you were taking with you only about one week's water supply and that there was probably not

enough water available for you and the other twenty thousand Israelites in the Sinai Peninsula until you reached the head of the Gulf
of Aqaba.

So what would you have done? Travel only a meager ten miles a
day? Or would you rather have gone flat out, marching both by day
and by night (Exodus 13:21) until you arrived at the head of the Gulf
of Aqaba, where there was plentiful water and where you were now
outside the Egyptian-controlled Sinai Peninsula? I know what I would
have done!

So I suggest the Israelites marched flat out. Nothing less than the
survival of an emerging nation was at stake. Young children and the elderly would have been carried on the backs of donkeys. The majority
of the twenty thousand Israelites, plus the majority of their animals,
would easily have been able to travel at two miles per hour for a long
period of time, which corresponds to walking one mile in thirty minutes, which is relatively easy, even in rough terrain. Since the book of
Exodus implies that they traveled by both day and night (Exodus
13:21), then they probably traveled at least fourteen hours per day,
walking by night in the light of the moon. Remember that the Israelites must have been determined and desperate. They knew that if
they could reach the Gulf of Aqaba they would have water and they
would be relatively safe. Marching at two miles per hour for fourteen
hours would mean covering twenty-eight miles per day. I believe this is
realistic in the circumstances: the Israelites must have been on a "high"
at leaving Egypt and also terrified that Pharaoh would chase after them.

So, if the Israelites covered twenty-eight miles per day, the 180-mile
journey from Succoth to the Gulf of Aqaba would have taken about
6.5 days. This is consistent with the six-day journey time Arab historians give for Muslim pilgrims marching from the head of the Gulf of
Suez to the head of the Gulf of Aqaba along the Hajj route from
Egypt to Mecca. If my time estimates are correct, since in chapter 11 I
suggested that it took one day to travel from Rameses to Succoth,
then the total journey time from the start of the Exodus at Rameses to
arriving at the Gulf of Aqaba would have been about seven or eight
days. I do not think it was less than seven days, and perhaps it was several days more; the time isn't critical, but my best estimate of the journey time is seven or eight days.

So here we have a clever piece of planning by Moses. He asks Pharaoh for permission to take the Israelites on a three-day journey into the desert to offer sacrifices to their God. This enables the Israelites to carry with them a seven-day supply of water (three days out, one day for sacrifices, three days back) without arousing the suspicion of the Egyptians when they leave Egypt. However, Moses has no intention of returning, and he leads the Israelites across the Sinai Peninsula, marching both by day and by night, to the head of the Gulf of Aqaba, a journey that he knows will take about seven days, since he had done it previously himself. Hence the Israelites take with them exactly the right amount of water to get them to the Gulf of Aqaba. They can then get fresh water in Aqaba where it is plentiful: a brilliant plan.

Trapped by Pharaoh

Moses' clever plan was never executed to completion because Pharaoh's armies caught up with the Israelites just before they reached the freshwater at Aqaba. The book of Exodus says that the Israelites "were terrified" (Exodus 14:10) because Pharaoh had trapped them. It has never been satisfactorily explained how Pharaoh so totally trapped the Israelites that they had no option but to cross the Red Sea. In order to explain this we have to understand the detailed geography of the situation and the clues provided in the Exodus account.

The ancient trade route from Tell el-Maskhuta (ancient Succoth) to the head of the Gulf of Aqaba passed through Nakhl (also spelled Nekhl) somewhat more than halfway along the route (map 3.1, pg. 30). The word *nakhl* means palm tree, so it must have had at least one palm in the past, but no palms grow there now. According to Jarvis, in *Yesterday and Today in Sinai,* published in 1931, at Nakhl "water is plentiful but unpleasant, though not harmful to health." This description reminds one of the coffee served on many airlines! It is possible that some Israelites topped up their water supplies at Nakhl with this unpleasant water, and it may have been useful for the flocks, but it would not have been nearly enough for twenty thousand people.

The next significant place along the old trade route was Thamad (also spelled Themad) and after that Ras al-Naqb (also written Nagb), where the high ground on the plateau of el Tih starts to descend to

15.2. Very steep part of the ancient trade route, now surfaced, between Egypt and the head of the Gulf of Aqaba, between Ras al-Naqb and the Gulf to Aqaba.

the low ground around the head of the Gulf of Aqaba (map 3.1, pg. 30). Ras al-Naqb is close to the modern Netafim border crossing between Israel and Egypt. The ancient trade route descends from Ras al-Naqb very steeply indeed, dropping down from a height of 2,500 feet on the plateau of el Tih to sea level at the Gulf of Aqaba in only three miles. At the bottom the route crosses the Wadi Masri (modern Wadi Shlomo) and emerges on the western side of the Gulf of Aqaba about three miles southwest of modern Eilat (see map 12.3, pg. 181).

I asked Alfonso to drive Sarah and me up this ancient trade route, starting from Eilat. Even though the road has been much improved since the time of the Exodus and partially surfaced with modern materials for some of its length, it is still a very steep climb, and a four-wheel-drive vehicle is essential. We got out of Alfonso's jeep and walked up and down part of this ancient road to get a feel for just how steep it is (see photograph 15.2, above).

Jarvis, in *Yesterday and Today in Sinai,* writes, "The pass from the Ras el Nagb is dangerous and rough and, in parts, the gradient is one in three with an indifferent surface, though some of the worst places have been tarred." Jarvis adds, "The descent should not be attempted unless the brakes are in perfect order and the driver has every confidence in himself and his car." Why am I dwelling on the difficulty of descending from Ras al-Naqb down to the Gulf of Aqaba? For a very good reason! Having walked down this ancient trade route myself, I am certain that Moses and the Israelites could have walked down it, even with their flocks, but I am equally certain that Pharaoh's horse-drawn chariots could not have come down it. It would have been impossible for them.

It is time we returned to the account of the entrapment in the book of Exodus. Exodus 13:20 states, "After leaving Succoth they camped at Etham on the edge of the desert." I have previously identified Etham with a district around the head of the Gulf of Aqaba, extending around both sides of the gulf. I suggest that the camp referred to in Exodus 13:20 was around Ras al-Naqb, since I believe Moses would have wanted to assemble the Israelites at the top of the steep descent, to give the slow walkers some opportunity to catch up and to prepare the Israelites, who had previously been walking in a group about twelve miles across, for the steep descent they now had to make, which would have meant walking with no more than ten people across.

We then come to a very curious change of direction that puzzles all biblical scholars: for some reason the Israelites turned back. Exodus 14:1, 2 states, "Then the Lord said to Moses, 'Tell the Israelites to turn back and camp near Pi Hahiroth, between Migdol and the sea. They are to camp by the sea, directly opposite Baal Zephon.'" Notice once again the precision of the geography. The writer is trying to describe the exact place the Israelites turned back and camped after Etham. It was between Migdol and the sea, near Pi-hahiroth and opposite Baal Zephon. In modern language, the writer is specifying the place the Israelites camped in terms of triangulation—giving the position of the campsite relative to three other nearby places. A really modern analogy would be locating a position using global positioning satellites! Although from the above description the original readers would have known precisely where the Israelites camped, sadly, the sites Pi-hahiroth, Migdol, and Baal Zephon are all unknown today (also the spelling is confusing: the NIV has Pi Hahiroth, whereas Pi-hahiroth is more usual).

However, I would like to focus on the Israelites turning back. Why did they do this? There must have been a reason. You don't turn back when an army may be pursuing you! First, note that the Exodus text says that they were by the sea. This implies that they were at sea level. If we have the correct route so far, then the Israelites must have descended down the steep part of the route from Ras al-Naqb and were now at the bottom, where the modern Wadi Shlomo (ancient Wadi Masri) runs into the Gulf of Aqaba (see map 12.3, pg. 181). (The Texas Ranch and a famous house called Williams House are now located at this point.) The geography at this point is like a T junction, with the Wadi Shlomo meeting the Gulf of Aqaba. But which way were the Israelites to turn at this junction? There were two possibilities. They could either turn left and walk northeast along the side of the Gulf of Aqaba up to the head, only three miles away; or they could turn right and walk southwest down the Gulf of Aqaba toward modern Taba and then on toward Sharm el-Sheikh. Exodus 14 tells us which way they went at this T junction: they turned back. Back with respect to what? It must be either as compared with the road they had been taking or with respect to the pillars of fire and of cloud, which were "in front of the people" as described at the end of Exodus 13. Either way, turning left at the junction and walking up to the head of the Gulf of Aqaba fits "turning back." We look at this in a little more detail below.

Exodus 13:22 states, "Neither the pillar of cloud by day nor the pillar of fire by night left its place in front of the people," and this is immediately followed by Exodus 14:1, 2, about the Israelites turning back (remember that there were no chapter divisions in the original Hebrew text). If the Israelites had turned right at the end of the Wadi Masri and had headed down the Gulf of Aqaba toward Taba and Sharm el-Sheikh, then the pillars of cloud and of fire from Mount Sinai in Arabia would still have been ahead of them—not directly ahead, but ahead on their left. However, if the Israelites had turned left at the end of Wadi Masri and headed northeast up the Gulf of Aqaba toward its head, then the pillars of cloud and of fire would have been behind them, at their back and to the right. Since Exodus 14 says that the Israelites turned back, this must mean that they turned left and walked up toward the head of the Gulf of Aqaba, where they camped.

It made sense to camp again so they could regroup after coming down the steep descent from the plateau of el Tih. That the pillar of cloud was now behind the Israelites is explicitly stated in Exodus 14:19: "The pillar of cloud also moved from in front and stood behind them [the Israelites]." However, in my interpretation it is the Israelites who turned back, thus placing the pillar of cloud, arising from the top of Mount Sinai, behind them. The Israelites "turned back" not because they had lost their way, but because the geography demanded it. "Turning back" was the way to the head of the Gulf of Aqaba, where the Israelites would find freshwater before their journey into Midian.

So we now have the Israelites camped close to the head of the Gulf of Aqaba on the western side, near Pi-hahiroth, Migdol, and Baal Zephon. As I said above, the location of these places is unknown, and I don't want to spend as much time trying to locate each of these as I did locating Etham! Perhaps a reader of this book would like the challenge of identifying these sites, which I am sure must be around the head of the Gulf of Aqaba. Let me provide a few clues.

Migdol is a Semitic word meaning "fortress" or "tower" or "watchtower," and various forts in Egypt, on the Egypt–Sinai Peninsula border, and elsewhere, were called Migdol. In addition, in Jerusalem there is the Migdol David, "Tower of David." Hence Migdol is not a very specific name. However, to have a fort or a watchtower around the head of the Gulf of Aqaba makes sense because this was a very strategic site. As we have seen, three ancient trade routes met at Aqaba; there was abundant freshwater at Aqaba; Midian, Edom, and the Sinai Peninsula joined together at Aqaba; there was a large copper mine at Timna, north of Aqaba; Aqaba was an important port in pre-Islamic times. The crusaders built a fortress in Aqaba in the twelfth century A.D., which may have been built on the remains of an earlier fortress, and the fortress remains largely intact today. Today there are observation points on several of the Israeli mountains close to the head of the Gulf of Aqaba. Hence around the head of the Gulf of Aqaba is an ideal location for Migdol, a fortress or watchtower.

Baal Zephon literally means "God of the north," and it is the name of a Canaanite god associated with storms. At Ugarit, Baal Zephon is known to have been associated with Mount Cassius, whose peak thrusting through cloud on the northern horizon was thought to be the seat of the storm god. Since violent storms are relatively common on the Gulf of Aqaba (see the next chapter), and since the head of the Gulf of Aqaba is to the north, to have a shrine to Baal Zephon at the head of the Gulf of Aqaba would be appropriate, possibly in one of the tall mountains nearby.

The meaning of *Pi-hahiroth* is uncertain, but scholars have made various suggestions. One is that it means "House of the goddess, Hathor." The Egyptians built a temple to Hathor at Timna, 15 miles north of the head of the Gulf of Aqaba, so Hathor was certainly worshiped near here, and perhaps there was a shrine to Hathor near the head of the Gulf of Aqaba. Another possibility is that Pi-hahiroth means "the mouth of the canal(s)." If this interpretation is correct, then possibly it would have been applied to the head of the Gulf of Aqaba, which might have been thought of as the "mouth" of the gulf. Interestingly, five miles north of Eilat an ancient water system has been found, dating back to the Middle Ages, where the farmers dug wells close to the mountains to obtain fresher water and then channeled this water in underground canals to their farms. Perhaps this canal system builds on an earlier tradition of canals nearer the head of the Gulf of Aqaba, channeling very fresh water down from the mountains. So the name Pi-hahiroth is not out of place in the region around the head of the Gulf of Aqaba, but further evidence is needed for a positive identification.

I will now return to the entrapment by Pharaoh.

When the king of Egypt was told that the people had fled, Pharaoh and his officials changed their minds about them and said, "What have we done? We have let the Israelites go and lost their services!" So he had his chariot made ready and took his army with him. (Exodus 14:5–6)

We do not know how long it took Pharaoh to realize that the Israelites had fled and were not coming back. Moses had probably hoped he would have a seven-day lead over Pharaoh because Pharaoh expected the Israelites back after seven days (three days out, one day for sacrifices, and three days back). However, I think Pharaoh was shrewder than this. As soon as he realized that Moses and the Israelites had left Egypt on the major trade route to the head of the Gulf of Aqaba, and as soon as he was told that they were marching by both day and night, he no doubt would have known that they intended leaving for good. So Pharaoh and his troops probably set off in pursuit only a few days after the Israelites had left.

But there was a problem. Pharaoh had with him "horses and chariots, horsemen and troops" (Exodus 14:9), yet Pharaoh knew that his horse-drawn chariots could not descend the very steep slope from the el Tih plateau to the sea, starting at Ras al-Naqb. For a great leader like Pharaoh, problems were opportunities, so I suggest he devised the strategic pincer plan set out below.

Lucas, in *The Route of the Exodus,* describes an alternative route from Egypt to the Gulf of Aqaba that avoids the steep decline at the Ras al-Naqb. This route leaves the ancient trade route at el Thamad (see map 12.3, pg. 181) and goes northeast to el Kuntilla and then farther northeast to the Arabah.

The route then comes down the Arabah to the head of the Gulf of Aqaba. This route is sketched on the map. This route is about a hundred miles longer than the direct route, but Lucas calls it "an easy route." So I suggest that Pharaoh's forces split up at el Thamad, with the horses and chariots going northeast on the longer but easier route and then coming south down the Arabah, and the foot soldiers continuing along the ancient trade route to Aqaba, hot on the footsteps of the Israelites.

No doubt the Israelites planned to walk around the head of the Gulf of Aqaba after they had camped by the head of the gulf on its western side, but Pharaoh was too fast. He trapped them brilliantly and totally. His horses and chariots came down the Arabah and blocked the Israelites from walking around the head of the gulf. His foot soldiers were behind the Israelites so they couldn't retreat. Mountains were to the west of the Israelites, and the water of the Gulf of Aqaba was on their east (see map 12.3, pg. 181).

The Israelites were hemmed in with nowhere to go. What a superb military maneuver by Pharaoh! Surely he had won decisively.

Here's how the book of Exodus describes the entrapment: "The Egyptians . . . pursued the Israelites and overtook them as they camped by the sea" (Exodus 14:9). How could the Egyptian army have overtaken twenty thousand Israelites camping in the confined space between the sea on their east and the high mountains on their west? I believe *overtook* here refers to the Egyptians' horses and chariots taking the longer route around the Israelites and then coming down the Arabah so they were ahead of the Israelites. The Israelites were certainly then overtaken. Exodus 14:10 states, "As Pharaoh approached, the Israelites looked up": they looked up because Pharaoh in his chariot was ahead of them. "And there were the Egyptians marching after them" (Exodus 14:10): this refers to the foot soldiers who were behind them. Thus the book of Exodus describes the Egyptians *both* as having overtaken the Israelites and also as being "after them," and my interpretation is consistent with this, with Pharaoh and his horses and chariots ahead of (that is, to the north of) the Israelites and his foot soldiers behind (to the southwest of the Israelites).

The effect on the Israelites was devastating. "They were terrified. . . . They said to Moses, 'It would have been better for us to serve the Egyptians than to die in the desert.'" The Israelites must have felt like a nut in a pair of nutcrackers: about to be crushed by the Egyptian army, which was both in front of them and behind them.

So the situation seemed utterly hopeless. The Israelites were totally trapped with no way out. Or was there? The next chapter describes what is probably the greatest miracle in the Old Testament, the crossing of the Red Sea and the drowning of Pharaoh's army. Can we reconstruct what really happened in this event three thousand years ago? Is there a scientific mechanism that fits the description in the Bible? For me, the next chapter is one of the most memorable in this book.

CROSSING THE RED SEA

Then Moses stretched out his hand over the sea, and all that night the Lord drove the sea back with a strong east wind and turned it into dry land. The waters were divided and the Israelites went through the sea on dry ground, with a wall of water on their right and on their left. . . . Then the Lord said to Moses, "Stretch out your hand over the sea so that the waters may flow back over the Egyptians and their chariots and horsemen.". . . The water flowed back and covered the chariots and horsemen—the entire army of Pharaoh that had followed the Israelites into the sea. Not one of them survived.

Exodus 14:21–22, 26–28

The Red Sea crossing is, I believe, the greatest miracle in the Old Testament. The Israelites had arrived at the Red Sea but were now doomed, trapped by Pharaoh's chariots and horsemen barring the way in front of them to the north and his Egyptian foot soldiers blocking retreat routes behind them to the south. The helpless Israelites were about to be crushed between the jaws of Pharaoh's military vice. They couldn't escape sideways because of a wall of tall mountains immediately to the west and the waters of the Gulf of Aqaba to the east. There was absolutely no escape route. Then the miracle happened. A strong wind blew all night, the waters were driven back, and the Israelites crossed the Gulf of Aqaba on dry land. And then another miracle happened. The wind suddenly stopped, and the waters returned and drowned the Egyptian army that was pursuing them. In twelve awesome hours, from evening to morning, the tables had been turned. It was the Egyptians, not the Israelites, who were doomed and defeated. Now the Israelites were free and a nation was born. The crossing of the Red Sea marked a defining moment in history.

No one has ever given a convincing scientific explanation for the crossing of the Red Sea that fits the description in the book of Exodus. However, I believe we can now do this using modern science. After three thousand years we can now understand how the greatest miracle in the Old Testament happened. And what a miracle of timing it was! The Israelites were within hours, if not minutes, of being crushed, captured, or killed, and then, when all seemed lost, deliverance came. Once again, imagine you were there as one of the Israelites. Your emotions would have gone from total terror before the crossing to indescribable elation afterward. But how did this amazing miracle really happen?

Natural Mechanisms for the Crossing of the Red Sea

Let's start by looking briefly at natural mechanisms proposed by others for the crossing of the Red Sea. A number of people (for example, the scholar Hans Goedicke, professor emeritus of Near Eastern Studies at John Hopkins University in Maryland, and the more popular writer Ian Wilson, in his book *Exodus: The True Story Behind the Biblical Account)* claim that the crossing of the Red Sea was made possible by a huge tidal wave called a tsunami, which resulted from the eruption of the volcano Santorini, a Greek volcanic island in the Mediterranean. I think we can dismiss this idea because the eruption of Santorini occurred well before the events of the Exodus. Scholars are, in fact, divided on the exact date that Santorini erupted. Tree ring dating clearly indicates a massive volcanic eruption in 1628 B.C. (and, yes, we really can be that precise because each year an extra tree ring grows, so by counting the rings we get dates accurate to one year). For a period of about seven years following 1628 B.C., tree rings from trees as far apart as California and Ireland are exceptionally narrow, indicating a massive disturbance in the climate at that time. The most likely candidate is the eruption of Santorini, the ash cloud from which would have caused global cooling. However, the atmospheric disturbance could have been due to another volcano, in which case archaeologists believe that Santorini probably erupted in about 1500 B.C., based on the style of pottery that was destroyed in the Santorini eruption. Radiocarbon dating from grain and timber samples found at Akrotiri, on the island of Santorini, suggests that the eruption occurred during the period 1650 to 1500 B.C. All dating methods therefore reveal that the date is much earlier than the probable date of the Exodus (1250 to 1300 B.C.). No serious archaeologist or volcanologist believes that the great eruption of Santorini was that late.

Another suggested mechanism is that the Red Sea crossing was made possible by a tsunami caused by an underwater volcanic eruption in the Red Sea that sent huge tidal waves up the Gulfs of Aqaba and Suez. The problem with this explanation is that it simply does not fit the Exodus account. A tsunami would cause rapid flooding followed by rapid recession of the water. The whole point of the Exodus account is that these events happened the other way around: first the water receded, enabling the Israelites to cross, and then it returned, drowning the Egyptian army. So we can rule out a tsunami, due to Santorini or any other volcano, as the mechanism for the Red Sea crossing.

A further suggestion is that the crossing was made possible by a very low tide followed by a very high tide. There are two difficulties with this suggestion. First, tides don't form walls of water as described in the Exodus account. Second, although in some locations in the world the tide can come in rapidly because of how the land lies, and people can be trapped and drowned, this is not the case in the Gulfs of Suez and Aqaba, where the tide comes in slowly.

So if there is a natural explanation of the crossing of the Red Sea, it has to be different from those given above. In fact, the Bible tells us that there was indeed a natural mechanism, and it also tells us what that mechanism was: a strong east wind that blew all night (Exodus 14:21). This can lead to a phenomenon called wind setdown, which has been proposed by Professors Doron Nof and Nathan Paldor for the crossing of the Red Sea, which they took to be the Gulf of Suez. So what is wind setdown?

The Wind Setdown Mechanism

I've just interrupted writing this chapter to perform a very simple experiment. If you take a glass, fill it to the brim with water, and blow across the surface of the water, then water is blown from one side of the glass to the other and some of it is blown out of the glass altogether. The same effect, on a much bigger scale, occurs when a strong wind blows across a large body of water. Oceanographers call it "wind setdown" when the water is blown away from the shore and "wind setup" when water is blown onto the shore. An alternate name sometimes used for wind setup or setdown is wind tide.

Wind tides are well known to oceanographers. For example, a strong wind blowing along Lake Erie, one of the Great Lakes, has produced water elevation differences of as much as sixteen feet between Toledo, Ohio, on the west and Buffalo, New York, on the east. This is a huge difference. Relatively recently, on February 17, 1998, a strong wind blowing along Lake Erie produced a water level difference of five feet.

On the Caribbean coast, strong winds can cause water level heights to vary by over fifteen feet. These large changes in water level during storms usually occur not only as a result of high winds blowing back the water but also because of changes in the atmospheric pressure that are common in storms. Reservoirs and dams have to be designed taking into account these wind setup effects.

There is an interesting article by Christopher Letts in the April 5, 1995, issue of the *Hudson River Almanac*. In it Letts says,

> We had a "blow-out tide" with winds up to 30 miles per hour from the north-west. Croton Point reef was exposed for 200 yards, something I had never seen before in 20 years of exploring the point. . . . The tide was low enough to expose the old piers. . . .

The almanac then adds the following explanatory note: "Blow-out Tide is a colloquial phrase used to describe an unusually low tide. They occur rather infrequently when wind, tide and other climatic elements combine to produce unusually prolonged seaward flow, resulting in large areas of exposed river bottom. . . ." There are many well-documented records of wind setdown effects around the world causing water levels to drop by several yards. If the water is on a sloping shoreline, then water is pushed back so that hundreds of yards (or meters) of shoreline is exposed. The reverse effect happens in wind setup.

If a strong wind blows from the southeast up the Gulf of Suez, then wind setup occurs and the sea level at the head of the Gulf of Suez can rise by about six feet (about two meters). This causes water from the Gulf of Suez to go about five miles northward into the Suez Canal, which was dug in the nineteenth century A.D. and which is joined to the Gulf of Suez. There are reports that Napoleon was almost killed by a "sudden high tide" while he was crossing shallow water near the head of the Gulf of Suez. Presumably this tide was due to wind effects as described above.

From my investigations, and from the above examples, I believe the only natural mechanism capable of explaining the events of the Red Sea crossing is a strong wind, which is precisely the cause given in the book of Exodus. I would therefore like to explore this mechanism further. Some biblical scholars accept that a strong wind was the cause, but because they are unaware of the wind setdown phenomenon, their conclusions are incorrect. For example, Hyatt, in his well-known commentary, *Exodus,* writes, "If we turn now to discuss the manner in which the Israelites crossed the sea, we may conjecture that it took place as follows. A strong, hot wind from the E. or NE. blew for several days, and dried up the water in a marshy lagoon around the southern end of Lake Menzaleh, which was the 'sea' the Israelites were to cross." Notice how Hyatt has to have his wind blowing for several days, whereas the book of Exodus is explicit that it blew for one night. Notice also how Hyatt's wind dried up a lagoon, whereas the book of Exodus says the Red Sea was driven back, just as we expect with wind setdown. Hyatt then has a hard time explaining how the Egyptian army was subsequently drowned. It is not easy to drown an army in a dried-up lake, so Hyatt then has to propose a downpour of rain that drowned the Egyptians. If only Hyatt had known about wind setdown, he could have saved himself from unlikely speculations.

From the examples I have given above of wind setup and setdown in Lake Erie, at Croton Point, and even in the Gulf of Suez, it is clear that a strong wind can cause substantial changes in water level and result in the water being pushed back for large distances. For significant effects, a strong wind has to blow for a number of hours, because the water is pushed back gradually, and this is precisely what the book of Exodus records: "All that night the Lord drove the sea back with a strong east wind and turned it into dry land" (Exodus 14:21). These biblical words really couldn't be a clearer description of wind setdown.

As we will see later in this chapter, wind setdown can also explain "walls" of water and, in addition, how Pharaoh's army could not escape and was drowned.

You get substantial wind setdown effects only over long stretches of water, such as Lake Erie. This is because a strong wind has to blow down a long stretch of water in order to build up a big effect. However, and this is very important, none of the inland lakes in the Sinai Peninsula, for example, Lake Timsah or the Bitter Lakes, is long enough for wind setdown to produce a significant effect. Since I've argued earlier that wind setdown is the only plausible natural mechanism to explain the Red Sea crossing, and since this mechanism produces negligibly small wind setdown in the inland lakes in the Sinai Peninsula, this is yet another reason for ruling out all these inland lakes as the site of the Red Sea crossing. However, both the Gulf of Suez and the Gulf of Aqaba are long enough to produce a substantial wind setdown effect: the Gulf of Suez is 194 miles long, and the Gulf of Aqaba is 112 miles long. These are the only two candidates for the Red Sea crossing site, if the mechanism was wind setdown.

Do we have any evidence to rule out one of these to leave a unique site? Exodus 14:21 states, "The Lord drove the sea back with strong east wind." As I said earlier, the ancient Hebrews used only the four directions, north, south, east, and west, and didn't use intermediate directions like northwest. So an "east wind" can refer to any wind direction from northeast to southeast. Also, we know from other evidence that when the ancient Hebrews referred to an east wind, they meant a wind from the east, just as we do today.

A wind from the east, northeast, or southeast, would have blown *across* the Gulf of Suez, not *along* it (see map 1.3, pg. 10), and hence would not have caused significant wind setdown on the Gulf of Suez. On the other hand, a wind from the east, particularly from the northeast, would have blown straight down the Gulf of Aqaba, exactly as required for wind setdown to occur. The high mountains on either side of the Gulf of Aqaba would have helped funnel this wind all along the Gulf of Aqaba. Thus I believe the description in the book of Exodus of the Red Sea being blown back by a strong east wind enables us to determine uniquely where the Red Sea crossing occurred: it was at the Gulf of Aqaba. That fits with all the evidence discussed in earlier chapters, for example, that Etham was located around the head of the Gulf of Aqaba. Thus we have a unique solution to the problem of the location of the Red Sea crossing: it occurred at the head of the Gulf of Aqaba.

Wind Setdown in the Gulf of Aqaba

As I mentioned earlier, the problem of wind setdown in a long, narrow body of water has been solved and applied to the Gulf of Suez by two distinguished scientists, Doron Nof, who is in the Department of Oceanography at Florida State University, and Nathan Paldor, at the Institute of Earth Science at the Hebrew University of Jerusalem. Their paper, "Are There Oceanographic Explanations for the Israelites' Crossing of the Red Sea?" was published in 1992 in the *Bulletin of the American Meteorological Society.* It is an excellent paper, but it doesn't consider wind setdown in the Gulf of Aqaba, since almost all scholars overlook the Gulf of Aqaba as the site of the Red Sea crossing. Instead, the paper first rules out inland lakes in the Sinai Peninsula as the Red Sea crossing site, as I have done, because they are not long enough for appreciable wind setdown to occur. Then it deals exclusively with wind setdown in the Gulf of Suez, even though the authors recognize that the east wind specified in the Bible is in the wrong direction for wind setdown to occur in the Gulf of Suez! The authors state, "The apparent discrepancy between our choice of a north-westerly wind and the biblical description of an east wind prior to the crossing is attributed to local variability of the wind." My view is that since the book of Exodus deliberately specifies that the wind was an *east* wind, then this is a key clue that we shouldn't ignore. For wind setdown to occur on the Gulf of Suez, a *northwest* wind is required so that the wind blows down the length of the gulf. For wind setdown to occur on the Gulf of Aqaba, a *northeast* wind is required since it has to blow down the length of *this* gulf. Hence the east wind clue in the book of Exodus is, I suggest, clearly pointing us to the Gulf of Aqaba as the site of the wind setdown event that made the Red Sea crossing possible.

How unusual an event is a northeast wind down the Gulf of Aqaba? An article called "Physical and Chemical Oceanography of the Red

Sea," published by S. A. Morcos in 1970 in a series called *Oceanography and Marine Biology: An Annual Review,* gives a wealth of information about the Red Sea. For example, it states that the prevailing wind in the northern part of the Red Sea is north to northwest all year round, except in the Gulf of Aqaba, where the prevailing wind is east of north. Hence the east wind described in the book of Exodus, which we can deduce was a northeast wind because it caused wind setdown at the head of the Gulf of Aqaba, was not a special wind; it was the prevailing wind. What was unusual about it was its strength and duration: it lasted all night. "All that night the Lord drove the sea back with a strong east wind" (Exodus 14:21). I am reminded of the plagues of Egypt, which we showed were natural events but of an unusual intensity.

How common are strong winds on the Gulf of Aqaba? They appear to be reasonably common because they are referred to by various explorers. For example, J. S. Stephens, in *Incidents of Travel in Egypt, Arabia Petraea and the Holy Land,* published in 1837, describes a hurricane at the Gulf of Aqaba in these words:

> The sun was now obscured: a strong wind came down the sea directly in our teeth; the head of the Gulf of Aqaba was cut off from our view; the sea was troubled, and the white caps were dancing on its surface; the dark mountains looked darker and more lonely; while before us a rainbow was forming on the point of Aqaba, which threw itself across the gulf to the east, marking in the firmament with its rich and varied colours, the figure of the crescent. Soon after we were in the midst of a perfect hurricane. . . . I listened to the fierce whistling of the wind and the cracking of thunder among the mountains.

According to the account in the book of Exodus, a strong wind blew down the Gulf of Aqaba all night. We have to think of this wind as blowing over the surface of the water along the entire length of the gulf and forcing the water back, just as blowing across the water in a glass of water forces the water back. As the wind continued to blow down the gulf, the water was forced farther and farther back until what scientists call a "steady state" was reached, a point at which the water could be forced back no farther, however long the wind blew. It requires a strong wind to blow for a number of hours before this steady state is reached, and the biblical description of the wind blowing all night is consistent with this.

I have done some calculations and made an approximate estimate of wind setdown in the Gulf of Aqaba. If we assume that the wind was very strong, a hurricane as described by Stephens, traveling at 80 miles per hour, then wind setdown pushes back the sea for a distance of 800 yards. Of course, we don't know the actual distance the water in the Gulf of Aqaba was pushed back at the time of the Exodus. If the wind was stronger than 80 miles per hour, then wind setdown would have forced the sea back farther than 800 yards; on the other hand, if the wind was less strong, then wind setdown would have resulted in less than 800 yards of shore being uncovered. However, in a storm, there are usually large changes of atmospheric pressure, and these usually act to increase the effects of wind setdown. Thus the combined effects of changing atmospheric pressure and wind setdown could well have meant that the water of the Gulf of Aqaba receded by about one mile, enabling the Israelites to walk across on dry land (the sand would drain rapidly and the wind would dry it out), just as described in the book of Exodus.

A Wall of Water

The book of Exodus twice describes the water as being like a "wall" when the strong east wind drives back the water. Exodus 14:22 states, "The Israelites went through the sea on dry ground, with a wall of water on their right and on their left." Exodus 15:8 is even more explicit: "By the blast of your [God's] nostrils the waters piled up. The surging waters stood firm like a wall." Virtually all scholars regard the word *wall* here as picture language. For example, Houtman's commentary on Exodus states, "Water, which as a liquid is never rigid, through God's instrumentality has the hardness and thickness of a high wall." Also, "The point here is that the water serves the same function as a city wall." Since water is a liquid that flows, it seems scientifically impossible that it could stand up like a wall.

However, rather remarkably, the scientific paper of Nof and Paldor shows that the water that is pushed back rises up vertically from the seabed at the receding point, just like a wall. How high is this wall? Well, it depends upon the wind strength and atmospheric conditions, but for a hurricane in the Gulf of Aqaba that pushes the water back about 800 yards, I've calculated that the height of the wall of water is approximately four feet. This height could easily be doubled to about eight feet by changes in atmospheric pressure. Thus the biblical description, "The waters piled up, the surging waters stood firm like a wall," is a remarkable eyewitness type of description of what the mathematics reveals to be the case for water pushed back by a very strong wind (see figure 16.1, below).

A Wall of Water on Both Sides

As we have just seen, Exodus 14:22 states, "The Israelites went through the sea on dry ground with a wall of water on their right and on their left." This seems really tricky to explain. How can wind setdown produce water on *both sides* of the Israelites? Well, as Nof and Paldor point out, this is possible if there is a ridge of higher land running across the top of the gulf, as shown schematically in figure 16.2. The wind pushes the water down the Gulf of Aqaba, leaving the ridge of higher land exposed, and the Israelites walk across this with water on their right and on their left.

The photograph of modern Eilat shown on the next page (16.3) is very suggestive. It is clear from the photograph that there are two regions of higher land lying above the present-day shoreline. As

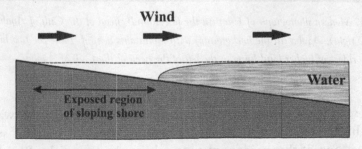

16.1. *Diagram of wind setdown. The water is blown back, exposing a region of the sloping shore (normal waterline drawn dotted).*

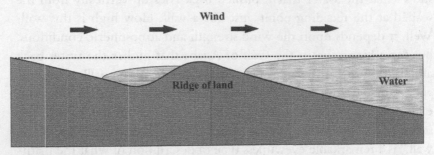

16.2. *Water on both sides of a ridge of higher land. Normally the ridge is submerged below the waterline (drawn dotted).*

16.3. *Modern photograph of Eilat (in the foreground), head of the Gulf of Aqaba (on the right), Aqaba (in the background) with mountains behind. Note the two large ridges of higher land lying to the left of the head of the Gulf of Aqaba.*

we've seen in an earlier chapter, three thousand years ago the water came higher up the Gulf of Aqaba than it does today, and I suggest that one of these ridges may have been the site of the Red Sea crossing.

Drowning Pharaoh's Army

The miracle of the Red Sea crossing had two parts: first, the Israelites crossed on dry land; second, Pharaoh's army was drowned. Let us hear again the Exodus account of the drowning of Pharaoh's army: "Moses stretched out his hand over the sea, and at daybreak the sea went back to its place. . . . The water flowed back and covered the chariots and horsemen—the entire army of Pharaoh that had followed the Israelites into the sea" (Exodus 14:27, 28).

At first sight, the drowning of Pharaoh's army is more difficult to understand than the Israelites' crossing of the Red Sea on dry land. The book of Exodus tells us that it was daybreak, so why didn't the Egyptian army see the water of the Gulf of Aqaba flowing back, and why didn't they escape? If their chariot wheels were stuck in the clay at the head of the Gulf of Aqaba, then why didn't the soldiers jump out and run? The clear implication of the Exodus account is that there wasn't time. "The Lord swept them [the Egyptians] into the sea" (Exodus 14:27); "The horse and its rider he has hurled into the sea" (Exodus 15:1); "Pharaoh's chariots and his army he has hurled into the sea" (Exodus 15:4). The picture in the book of Exodus is of a rapidly returning high wave, which knocked over the Egyptian horses and their riders suddenly and with great force. Is this possible scientifically? Or is the book of Exodus wildly exaggerating and using poetic language here?

As we have seen, for appreciable wind setdown effects to occur, a strong wind must blow for a number of hours, gradually forcing the water back. This phenomenon is well documented for long, narrow stretches of water such as Lake Erie, and it fits perfectly the biblical account of the water of the Red Sea being driven back so the Israelites could cross on dry ground. However, when a very strong wind blows steadily for several hours and then stops, it usually stops blowing gradually over a period of hours, and the water that was blown back slowly returns to its previous position, causing no threat to humans.

What happens if the very strong wind suddenly stops blowing? This, I think, is the implication of the Exodus account. The strong wind started when "Moses stretched out his hand over the sea" (Exodus 14:21), and it blew all night. Then at daybreak, for a second time, "Moses stretched out his hand over the sea" (Exodus 14:27), and the implication is that the wind suddenly stopped. What happens to the large volume of water that has been blown back? Does it return slowly or rapidly?

Nof and Paldor have performed a mathematical analysis of this for the Gulf of Suez, and what happens is quite remarkable. The water returns as a fast-moving vertical wave called a "bore." I've calculated the speed of this returning wave for the case of the Gulf of Aqaba and for water that has been pushed back by a hurricane wind to a height of eight feet. The speed of the returning wave if the wind stops suddenly is eleven miles per hour (sixteen feet per second). Just think of a literal wall of water running up the Gulf of Aqaba at eleven miles per hour. It would cover the entire "dry" area of shore, about one mile wide, from which the water had been blown back, in only five minutes.

The biggest bore in the world (apart from certain people!) is the Hang-chou-fe in China. At spring tides the bore wave can reach a height of twenty-five feet and travel up to fifteen miles per hour. The roar of its advancing can be heard from fourteen miles away. The bore wave I am suggesting occurred at the time of the Exodus is modest by comparison. Another example of a bore wave is the Severn Bore in England, which has a height of up to nine feet. Thomas Harrel in 1824 described this bore wave as follows: "When the boar [his spelling] comes, the stream does not swell by degrees, as at other times, but rolls in with a head . . . foaming and roaring as though it were enraged by the opposition which it encounters." Three thousand years ago, the sound and sight of the approaching wall of water must have been truly terrifying to the Egyptians. In our modern society we are used to fast cars and even faster planes, so a wall of water traveling at eleven miles per hour may not seem very fast. It is the sort of speed many people do when cycling. I can assure you, however, that a wall of water traveling at eleven miles per hour, or sixteen feet per second, would knock over a horse and its rider and hurl them into the sea, just as described in the book of Exodus. The wall of water would travel up the dry sand, overshoot, and the water would then come rushing back, dragging the knocked-over horses and their riders back into the depths of the Gulf of Aqaba. This is how the book of Exodus describes these events: "Pharaoh's chariots and his army he has hurled into the sea. The best of Pharaoh's officers are drowned in the

Red Sea. The deep waters have covered them; they sank to the depths like a stone" (Exodus 15:4–5). The natural mechanism of wind set-down followed by a wall of water rushing in, I believe, fits perfectly the description of events in the book of Exodus.

Was Pharaoh Drowned?

There is a widespread popular belief that Pharaoh was drowned in the Red Sea along with his army. The book of Exodus nowhere explicitly says this, but some passages may appear to imply it, for example, "The water flowed back and covered the chariots and horsemen—the entire army of Pharaoh that had followed the Israelites into the sea. Not one of them survived" (Exodus 14:28).

So did Pharaoh die? The book of Exodus describes at length the drowning of the Egyptian army, devoting as many as thirty verses to this (Exodus 14:23–15:21). However, nowhere is it stated that Pharaoh himself was drowned. Of particular importance, I believe, is the statement, "The best of Pharaoh's officers are drowned in the Red Sea" (Exodus 15:4). Surely, if Pharaoh himself had died, the writer could not have resisted mentioning it here, since the death of Pharaoh would have been so important. The very fact that the book of Exodus refers to the best of Pharaoh's officers drowning but nowhere refers to Pharaoh himself drowning is strong evidence to me that Pharaoh did not die. I suggest that he probably didn't follow the Israelites into the Red Sea but let his army go ahead with the intention of recapturing these runaway slaves and bringing them back to him.

Of course, if Pharaoh had drowned in the Red Sea, this would be a useful clue to help find out who the Pharaoh of the Exodus was and hence to date the Exodus. As I have argued earlier, I think the most probable Pharaoh at the time of the Exodus was the great Ramesses II. However, I believe he didn't die in the Red Sea. He lived and reigned for many years after the events of the Red Sea crossing (we know from Egyptian texts that Ramesses II reigned for sixty-six years and died at the age of ninety-two).

Some readers may feel that this ruthless Pharaoh who had mis-treated the Israelite slaves deserved to die in the Red Sea and that God should have made it happen! Well, it is not for us to question the motives of God, but I can tentatively suggest why I think it was actually in the Israelites' best interests for Pharaoh to survive. Following on from the ten plagues, I believe the Red Sea crossing would have finally taught Pharaoh a lesson he would never forget: that the God of the Israelites really was more powerful than all the Egyptian gods. He would know he must never tangle with the Israelites again. So, as long as this Pharaoh ruled Egypt, I believe the Israelites were safe from the Egyptians. And indeed, history records this to be the case. There is no record in the Bible or anywhere else of the Egyptians attacking the Israelites after the failed attack at the Red Sea until Ramesses II's son, Merenptah, attacked the Israelites in Canaan in about 1210 B.C. This event was recorded by the Egyptians on a large granite stele, now in the Egyptian Museum in Cairo. (A stele is an upright slab with inscriptions on it, rather like a gravestone.) The stele was discovered by the Egyptologist Flinders Petrie in 1896, in Merenptah's mortuary temple in Thebes (modern Luxor). This monument has sometimes been called the "Israel Stele" because it is the earliest surviving Egyptian text to mention the people of Israel (in a list of cities, peoples, and states defeated by Merenptah).

Incidentally, many people doubt the historicity of the Exodus because Egyptian texts do not refer to this event at all. However, the fact is that Egyptian texts boast of Egyptian victories but rarely mention Egyptian defeats! For example, historians now accept that the famous Battle of Qadesh, in about 1274 B.C., in which Ramesses II fought the Hittite king Muwatallis, ended in stalemate. However, both sides claimed a great victory in their texts describing the battle. It would therefore be surprising to find Egyptian texts referring to the Exodus and to the defeat of the Egyptian army at the Red Sea by a bunch of Israelite slaves. This humiliating incident was best forgotten by the Egyptian scribes who kept records of the deeds of the pharaohs, although I suggest that it would have been indelibly inscribed on the heart of the pharaoh.

Ramesses II reigned from about 1279 to 1213 B.C. This extraordinarily long reign meant that at least twelve of his sons died before him, until Merenptah took over as pharaoh in about 1213 B.C. The Exodus probably happened in the early years of the reign of Ramesses II, since

Exodus 2:23 and 4:19 record that Moses left Midian and returned to Egypt when he heard that the men who had wanted to kill him had died. Thus, following the Red Sea crossing, the Israelites probably had about sixty years free from attack by Ramesses II and his army: a useful time for establishing themselves as a nation.

How Long Did It Take for the Israelites to Cross the Red Sea?

The Exodus account has the Israelites crossing the Red Sea in less than one night. Is this plausible? I have estimated earlier that the strong wind plus changes in atmospheric pressure may have forced the Red Sea back for about one mile. It may have been greater or less than this, depending on the wind strength and the pressure, but one mile is a plausible figure. Imagine the Israelites crossing this one-mile-wide strip of land almost shoulder to shoulder. If each person occupied a width of about one yard, then about two thousand Israelites could stand shoulder to shoulder in the front row of those going across. If there were about twenty thousand Israelites at the Exodus, and if the rows were one yard apart, all the twenty thousand Israelites could have been contained in a broad column one mile wide and ten yards deep. Of course, the crossing wouldn't have been nearly as orderly as this: I am looking here at how feasible it was.

The present-day width of the Gulf of Aqaba at its head is about three and a half miles. I have argued that three thousand years ago the waters of the gulf extended farther north, and I suspect the distance across at the head was then narrower, from my inspection of the land in 1999 and 2001. However, let us assume that the Israelites had to cross three and a half miles to get from the west side of the head of the Gulf of Aqaba to the east side. They had animals to get across plus children and old people, and an extremely strong crosswind was blowing. Fortunately, it wasn't a head wind! I believe the Israelites would have linked arms and grabbed hold of their animals as they battled through the fierce crosswinds, one step at a time. Given these ferocious conditions, my best guess is that it probably took the Israelites two to three hours to cross the Red Sea.

The Egyptians then followed but their chariot wheels came off (or jammed, according to the Septuagint), I suggest, because they got stuck in the patch of thick clay that I and others have found at the head of the Gulf of Aqaba. Since the chariots were probably leading the Egyptians across, the rest of the Egyptian army piled up behind, both the horses and the foot soldiers. Then came daybreak (about 6 A.M.), and Moses stretched out his hand over the sea again. The wind suddenly stopped, the water came rushing back as a wall or bore, and the Egyptians were knocked over, swept back into the sea, and drowned. What a spectacular climax to the story! Picture the scene, and imagine the sense of wonder and awe at the remarkable events the Israelites had just witnessed.

Hence we have a consistent set of natural explanations for the Red Sea crossing, which fit the account in the book of Exodus very well. In fact, they fit so well that I think there can be little doubt that the Red Sea crossing was made possible by wind setdown at the head of the Gulf of Aqaba. Our modern scientific understanding of wind setdown, together with the description in the book of Exodus, therefore enables us to specify the exact location for the Red Sea crossing: the head of the Gulf of Aqaba. Virtually no modern scholar believes this was the location. If the arguments in this chapter are accepted, then a major rethinking of the events of the Exodus will be required.

In the next chapter the Israelites leave the Gulf of Aqaba and head for Mount Sinai. Along the way a remarkable thing happens: Moses turns bitter water into sweet water using a piece of wood. Does this event have a natural explanation? What route did the Israelites take? Also, in the next chapter we will tentatively identify a complete sequence of places the Israelites camped at using clues in the biblical account.

PART FIVE

DISCOVERING
MOUNT SINAI

SEVENTEEN

TURNING BITTER
WATER SWEET

*When they came to Marah, they could not drink its water because it
was bitter. (That is why the place is called Marah.) So the people
grumbled against Moses, saying, "What are we to drink?" Then
Moses cried out to the Lord, and the Lord showed him a piece of wood.
He threw it into the water, and the water became sweet.*

Exodus 15:23–25

Perhaps it is because of the classic film *Lawrence of Arabia* that we
think of Arabia as a country of vast, waterless deserts of shifting
sands. My wife gave me the video of *Lawrence of Arabia* for my
birthday in 2002, and from the credits at the end of this epic film it
seems that none of it was actually shot in Arabia! It was all made in the
deserts of Morocco, in Rum in present-day Jordan, with its magnificent rock formations, and in the Shepperton Film Studios.

I needed to find out what the landscape of Arabia was really like at
the time of Moses, three thousand years ago, because the remaining
chapters of this book, which take us from the head of the Gulf of
Aqaba to Mount Sinai (the real one) are all set in Midian in Arabia.
Modern Arabia, called Saudi Arabia, has changed dramatically in recent years, largely because of its oil wealth, and great cities have developed. However, my belief is that if you go back a hundred years, the
Arabian landscape was much the same as it was three thousand years
ago, because the country was tribal one hundred years ago, there were
very few roads, and the evidence we have suggests that the climate has
not changed greatly in the last three thousand years. I consulted with a
Saudi Arabia expert, the former diplomat Henry St. John Armitage,

over this. St. John Armitage lived in Saudi Arabia for many years and is very knowledgeable about its history and geography. He confirmed to me, "Midian has changed little in terms of its 'countryside' in the last three thousand years."

So what was Arabia like a hundred years ago? The intrepid explorers I've mentioned earlier, people such as Burton, Wallin, and Doughty, tell us in their vivid writings. To be sure, Arabia contained (and still does) some vast deserts: for example, one of these is called the Empty Quarter, because it occupies about one-quarter of Arabia and is almost devoid of human habitation. However, although Arabia receives little rainfall and on average is very dry, explorers tell us that there were oases with palm trees and freshwater springs dotted about, also some rivers, and very, very occasionally regions of really luxurious plant growth with a wide variety of different trees, shrubs, and flowers. From archaeology we know that parts of Arabia three thousand years ago supported wealthy, flourishing tribal societies.

Today the wealth of a country is based on manufactured goods, property, natural resources such as oil, and financial investments such as stocks and shares. Three thousand years ago wealth arose mainly from natural resources, and people traded gold, incense, spices, and precious stones: Arabia had all of these, particularly incense in south Arabia (modern Yemen) and gold in Midian. So trade routes developed to carry these desirable goods from Arabia to places such as Egypt and Damascus in modern Syria. Along the trade routes were designated stopping places, guarded by local tribesmen, where it was safe to rest and sleep, for a fee of course, and where food and water were usually available, again at a price. Ancient trade routes were somewhat like modern toll roads: each time you passed a toll point (stopping point) you paid a fee and were allowed to proceed to the next toll point.

As far as we know, there were no signposts, although the trade routes may have been marked and the trodden-down pathway would normally have been clear. To stray off a trade route, as I've said before, was fraught with danger. If you were a stranger to the region, and you traveled off a trade route, you wouldn't know when you could next find water or if the track you had taken might peter out or hit an impassable cliff face.

So I believe that Moses and the Israelites would have kept to trade routes, or known tribal routes, as much as possible in their journey to

Mount Sinai. Whether they paid their tolls, or whether the local tribesmen guarding the stopping places fled at the sight of twenty thousand Israelites, I don't know. My guess is that the relationships with the local tribes were usually friendly, although we will see in the next chapter an example of when they were not, which resulted in a pitched battle.

So where did Moses and the Israelites go after crossing the Red Sea at the head of the Gulf of Aqaba? There were two main thirteenth-century B.C. trade routes through Midian, as shown in map 4.1, pg. 46. The first goes south from Aqaba through Madian (modern al-Bad'), the second runs almost parallel to this and goes farther east through Tabuk. In addition, there were ancient routes linking the head of the Gulf of Aqaba with the major settlements of Qurayyah and Tabuk. Can we say which of these routes the Israelites took? I think we can because the book of Numbers provides a key clue. Numbers 33 lists the stages in Israel's Exodus journey. Some days after crossing the Red Sea, Numbers 33:10 states that the Israelites camped by the Red Sea. As we've seen in an earlier chapter, this text has puzzled biblical scholars for years. However, it makes perfect sense if the Red Sea crossing occurred at the head of the Gulf of Aqaba and the Israelites then traveled south along the trade route through Madian (al-Bad'), because this trade route moves inland away from the coast of the Gulf of Aqaba and then returns to the Red Sea coast farther south at Ainuna (see map 4.1, pg. 46).

I will look at this in more detail later in the chapter. As I said earlier, archaeology reveals that this trade route existed in the thirteenth to twelfth centuries B.C., at the time of the Exodus.

This chapter is largely a geographical detective story about discovering the route of the Exodus. But along the way, some amazing things happen, like Moses turning bitter water sweet using a piece of wood. Impossible? Well, read on!

The Exodus Route After the Red Sea Crossing

"Then Moses led Israel from the Red Sea and they went into the Desert of Shur. For three days they travelled without finding water" (Exodus 15:22). I believe this verse contains an interesting clue: the

Israelites traveled for three days without finding water. Why is this a clue? Because if they were on a trade route, then normally the stopping places, a day's journey apart, contained drinking water. So the implication of this verse is that, on this part of the journey, unusually the stopping places contained no drinking water. Is this consistent with what we know about the trade route going south from the head of the Gulf of Aqaba?

Musil, in *The Northern Hegaz,* describes the stopping places on this ancient trade route. The first stopping place, one day's journey from the head of the Gulf of Aqaba, was Haql (also spelled Hakl). Haql is on the coast of the Gulf of Aqaba, twenty-five miles southwest of the head of the gulf (see map 4.1, pg. 46).

Musil writes, "The water [at Hakl] is either salt or brackish and causes violent fever." So although the water may have been adequate for the Israelites' flocks, the Israelites themselves wouldn't have wanted to drink it. So, there was no drinking water at Haql.

The trade route then moves inland, and Musil gives the next traditional stopping place, a day's journey from Haql, as as-Saraf, about twenty-five miles south of Haql (see map 4.1, pg. 46). Musil does not mention whether there is water there or not, but the archaeologist David Hogarth, in his *Handbook of Hejaz,* published in 1917, dismissively writes of this place, "No water." So there was probably no water there for the Israelites to drink.

According to Musil, the next stopping place, a day's journey from as-Saraf, was Mughayir Shu'ayb, meaning the Caves of Jethro, which I described in chapter 4. These caves were part of ancient Madian, modern al-Bad', believed to have been the old capital of the land of Midian. This place is twenty-five miles south of as-Saraf (map 4.1, pg. 46), and here Musil tells us there was plentiful drinking water. He describes his visit there as follows: "On all sides there are springs of various sizes, the water of which flows together and forms a stream. . . . Some men and women were watering goats and camels and filling their skin bags." So if the Israelites had gone south along this trade route from the head of the Gulf of Aqaba, they would have traveled for three days before finding drinking water (one day to Haql, one to as-Saraf, and one to Madian), just as described in Exodus.

The book of Exodus calls the desert they walked through the Desert of Shur. We've already seen in chapter 14 that *shur* is Hebrew for "wall," and I've argued that Shur was the name of the region around the head of the Gulf of Aqaba, so called because the mountains on each side of this rift valley look like walls. So I suggest that the Desert of Shur was the name the Israelites gave to the desert they entered that ran down the eastern side of the Gulf of Aqaba, since this is indeed bordered by a wall of mountains. The name Desert of Shur fits well this geographical landscape.

The Mystery of Marah

"They went into the Desert of Shur. For three days they travelled in the desert without finding water. When they came to Marah they could not drink its water because it was bitter" (Exodus 15:22, 23). We have a problem! I've just argued that the Israelites were traveling south on the trade route from the head of the Gulf of Aqaba, and if this is correct, then after three days' journey they should have reached ancient Madian, where, according to Musil, freshwater was plentiful. However, according to the book of Exodus, it was not Madian but a place called Marah that was three days' journey after the Red Sea crossing, and the water there was bitter. Was Marah the same place as Madian? Can we find out after three thousand years?

Marah is a Hebrew word meaning "bitter." In fact, the book of Exodus specifically tells us this: "When they came to Marah, they could not drink its water because it was bitter. (That is why the place is called Marah.)" (Exodus 15:23) Since *Marah* is a Hebrew word, do we have any hope of locating on a map of Arabia the place the Israelites called Marah? I think we do, and let me try to explain the way I went about solving this problem.

The book of Exodus records that some places along the Exodus route were named by the Israelites themselves because of things that happened to them there. For example, Exodus 17:7 states, "He [Moses] called the place Massah [Hebrew for testing] and Meribah [Hebrew for quarreling] because the Israelites quarrelled and because they tested the Lord." In this example, Massah and Meribah are clearly names that Moses invented for a place because of what happened there, and I think it would be pointless to try to find Arabic equivalents of these names on a map of Arabia.

However, I believe the case of Marah is different, because Exodus 15:23 states, "That is why the place is called Marah." My interpretation of this is that Moses didn't invent the name Marah, meaning bitter, for the place, but rather that the place was already called bitter by the local Midianites, and the Israelites then called it by the Hebrew word for bitter, Marah.

What does the Bible mean by the description "bitter water"? In the ancient world, bitter water was usually another name for salty water. For example, the Bitter Lakes in the Sinai Peninsula are so called because their water is slightly salty (because of salt deposited in ancient times by the Red Sea). The Arabic words for salt are *malh* and *milh,* and *malih* and *milhi* both mean "salty." For example, the Dead Sea in Arabic is *Bakhr el-Melkh,* meaning "the Salt Sea," and there is today a salty spring 180 miles southwest of Dongola in the Sudan called Bir-el-Malha. The Arabic *murr* means "bitter," and *mirra* means "gall." These words are all related since the consonants *l* and *r* are sometimes interchanged in Arabic.

How are we to locate the place the Israelites called Marah on a map of Arabia? This is where the story really starts to be intriguing. As we have seen, the book of Exodus implies that Marah was three days' journey from the Red Sea crossing site. If the Israelites traveled south through Midian along the ancient trade route from the head of the Gulf of Aqaba, then I have shown that three days' journey would have taken them to ancient Madian, modern al-Bad'. Hence if my theory is correct, the place the Israelites called Marah should be what the Arabs called Madian. However, the consonantal form of Madian, *m-d-n,* differs significantly from *m-l-h,* meaning salty, so my theory seems not to work. In addition, although we can deduce from texts written two thousand years ago by Josephus, Ptolemy, and Eusebius that modern al-Bad' was called Madian, we don't know whether or not the place was called Madian a thousand years earlier at the time of the Exodus. So my theory seems impossible to pursue any further.

Or does it? Imagine my amazement on rereading Musil's *The Northern Hegaz* to see Musil's sketch map of ancient Madian (which I reproduced in chapter 4; see map 4.3, pg. 55) showing that it contains the archaeological remains of four settlements about a thousand yards apart, and that one of these four ancient settlements was called al-Malha (the same name as the modern salt spring in Dongola, mentioned above). Musil states in his book that ancient Madian dates from at least Nabataean times (that is, from about 100 B.C.). But as we saw in chapter 4, a more recent archaeological survey of al-Bad' (ancient Madian) in 1981 discovered a substantial quantity of the distinctive Midianite pottery there, which has been dated to the thirteenth century B.C. We also saw in chapter 3 that the most probable date for the Exodus was in the thirteenth century B.C. So Madian was a significant Midianite settlement at the time of the Exodus. In addition, since there was a settlement called al-Malha in Madian, it is possible that at the time of the Exodus, ancient Madian could have been called al-Malha, or an earlier Midianite word meaning salty or bitter. I suggest the Israelites then took over this name and called the place Marah, the Hebrew word for bitter.

I wondered if any other explorers had discovered anything interesting about al-Malha, and I opened my battered secondhand copy of *The Land of Midian,* written by the relatively modern British explorer H. St. John Philby in 1957. Philby visited ancient Madian, modern al-Bad', which he calls Bad'a, and he describes his time there as follows:

> It was astonishing that my companions, all of whom had passed through Bad'a before on their way between Tabuk and Dhuba, had never taken the trouble to visit the scenes of Jethro's activities, celebrated in the Quran, let alone the traditional sites associated with Moses. . . . The tiny oasis of al Maliha . . . lay about 1000 yards from the Mughayir [the caves of Jethro].. . . In the oasis were a number of wells, about 3½ fathoms in depth, with water so sweet that it is compared in local estimation with the Nile. Hence its name [al Maliha], meaning "the salt well" on the *lucus a non lucendo* principle.

How fascinating! Let's look at what Philby is saying. He is saying that in modern al-Bad', a thousand yards from the "caves of Jethro," there is an oasis called al Maliha. Musil places al-Malha a thousand yards from the caves of Jethro, and I have no doubt that "Maliha"

(Philby) and "Malha" (Musil) are the same place (note the identical consonants). Philby also says that the water there is wonderfully fresh and sweet, in agreement with Musil, who states that the water at Madian is fresh and plentiful.

However, and here is the really interesting point, Philby clearly has problems understanding why the place is called al-Maliha, "the salt well," when the water from the wells is particularly fresh and sweet, so he says that the name was given on the *lucus a non lucendo* principle. Although I learned Latin at school, I had to look up the meaning of this phrase in a dictionary. It means a self-contradictory statement, since in Latin *lucus,* meaning "grove," is derived from *lucere,* meaning "shine," and light doesn't shine in a shady grove. It is like deliberately saying black is white. So Philby is suggesting that the Midianites deliberately called a well with wonderfully sweet water by the name of *al Maliha,* meaning "the salt well," as a sort of bizarre joke. I may be wrong, but I don't think that ancient Midianites would make a joke like this about something as precious to them as freshwater.

Is there an alternative explanation? I think there may be. Philby states that the oasis of Maliha is in a valley at the foot of some cliffs, and this local geography may provide a key clue as to why the place is called the salt well. How does a well get its water? Normally, wells draw up water from the ground, called groundwater. Groundwater is stored naturally below the earth's surface, and it forms about 20 percent of the freshwater used in the United States. Most rainwater is absorbed by the ground and fills up the tiny spaces between soil particles. However, in a heavy storm, excess water runs over the top of the soil, carrying with it pollutants it encounters. Stormwater cascading down cliffs can contain dissolved mineral salts from the rocks, and if there is a well near the foot of the cliffs, this salty water can flow into the well. Normally the water in the wells at Maliha is very fresh and sweet, as described by both Philby and Musil. However, I suggest that after a violent storm mineral salts are washed down from the nearby cliffs into the valley and the water in the wells becomes salty. This is a logical reason for calling the place Maliha or Malha, "the salt well." Another possibility may be that the name Malha arises from an ancient tradition that Moses and the Israelites found bitter water here.

Now picture Moses leading the Israelites to Malha. They had been traveling for three days without finding water and were becoming desperate. However, Moses, who I believe had lived here before with Jethro, would have known how good the water at Malha usually was, and he would have told them, "Don't worry. There is wonderful water at the bitter well, despite its name. It is as sweet as the Nile." So when the Israelites arrived at Malha they rushed to the well to drink deep of its wonderful water, only to find it was bitter. So the Israelites called the place Marah, Hebrew for "bitter," following the existing Midianite name meaning "salty" or "bitter." Why was the water bitter? Only three or four days previously the water of the Gulf of Aqaba had been blown back by a hurricane wind, which is usually associated with a storm, and I suggest that it was this storm that had washed mineral salts down from the nearby cliffs into the well.

So a consistent story emerges. Biblical Marah may be ancient Malha in Midian. I can think of only one argument against this. In chapter 4 I gave reasons for believing that Jethro, Moses' father-in-law, probably lived in Madian. But if Jethro had lived there, surely he would have been mentioned in the story. However, since the Bible calls Jethro "the priest of Midian," he probably covered a wide territory, perhaps all of Midian, and I suggest he happened to be away from home when Moses and the Israelites were there. However, if the family of Jethro did indeed live in Madian, then Moses would undoubtedly have explained to them all that had happened, and that, as instructed by God, he was heading for Mount Sinai. This may explain how "Jethro, the priest of Midian and father-in-law of Moses, heard of everything God had done for Moses and for his people Israel" (Exodus 18:1), and how Jethro came to visit Moses near Mount Sinai one to two months after Moses had passed through Marah (Malha).

How Did Moses Sweeten the Water?

"When they [the Israelites] came to Marah they could not drink its water because it was bitter, . . . and the Lord showed him [Moses] a piece of wood. He threw it into the water and it became sweet" (Exodus 15:23, 25).

In this book I've suggested that the miracles of the Exodus were natural events but nevertheless still miracles because of the timing. So can science explain how throwing a piece of wood into a well of salty water could produce sweet-tasting water? Very tentatively, I can suggest two possible explanations.

The first involves charcoal. Only some varieties of trees produce good charcoal when they are burned, and one of these is a species of acacia called the *Acacia seyel* tree. Wallin, in his book *Travels in Arabia* (1845 and 1848), says that the wood of the *Acacia seyel* tree produces "the best kind of charcoal for fuel." Now it is clear from the books of Wallin, Musil, and others that this acacia tree is common in Midian, and burning wood for charcoal is a traditional practice that goes back thousands of years. Hence it is not unlikely that there was some burned acacia wood, covered with a layer of charcoal, lying about in ancient Marah, and I suggest it was this wood that Moses threw into the salty well at Marah to purify it.

Charcoal has been used for many years to purify water. There is a fascinating old book I have unearthed, *On the Stowage of Ships and Their Cargoes,* published in London in 1869, in which Robert White Stevens writes, "A pound of charcoal thrown into a cask of water, twelve hours before use, will purify it." Charcoal removes salty and other bad-tasting molecules from water by adsorbing them onto the surfaces of all its tiny pores. Charcoal is extremely effective in doing this, and we even use charcoal today in water filters.

It's worth remembering that the water at Marah was normally fresh and sweet, and I've suggested that it was only on rare occasions that mineral salts making the water taste bitter were washed down from the nearby cliffs. The degree of saltiness may have been relatively small. A large piece of burned acacia wood covered with charcoal could therefore have sweetened the water rapidly and effectively.

Of course, it is unlikely that twenty thousand Israelites drank from one well! Although when the Israelites traveled across the broad el Tih plateau of the Sinai Peninsula, I suggested that they would have traveled in a widely spread out group, the ancient trade route from the head of the Gulf of Aqaba to south Arabia is quite narrow in places, and so the Israelites would have traveled in a much longer column after the Red Sea crossing. I suggest that the first Israelites to arrive in Marah drank from the well and found it to be bitter because of the runoff of water into it from the nearby cliffs. Moses then sweetened the water, and the Israelites would have drunk until the well was empty. They then would have dug fresh wells to obtain more water, which, if farther from the cliffs, would have been naturally sweet through normal filtering of water through the soil.

At the start of this section I mentioned two possible explanations for wood sweetening water. Charcoal-burned wood is one possibility, but it is worth mentioning that certain trees are known to be water purifiers and desalinizers without being burned. For example, in Sri Lanka, wood from the kumbuk tree (*Terminalia arjuna*) is used to line the inner walls of wells because it purifies and desalinizes the water. In addition, charcoal-burned wood is often added to the wells to reduce further the salinity of the water. However, I have not been able to find out if any of the trees in Midian are natural water purifiers. What is clear is that charcoal-burned *Acacia seyel,* which is common in Midian, would be an excellent purifier. Thus there is a tentative scientific explanation for how Moses sweetened the water with a piece of wood.

The Route to Mount Sinai

My father loved routes and maps. When I was a child, whenever we went on a long car trip, he would write to an auto organization called the Royal Automobile Club and request two routes from them, one the fastest and the other the most scenic. He would then spend long hours poring over these routes before deciding which one to use. My mother, on the other hand, just wanted to get to our destination and didn't care about the route. So some people are really interested in routes, and others find them boring. If you are interested in routes, then please read on because we are now going to reconstruct a key part of the Exodus route for the first time. However, if you are one of the many people who find routes rather boring, then you might like to fast-forward to the next chapter. However, I hope some readers will stay with me because I think that the Exodus route is a fascinating puzzle.

Where did the Israelites go after leaving Marah? Here are the place-names, in the exact order they occur, in both Exodus and Numbers, starting from Marah and ending at Mount Sinai.

EXODUS 15:23–19:2	NUMBERS 33:9–15
Marah	Marah
Elim	Elim
Desert of Sin	Red Sea
Traveled from place to place	Desert of Sin
Rephidim	Dophkah
Massah	Alush
Meribah	Rephidim
Desert of Sinai	Desert of Sinai
Mount Sinai	

At first sight these two lists of stopping places look very different, and many biblical scholars believe they are contradictory. However, we have demonstrated many times in this book just how accurate the Old Testament writings are about the Exodus, so we should not accept too readily that they have now become inaccurate. Let's do a simple analysis of the above two lists.

The first point to note, as we've said earlier, is that Massah and Meribah were not existing place-names but Hebrew names given by Moses to a certain site because of particular events that occurred there. I believe this explains why the book of Numbers does not mention them. We can therefore ignore these two names as places we can hope to find on the route.

After leaving Elim, the book of Numbers states that the Israelites "camped by the Red Sea" (Numbers 33:10), whereas the book of Exodus ignores this campsite. The fact that no place-name on the Red Sea is mentioned suggests that there may not have been one—that it was simply an unnamed campsite and this could explain why the book of Exodus does not mention it. However, there must have been an important reason for including an unnamed site in the book of Numbers, and I will return to this later.

Both Exodus and Numbers record the Israelites camping in the Desert of Sin. Exodus states that, after leaving the Desert of Sin, the Israelites traveled "from place to place" (Exodus 17:1), whereas Numbers names these places as Dophkah and Alush. Both Exodus and Numbers refer to Rephidim and the Desert of Sinai. Numbers does not refer to Mount Sinai in the list of campsites because the Israelites didn't camp on Mount Sinai itself; they camped in the Desert of Sinai surrounding Mount Sinai.

This simple analysis of the routes given in Exodus and Numbers enables us to put together an overall route list, which is a synthesis of the place-names in both Exodus and Numbers, as follows:

Marah

Elim

Red Sea

Desert of Sin

Dophkah

Alush

Rephidim

Desert of Sinai

Mount Sinai

Can we reconstruct this route from clues given in the Bible? We've just left Moses and the Israelites at Marah, so where was Elim, the next recorded stopping site?

Elim

Elim must have had a good supply of freshwater since this time there were no complaints from the Israelites about the water. This is what the book of Exodus records: "Then they [the Israelites] came to Elim, where there were 12 springs and 70 palm trees, and they camped there near the water" (Exodus 15:27). Can we identify Elim? According to Houtman's commentary on Exodus, *elim* is a Hebrew word meaning "big trees." So Elim may have been the name given by the Israelites to this site because of the tall, well-watered trees there.

From ancient sources quoted by Musil in *The Northern Hegaz*, we know that the next stopping place on the trade route to south Arabia after Madian, modern al-Bad', was at an oasis called Ainuna (also transliterated Ajnuna or Aynunah), about thirty miles south of Madian (map 4.1, pg. 46). Could this be the place the Bible calls Elim? What do we know about Ainuna?

Musil visited Ainuna and describes it as follows:

> We saw to the southeast the green palm groves in the oasis of Ajnuna. . . . The oasis of Ajnuna is famed for its good, fresh water. . . . At ten o'clock we entered Wadi Ajnuna, two kilometers broad, which might easily be transformed into one great palm garden.

In all of my travels I cannot recall seeing a river or a riverbed over a mile wide, and yet here is one in Arabia, of all places. This immense wadi was formed, not by trickles of water, but by torrential floods. Clearly Ainuna is a very well watered place. Ancient Ainuna is a few miles from another oasis called Sharma (map 4.1, pg. 46), which Philby visited and described in *The Land of Midian* as follows: "Ainuna itself appears to have been a place of considerable importance. . . . The spring and oasis of Sharma must be of great antiquity."

Musil records that a text written by the Arab al-Ya'qubi states that in his time (about A.D. 890) the settlement of Ainuna was inhabited, that it had palm gardens, and that buried gold was being sought there. Musil also encountered, near Ainuna, an Arab who said, "If we belonged to the Egyptians or the English, all the settlements on our coast would flourish. Our oases would be capable of feeding thousands of people." Many people don't believe the Exodus story because they say it would have been impossible for thousands of Israelites to have survived in the desert. These people make a good point, which has to be answered by those who take the Exodus story seriously, as I've done in this book. I myself have doubts about how the Israelites could have survived in the Sinai Peninsula if they had traveled to the traditional Mount Sinai. However, the descriptions of major oases in Arabia by explorers like Musil leave me in no doubt that twenty thousand Israelites could have survived along the Exodus route to the real Mount Sinai. Places like Ainuna had large quantities of freshwater.

The British explorer Richard Burton writes in *The Gold-Mines of Midian,* published in 1878,

We minutely inspected the Wadi Aynunah. . . . It is a true oasis, a perpetual spring bordered by *tall palms* [my italics]. . . . The Bedouin declare that, after the Nile, it [the water of Aynunah] is the best in the world.

Thus Ainuna, with its tall palm trees and plentiful excellent freshwater, fits admirably the description of Elim in the book of Exodus. In addition, Ainuna was the next stopping place on the trade route after Madian, and Elim was the next stopping place for the Israelites after Marah, a settlement in Madian. I therefore identify the Hebrew place-name Elim with Ainuna. Midianite pottery, dating from the thirteenth century B.C., has also been found at Ainuna by the archaeologist Peter Parr, so a settlement clearly existed there at the time of the Exodus.

The Camp by the Red Sea

We come now to the curious clue of the Red Sea campsite. Numbers 33 lists the campsites on the Exodus route all by place-names, except for one site: "They camped by the Red Sea" (Numbers 33:10). Why doesn't Numbers state the name of the place they camped at by the Red Sea? As I said before, I think the reason has to be that there was no significant named settlement at this site or else the book of Numbers would have given it. In addition, as I mentioned above, if there was no place with a name there, this may explain why the book of Exodus doesn't mention it.

But why does the book of Numbers mention this campsite-without-a-name at all, particularly since nothing is recorded as happening there? I've thought about this a lot and can think of only one possible reason: it is mentioned because here the Israelites changed routes. At this site on the Red Sea coast they left the trade route they had been following, which went from the head of the Gulf of Aqaba down to south Arabia, and they traveled inland. Let's think back to the instructions I gave to the American tourist wanting to travel from Cambridge to London. I told him to go from Cambridge to Trumpington to London. Trumpington is an insignificant tiny village outside Cambridge, but its significance on the route from Cambridge to London is that it marks a change of road: it is just outside Trumpington that the driver gets on to the M11 highway to London. In a similar way, I suggest the importance of the reference to the "camp by the Red Sea" is that it marks the Israelites' leaving the coastal trade route and heading inland. However, if the campsite isn't named, then how can we find it?

If biblical Elim was Ainuna, as I have suggested above, then traveling southeast from Ainuna along the ancient trade route, which follows the Red Sea coast, we come to a point where a major river or riverbed called the Wadi Tiryam comes down to the coast (see map 4.1, pg. 46), about twenty miles southeast of Ainuna.

The explorer George August Wallin, in *Travels in Arabia* (1845 and 1848), tells us that this place was the next campsite after Ainuna for the Muslim pilgrims on their way to Mecca from Egypt, and, as we have stated earlier, the pilgrim campsites were almost certainly based on the sites previously used by ancient traders carrying spices to Egypt and other places. Wallin says that in the Wadi Tiryam there are water wells. Musil calls the Wadi Tiryam the Wadi Terim. Interestingly, and I believe importantly, neither Musil nor Wallin refers to a named settlement where the Wadi Tiryam meets the Red Sea. So this site was the next campsite after Ainuna on the trade route, and hence it was also, I believe, the next stopping place for the Israelites after Elim, which I identify with Ainuna. I therefore suggest that the unnamed camp by the Red Sea was where the Wadi Tiryam meets the Red Sea.

Is there any evidence for an ancient route running along the Wadi Tiryam and meeting the coastal trade route? After very tentatively making the deduction in the paragraph above, I was browsing among the Arabian books in the Cambridge University Library during lunch one day when I came across a book by F. E. Peters, *Mecca: A Literary History of the Muslim Holy Land,* published in 1994. In the front of this book there is a small sketch map depicting the ancient trade routes of Arabia, drawn in solid lines, which I was familiar with, but I was intrigued to see a route drawn in a dotted line, marked "alternative route," which I had never seen on any map before. This route leaves the main coastal trade route just below Ainuna, goes inland, and ends near the ancient settlement of Dedan (modern al-Ula; see map 4.1, pg. 46). The map in Peters's book is small-scale, not very detailed, and it is difficult to see where this "alternative route" begins and ends.

I then found in the Cambridge University Library William Facey's book about central Arabia, *Riyadh—The Old City.* Figure 3 of Facey's book contains a sketch map titled "The pre-Islamic trade routes and cities of Arabia." This map again has a trade route linking the coastal trade route with the parallel inland route and appearing to start from near Ainuna and end near ancient Dedan. However, tantalizingly, the map is too small-scale to see exactly where this route starts.

I contacted William Facey for further details of this route, and he was very helpful, even sending me a copy of his original drawing of this figure. He told me he had used various sources in reconstructing it, particularly articles in *Atlal: The Journal of Saudi Arabian Archaeology.* I tracked this down in the university library, and there, in volume 5, was a more detailed map of the start of this trade route. Where did it start? From where the Wadi Tiryam runs into the Red Sea, precisely as I had deduced earlier. William Facey then emailed me: "Yes, Wadi Tiryam is the route, leaving the coast just south of Aynunah."

In science, it is always reassuring when a prediction comes true, and I now found this equally reassuring with the Exodus route. I had deduced from the biblical account that the unnamed camping site by the Red Sea must be where the Wadi Tiryam came down to the Red Sea. I had also deduced that this site had been recorded in the book of Numbers because it marked the spot where the Israelites changed routes, leaving the coastal trade route and going inland along the Wadi Tiryam. When I made this deduction I had no idea that there really was a trade route along the Wadi Tiryam because the books of the great explorers Musil, Wallin, Philby, and Doughty don't mention it at all. But this "minor" route, linking the major north-south coastal trade route with the major north-south inland trade route, really existed and has been found in the relatively recent archaeological surveys reported in *Atlal* in 1981.

Why did the Israelites leave the coastal trade route? As we have seen, Mount Sinai was a volcano, and the volcanoes in Midian are not on the coast but are inland (in Harrat Rahah and Harrat 'Uwayrid; see map 4.1, pg. 46), so the Israelites had to leave the coastal trade route and travel inland in order to reach Mount Sinai. Thus a logical, coherent story starts to emerge for the route the Israelites took to Mount Sinai.

The Wadi Sadr runs into the Wadi Tiryam (see map 4.1, pg. 46). Wallin writes about the Wadi Sadr as follows: "The Wadi Sadr . . .

affords plenty of water and contains some date-trees. . . . Wadi Sadr being one of the most fertile spots in as-Sahil, is a favourite dwelling-place with the Arabs here." So on this part of their journey the Is-raelites should have had no complaints about the water supplies, and indeed Exodus and Numbers record none here.

Incidentally, what does Wallin mean when he refers to as-Sahil above? Wallin states, "The land in this part of Arabia, between the sea and the chain of granite mountains which run parallel with the coast, at an average distance of 8 hours on foot (24 miles) from the beach, is known by the general name of as-Sahil (Sahil is Arabic for 'the shore')." Wallin adds, "The soil of as-Sahil is generally poor, affording only a scanty pasture." If the Israelites wished to head inland from the coast, then they had to cross at some stage the barren as-Sahil shore region, and traveling along the Wadi Tiryam, where the shore is less than ten miles wide, followed by the well-watered Wadi Sadr was clearly the way to go to maximize their supply of freshwater. No doubt this was the reason that this particular route was a trade route inland, connecting the coastal trade route with the major inland settle-ment of Dedan (modern al-Ula).

In this chapter I've reconstructed the route of the Exodus from the Red Sea crossing (the head of the Gulf of Aqaba) to the Wadi Sadr, which, as we will see in the next chapter, leads the Israelites to the Desert of Sin. At the start of this chapter I suggested that it made sense for Moses to lead the Israelites along known trade routes, as far as pos-sible. I've compared known stopping places along these trade routes with the campsites listed in the books of Exodus and Numbers, and in each case there is a close correspondence between the biblical descrip-tion of the campsite on the Exodus route and the description of the stopping site on the trade routes given by explorers who have visited them (who had no thought of their being sites on the Exodus route).

The descriptions given by explorers such as Musil and Wallin of the trade route stopping places that I've identified with biblical campsites fit not just one such site on the Exodus route, but a complete se-quence of such sites, and also in the correct order: Red Sea crossing site; traveling in the Desert of Shur for three days without finding drinking water; Marah with the bitter water; Elim with tall palm trees; the unnamed Red Sea campsite with a change of route. As we will see in the next chapter, my identification of the site of the Desert of Sin also fits the biblical description of this place in a remarkable way. I believe this good fit of a sequence of consecutive Exodus campsites with a sequence of consecutive trade route stopping sites inspires some confidence that my tentative identification of these sites is correct.

In the next chapter we'll think about quail, manna, and above all, dew! Why dew? Dew is familiar to most of us, but heavy dew is rare in deserts, and I believe the biblical description of heavy dew in the Desert of Sin is a key clue to where this desert was—a clue that has been ignored until now. We will also show why the Moon-god was so important in the ancient Middle East and we will give a natural explanation for obtaining water out of a rock.

EIGHTEEN

FROM THE CLUE OF THE DEW
TO WATER FROM A ROCK

The whole Israelite community set out from Elim and came to the Desert of Sin. . . . That evening quail came and covered the camp, and in the morning there was a layer of dew around the camp. When the dew was gone, thin flakes like frost appeared on the desert floor. When the Israelites saw it, they said to each other, "What is it?" For they did not know what it was. Moses said to them, "It is the bread the Lord has given you to eat. . . . Take an omer [about 2 quarts] for each person you have in your tent. . . ." The people of Israel called the bread manna.

Exodus 16:1, 13–16, 31

I will stand there before you by the rock at Horeb. Strike the rock, and water will come out of it for the people to drink.

Exodus 17:6

"DNA Traps Rape Killer 20 Years On" is the headline on page 31 of the *Daily Express* of April 11, 2002. I'm staying in London to attend a conference, and the newspaper has been left outside my hotel room door. The newspaper story is that a DNA sample recently taken from the mouth of a truck driver matched the DNA found twenty years ago on a murdered schoolgirl's jeans. So this tiny clue of microscopic DNA molecules has enabled police scientists to discover, beyond reasonable doubt, the identity of the killer, even though the crime was committed twenty years ago. Can we somewhat similarly use the tiny clues provided in the verses above from Exodus 16 to identify the lost Desert of Sin, even though the events recorded there occurred not twenty but more than three thousand years ago? And is water from a rock explicable scientifically?

Let's read again the words from Exodus at the start of this chapter and ask ourselves what are the key clues in this passage. Can you spot them? There are three obvious clues: the quail, manna, and water from a rock, but as we will see later in this chapter, all three can occur over quite a large region, so these clues are not specific enough to tell us where the Desert of Sin must have been. However, there are two less obvious clues, which biblical scholars have missed. First, there is the clue of the dew. Dew will be well known to readers as the moisture often found on grass in the morning, but heavy dew is rare in a desert. So I believe the biblical description of a *layer* of dew in the Desert of Sin is a key clue we need to follow up. The second important clue is the *large quantity* of the manna.

As we will see, manna is a natural substance that is not uncommon in the deserts of the Middle East. However, manna in large quantities is uncommon, and many biblical scholars have dismissed the two quarts per person of manna recorded in the book of Exodus as a hopeless exaggeration. But to do this, I believe, is to miss a key clue. It is precisely because the Israelites found large quantities of manna in the Desert of Sin that we can locate where this desert must have been.

But we are jumping ahead. In the previous chapter we left Moses and the Israelites traveling up the Wadi Sadr. Where did they go from there?

The Desert of Sin and the Clue of the Dew

The Desert of Sin is the next stopping place mentioned in the book of Numbers after the Red Sea campsite. So where was the Desert of Sin? Biblical scholars have no idea. The very useful *New Bible Dictionary* states in its entry "Sin, Wilderness of ": "As its position depends on the fixing of Mount Sinai, which is uncertain, it is impossible to determine the exact site." Well, let's try to do the impossible and find the Desert of Sin before we fix the position of Mount Sinai.

One evening I was reading Exodus 16, which describes what happened to the Israelites in the Desert of Sin, when I was struck by the following words: "That evening quail came and covered the camp, and in the morning there was a layer of dew around the camp. When the dew was gone . . ." (Exodus 16:13–14). I expect most people who read these words concentrate on the mention of quail. Well, what caught my eye was the dew!

I remembered a conversation I'd had a few years earlier with the physicist John Spence at Arizona State University. I've mentioned John in a previous chapter and said that he was a lover of classic cars. On old sports cars in England, rust is a major problem that is very expensive to repair, so I asked John how he coped with rust on his old MG and Jaguar cars. "Oh," he said, "in Arizona rust isn't a problem at all. Remember, this is desert country and the humidity can be as low as 2 percent. Airlines store their surplus planes in the Arizona desert because they don't rust there."

So if the humidity in deserts is usually low, I wouldn't expect a layer of dew to form there. And that's why I was surprised to read that in the Desert of Sin, "in the morning there was a layer of dew around the camp." Could these words be a key clue to the location of the Desert of Sin? Once again, let's turn to science to see if it gives some enlightenment.

Many readers will be familiar with the dew that they find on their lawns on cold evenings. But what is dew? All air contains a certain amount of water, but warm air can hold much more water than cold air. In many countries, including where I live in England, the amount of water vapor in the air, which we call the humidity, is often 50 percent or more. When evening comes and the daytime temperature falls, grass cools more quickly than the air above it. Moisture-laden warm air coming into contact with the grass is often cooled to a temperature at which its moisture condenses out, and it appears on the grass as the drops of water we call dew.

Now for the key point. The temperature at which dew is deposited, called the dew point, depends on the amount of water vapor in the air to start with. If this is very small, so the humidity is very low, then the temperature has to be very cold before dew will form. In a desert, the amount of water vapor in the air is usually low, and that explains why heavy dew is uncommon in a desert. So why was there dew in the Desert of Sin? Let's explore this mystery further. Perhaps the Israelites were in the Desert of Sin in the winter, when it can be cold at night, and this is the explanation of the dew. So when were the Israelites in the Desert of Sin?

The Israelites arrived in the Desert of Sin "on the fifteenth day of the second month after they had come out of Egypt" (Exodus 16:1) in their lunar calendar, which corresponds to April–May in our solar calendar. I've been in several deserts at night in April in the Middle East, and it was quite warm. The low humidity of desert air, coupled with the relatively warm desert nights in April and May, lead me to expect that heavy dew would be very unusual indeed in a Middle Eastern desert at that time of the year. Yet the book of Exodus specifically reports dew at that time in the Desert of Sin, and not just a few drops either: there was "a *layer* of dew around the camp" (Exodus 16:13). What a puzzle! Were these words written down long after the event, when the memory had faded and the imagination had been activated, so that in reality there never was any dew? Or was this the acute observation of an eyewitness, keen to write down what he must have known was a highly unusual event, thus providing us three thousand years later with a fascinating piece of information that, if only we could understand it, might provide us with a vital clue as to the location of the Desert of Sin?

Some months after asking these questions, I was reading *Travels in Arabia* (1845 and 1848), by the great explorer George Wallin, late one night in my study at home. My eyelids were closing and I was almost falling asleep, when I was suddenly awakened by the following words: "Dew also fell in the night, which I scarcely ever recollect having observed in Arabia, but only in the deserts near the Nile and on the shore of the Red Sea. It was also, I presume, owing to the partially humid state of the atmosphere, as indicated by the presence of dew, that diseases of the chest, of which I met with instances, sometimes occur here; similar affections being extremely rare in the interior of Arabia."

So Wallin is saying that dew is rare in desert lands, and in all of his extensive travels he only ever saw it in three places: near the Nile, on the shore of the Red Sea, and in the place in Arabia he was now writing from. Near the Nile and the Red Sea the air is close to large bodies of water, hence the humidity is relatively high, and that explains why Wallin had observed dew in these places.

Before accepting too readily the words of Wallin, I wanted to investigate further the presence of dew in deserts. The desert regions where

I would most expect to find dew are deserts high above sea level, because the temperature at night can drop dramatically in high places. I found that a detailed study has been made of dewfall in the highlands of the north Negev Desert, particularly at Avdat, over 1,800 feet above sea level (see map 4.2, pg. 52).

This is described in *The Negev,* by Michael Evenari, who states,

> The heaviest dew [at Avdat] was produced during September, October and November, the lightest in April and May. . . . The amount formed per dew night is small. Even on the heaviest dew night it does not amount to more than 0.35mm [0.01 inches].

The heaviest dew night was in November. From the figures given in the book I've calculated that the amount of dew in April–May, collected throughout the whole of the night at Avdat, was less than 0.003 inches, that is, less than three thousandths of an inch. Although this tiny amount of dew is vital to the survival of the sparse vegetation in the desert, such a very small quantity of water would certainly not form a *layer* of dew: it would be absorbed in the sand or soil and be invisible. So heavy dew in a Middle Eastern desert in April–May is not to be expected, even at a height of 1,800 feet.

Now for the really interesting question: Where was Wallin writing from when he was surprised by dew falling in the night? He was high up in an inland desert region of Midian, in northwest Arabia, called al-Hisma (also spelled Hesma). He had reached the desert of al-Hisma from the Red Sea by walking along the Wadi Sadr, following part of the very route I have just deduced the Israelites followed three thousand years ago (see map 4.1, pg. 46). How remarkable! Wallin was totally unaware that he was walking in the footsteps of Moses (if my reconstructed route of the Exodus is correct). Then at the end of the Wadi Sadr, Wallin found dew on the ground just as the Israelites had three thousand years earlier. So what do we know about the desert of al-Hisma?

Broadly speaking, we can divide the geographical regions of northwest Arabia (Midian) as follows (see map 4.1, pg. 46):

The low-lying land bordering the Red Sea is called the Tihama (from the Arabic word *taham,* which Burton, in *The Gold-Mines of Midian,* says means a "low unhealthy maritime region"). The seashore itself is called as-Sahil. Going inland (to the east) from the Red Sea, we first cross as-Sahil and then the Tihama (the Tihama includes the as-Sahil coastal region but is wider than this). We then come to a range of granite mountains called the Shifa (or Shefa). On the other side (east) of this mountain range is a high desert plateau (about 3,000 feet high) of sandstone covered with sand, called al-Hisma, and on the far side, east of al-Hisma, are huge volcanic lava fields and volcanoes in a region called al-Harrah, which means "the lava fields" (see map 4.1, pg. 46).

The Shifa mountain range is in fact a complex chain of mountains consisting of a series of "precipitous hills and valleys irregularly succeeding each other" (Wallin). The Israelites would have been able to cross this mountain chain only in a limited number of places, where natural passes have been cut by rivers. The Wadi Sadr has cut one such pass, and so by following this wadi the Israelites would have been able to cross the Shifa Mountains. The journey would have been slow and difficult but certainly possible. Wallin describes the general scene as follows: "The whole [picture] presents a gloomy, desolate aspect of ruin and desolation. The mountains of the [Shifa] chain on the coast side are exclusively granite, but further eastward, in the interior of the chain, dark brown sandstone succeeds." However, Wallin adds, "The ravines in the mountains are steep and rugged, but afford plenty of water," so the Israelites would have found water in the Wadi Sadr on their journey through the Shifa Mountains.

On the other (eastern) side of these mountains lies the high plain of the Hisma Desert. Wallin describes it as "a vast plain of soft and comparatively fertile sand" and adds, "The soil of the plain is that clean, soft sand called nufood (nafud), and which an Arab never ceases to look upon with predilection, from its constituting, in his idea, the proper element of his own and his forefathers' land. . . . As soon as we came in sight of its yellow plain, all the women of the clan exclaimed with evident delight, 'God be praised that we see the nufood again.'"

Wallin records that the Hisma is described by an Arabic writer as "a land in the desert, with high mountains, whose elevated peaks are generally enveloped in mist." Wallin also states that in the night it can be cold on the Hisma plain because of its high altitude (3,000 feet), and that the thermometer dropped to 41°F at sunrise when he was there in late February, compared to 52°F at sunrise on the coast. So we can now see why dew fell in the night in the Hisma Desert: the air was, in the words of Wallin, "partially humid," and it was also cold in the night because of the high altitude. Dew was therefore deposited from this humid air at night on the cold sand of the Hisma Desert.

I believe the "clue of the dew" given in the book of Exodus enables us to identify the Desert of Sin with the Hisma Desert. Wallin traveled extensively in the Middle East, and apart from the deserts near the Nile and the shore of the Red Sea, the only place he observed heavy dew in Arabia was in the Hisma Desert, near Wadi Sadr. I therefore believe this tiny clue of the heavy dew in April–May is like a DNA fingerprint, enabling us to identify, with reasonable confidence, the Desert of Sin with the Hisma Desert near Wadi Sadr. This identification also fits precisely the Exodus route we have tentatively deduced so far, in which we have Moses leading the Israelites up the Wadi Sadr toward the Hisma Desert (see map 4.1, pg. 46).

The Clue of the Manna

It was in the Desert of Sin that the Israelites first ate manna. But what was this strange substance called manna? Figure 18.1, on the following page, shows what a fifteenth century A.D. monk thought. Here are the key points as recorded in the book of Exodus:

> When the dew was gone, thin flakes like frost on the ground appeared on the desert floor. . . . Moses said to them [the Israelites], "It is the bread the Lord has given you to eat. This is what the Lord has commanded: Each one is to gather as much as he needs. Take an omer [about two quarts] for each person you have in your tent.". . . . Each morning everyone gathered as much as he needed, and when the sun grew hot, it melted away. . . . The people of Israel called the bread manna. It was white like coriander seed and tasted like wafers made with honey. . . . Moses said to Aaron, "Take a jar and put an omer of manna in it.

18.1. Manna: woodcut illustration from the 1478 Cologne Bible.

Then place it before the Lord to be kept for the generations to come."... The Israelites ate manna for forty years until they ... reached the borders of Canaan. (Exodus 16:14–16, 21, 31–35)

How mysterious! Here is an edible substance that disappears in a few hours when the sun becomes hot, yet if put in a jar it lasts for generations! Does the miracle of the manna have a natural explanation, like all the other miracles in the Exodus story we have considered? This time the explanation is well known to scholars, and here it is.

A number of trees and bushes contain a sweet, sugary sap. If the bark is cut, or bitten by an insect, this sap falls to the ground, solidifies, and can be eaten. Sometimes the insect feeds on the sap and then exudes droplets of a sticky substance that falls to the ground and can be eaten. Let me give some examples.

A species of ash tree called *Fraxinus ornus* grows widely around the coast of the Mediterranean. On the island of Sicily, which I visited in the spring of 2002, this tree is grown in plantations; the bark is deliberately cut, and the sweet sap exudes and solidifies as flakes. These sweet flakes are called manna, and they are sold as a delicacy. There is a species of the tamarisk tree that grows in the Sinai Peninsula and has the Latin name *Tamarix mannifera,* which is popularly called the "manna-tamarisk" tree. A scale insect with the Latin name *Gossyparia mannipara* (also called *Coccus manniparus*) bites the stems of the tamarisk tree, which then exude a sweet, sticky substance that falls to the ground and solidifies.

A botanist named Bodenheimer organized a manna expedition to the Sinai Peninsula to find out more about manna, and he published his findings in 1947. He saw for himself tamarisk trees being bitten by the insect referred to above and then exuding a resinous secretion that was about the same shape and size as a coriander seed. When it fell to the ground it was white. Bodenheimer ate some and wrote, "The taste of these crystallised grains of manna is particularly sweet. It is most of all like honey when it has been left a long time to solidify." So the biblical description of manna as being white, like coriander seed, and tasting like honey is exactly what Bodenheimer found. The Israeli guide I mentioned in an earlier chapter, Alfonso, told me that he had eaten manna and it tasted sweet like honey. The biblical description of manna fits so well the present-day manna that I believe we can say, beyond reasonable doubt, that the manna the Israelites ate in the desert was a natural substance produced by suitable trees.

Why do I write "produced by suitable trees"? Because manna is produced not only by the ash tree *Fraxinus ornus* and by *Tamarix mannifera,* but also by many different species of *Tamarix* and perhaps by other trees as well. For example, in the Grand Canyon there are fifty-four species of *Tamarix.* A leafhopper, *Opsius stactogalus,* feeds on the sap of these trees, and it then exudes droplets of a sugary substance that coats the ground below and that can be eaten.

We do not know which tree, and which insect, was responsible for the manna the Israelites ate in the Desert of Sin. No one has made a study of manna in Arabia, and there has been no really extensive botanical survey of Arabia, either. Sheila Collenette's *Flowers of Arabia* lists five species of tamarisk tree as growing in Arabia. *Tamarix mannifera* isn't one of these, but as we've seen above, this isn't important since all species of *Tamarix* contain a sweet sap. What is important is that the most likely source of the manna, a species of *Tamarix,* grows in Arabia.

But why did the manna melt away when the sun grew hot? Bodenheimer reported that the Bedouin hasten to gather up their "manna from Heaven" as early as possible in the morning before ants eat it up. Bodenheimer observed that the ants were inactive until about 8:30 A.M., but after this time, when the ground had warmed up, the ants rapidly ate the manna and all trace of it disappeared. Why does the Bible say the manna melted away if in fact ants were eating it? The Hebrew word the NIV translates as "melted away" can also mean "vanished," so the Bible is saying that the manna vanished when the sun grew hot, just as Bodenheimer observed. The Israelites may well have appreciated that it disappeared because it was being eaten since Exodus 16:20 says, "They kept part of it [the manna] until morning, but it was full of maggots." So perhaps ants eat manna in the Sinai Peninsula, and maggots eat it in the very different climate of the Hisma.

Why did the manna last for generations if kept in a jar? Most food goes moldy in a few weeks if kept in a jar. However, I am reminded of a story from my childhood. When I was a child I didn't like chocolate orange creams, which were chocolates with a soft orange center, but each year an aunt gave me a box of them for Christmas. So I carefully nibbled off the chocolate, which I did like, from all around the orange centers and put the centers in a jar. I didn't want to throw them away because they were a Christmas present from my aunt. I did this for a number of years, by which time the jar was full, and then I lost track of it. Many years later the jar turned up at the back of a cupboard. The orange centers were still there! They were now hard and dry but not moldy. The high sugar content had preserved them. So I suggest it was with the manna that lasted for generations: its high sugar content preserved it. (It would be interesting to test this idea using modern manna.)

The sap of the tamarisk tree is rich in carbohydrates, and so manna is an excellent source of energy-providing food. In England, hill walkers traditionally eat Kendal Mint Cake, which is very sweet and sugary, to provide them with lots of energy. I like to think of manna as the original Kendal Mint Cake or energy bar.

Tamarisk trees are scattered throughout the deserts in these regions, which explains how the Israelites ate manna for forty years when they were traveling. However, the Bible doesn't record that they ate a lot of manna all the time. It was in the Desert of Sin where the Israelites ate large quantities of manna: two quarts per person. I believe this is an important clue. Plenty of manna means there must have been large numbers of tamarisk trees in the Desert of Sin.

Is this reasonable? In my visits to the Sinai Peninsula I have seen tamarisk trees only dotted sparsely about. But listen to what Lawrence of Arabia writes in *The Seven Pillars of Wisdom* about a riverbed in Arabia, the Wadi Jizal, part of which is in the Hisma Desert, which I've identified with the Desert of Sin: "Jizal was a deep gorge some 200 yards in width, full of tamarisk sprouting from the bed of drifting sand, as well as from the soft twenty-foot banks." So tamarisk trees are plentiful in and around wadis in the Hisma.

At the Exodus there were about twenty thousand Israelites, and each one gathered as much manna as he or she needed. I believe that the "clue of the manna" is not that there was *some* manna in the Desert of Sin, but that there was *a very large quantity* of it. The Hisma Desert, particularly in the well-watered regions fed by streams from mountains, demonstrably had large numbers of tamarisk trees, which could produce plentiful manna. So I suggest the clues of the dew and the manna enable us to identify the Desert of Sin with the modern Hisma Desert, either all of it or a local region around where the Wadi Sadr runs into it.

A Tale of Quail

We've already seen that the book of Exodus probably provides the earliest recorded reference to an erupting volcano, to water filtration through sand, and possibly also to water purification through charcoal. Now we have what may be the earliest recorded mention of bird migration, or at least of the effects of bird migration: "That evening quail came and covered the camp [in the Desert of Sin]" (Exodus 16:13). Quail are one of the world's finest game birds. When the Israelites complained about the lack of meat to eat (Exodus 16:3), they were provided with some of the best meat in the world, and in great abundance: the quail covered the camp.

Some readers of this book may find it hard to imagine a flock of birds so numerous that they densely cover a camp much bigger than a football field and so stupid that they let themselves be caught. But this is precisely what the book of Exodus states and implies. If I'm correct, then as shown in chapter 8, there were about twenty thousand Israelites. Their tents would occupy a campsite much greater than the area of a large football field. The implication of the Exodus story is that the quail covered the campsite, were easily caught, and then provided plentiful food for all the Israelites. Is this realistic? What do we know about quail?

I needed to know not just about quail in general, but specifically about quail in Arabia. Did they exist there, for example? So I asked the Arabia expert William Facey. He said, "I only know of one book on the birds of Arabia, but it is excellent. It was written by Richard Meinertzhagen." So I visited Cambridge University Library and found *Birds of Arabia,* written in 1954 by Colonel Richard Meinertzhagen. Under the heading "Quail" he writes, "Birds have been observed almost throughout Arabia from mid-September to early May. It is believed they breed in Yemen [south Arabia]." So it is known that quail spend the winter in Arabia, particularly in southern Arabia. It is also well documented that other groups of quail stay in southern Africa over the winter.

In spring the quail migrate to Europe in order to escape the intense summer heat in southern Africa and Arabia. Meinertzhagen writes, "Spring passage lasts from the end of March to the end of April." At what time of year were the Israelites in the Desert of Sin? They arrived there on the fifteenth day of the second month, in their lunar calendar, after they had come out of Egypt (Exodus 16:1), corresponding to April–May in our solar calendar. So the time of year given in the book of Exodus corresponds precisely to when we know the quail migrate, demonstrating once again the accuracy of the Exodus account.

Let me make a short but important digression about the ancient Hebrew calendar. Before the Exodus, the Israelites had been in Egypt for several hundred years and almost certainly would have been forced to live by the Egyptian calendar. In fact, ancient Egypt at the time of Ramesses II had two calendars: a solar calendar for official purposes and a lunar calendar for fixing religious festivals. When the Israelites came out of Egypt it is clear from the Old Testament that they adopted a lunar calendar, which was probably similar to the Egyptian lunar calendar except that the month when the year started was changed. We know this from Exodus 12:1: "The Lord said to Moses and Aaron in Egypt, 'This month is to be for you the first month, the first month of your year.'" The Exodus from Egypt was so important for the Israelites that they fixed the first month of their lunar calendar as the month they came out of Egypt.

However, there is a problem with a lunar calendar. Each lunar month is either twenty-nine or thirty days long. So twelve lunar months total about eleven days less than a solar year. Some nations with lunar calendars did not worry about this: they were happy to let their lunar calendar roll on and become more and more out of step with the solar year. But for the Israelites it was important for both religious and agricultural reasons that their lunar calendar kept in step with the solar year. For example, the lambs had to be ready for the Passover feast each year, which was held on the fifteenth day of the first month; the first sheaves of barley were cut by the priests in a first-fruits festival on the sixteenth day of the first month, and so forth. So the Israelites had a "leap month" in their lunar calendar: they added an extra lunar month about every third year to keep their lunar calendar in step with the solar year. In a similar way, we add a leap day every four years to the month of February to keep our solar calendar in step with the true solar year.

Since the Passover feast was fixed on the fifteenth day of the first month, and the firstfruits festival of barley on the sixteenth, we know from this and other evidence that the first month of the Hebrew lunar calendar corresponded to March–April in our calendar. So that's how we know that when the Old Testament says the Israelites arrived at the Desert of Sin on the fifteenth day of the second month after they had come out of Egypt, this corresponds to April–May in our calendar. As I've said above, this was at just the right time for quail to have been flying over the Desert of Sin in their annual April migration.

The quail travel from southern Africa and Arabia by two broad routes. One group goes by the west coast of Africa to Spain, the other by the eastern Mediterranean to the Balkans. The quail passing over the eastern Mediterranean fly over northern Arabia and also over the

Sinai Peninsula and the Nile Valley. In the autumn they fly back again. After a winter of feeding, the quail are fat. Migration of these plump birds is such an effort that it is well documented that they fly in stages. They land in a group to eat insects and seeds and take a rest before flying on. When they have to cross a large body of water they always land before crossing and wait until the wind is blowing in the right direction to help carry them across. As we have seen, parts of the Hisma (Desert of Sin) are comparatively rich in vegetation and contain plenty of maggots to eat the manna, so it was an ideal place for the quail to stop and feed on their journey north.

But what about the huge numbers of quail implied by the Exodus account? Are these numbers plausible? The Roman writer Pliny, who lived in the first century A.D., describes quail coming into Italy in such large numbers, and so exhausted by their long flight, that if they sighted a sailing ship they settled on it in their hundreds and their weight would sink it. Meinertzhagen, in *Birds of Arabia,* states that in 1920 Egypt exported over three million wild quail for food. The Israeli guide, Alfonso, I mentioned in an earlier chapter told me, "One and a half billion birds every year migrate across Eilat, including quail." So the large number of quail in Exodus is no exaggeration. How would the Israelites have caught the quail? The Greek historian Herodotus, who lived in the fifth century B.C., records that the Egyptians caught quail with sticks, and there are other reports of Bedouin catching exhausted quail in spring and autumn by hand. So it would have been easy for the Israelites to have caught the quail. It therefore seems that the biblical story of the quail, although at first sight hard to believe, is in fact consistent with all we know about quail, even to the month of their migration. Once again, I find the accuracy of the Exodus account astonishing.

The Journey Time to the Desert of Sin

The Israelites started their Exodus journey "from Rameses on the fifteenth day of the first month" (Numbers 33:3) and arrived at the Desert of Sin "on the fifteenth day of the second month after they had come out of Egypt" (Exodus 16:1). Thus the journey from Rameses to the Desert of Sin took precisely one lunar month (twenty-nine or thirty days), leaving Rameses at full moon, the fifteenth day of the lunar month, and arriving in the Desert of Sin at the time of the next full moon. In terms of our solar calendar, they started out from Rameses in March–April and arrived in the Desert of Sin in April–May. Is this journey time consistent with the route we have deduced?

In an earlier chapter I suggested that the Israelites traveled by day and night from Rameses to the head of the Gulf of Aqaba, probably covering this distance in seven or eight days. However, after crossing the Red Sea, at the Gulf of Aqaba, and particularly after the drowning of Pharaoh's army, the Israelites could afford to relax, since their pursuers had perished. In addition, whereas the Israelites would have traveled many abreast across the plateau of el Tih on the Sinai Peninsula, the ancient trade route running south from the head of the Gulf of Aqaba was narrow in places, and the Israelites probably walked only two or three abreast for most of the time. The twenty thousand Israelites would then have walked in a column at least six miles long. I believe the Israelites would have walked fast between campsites, for reasons of water supply and also to minimize the risk of their long line of people being attacked by local tribesmen. However, when they camped, I suggest they would have stayed long enough to rest, regroup, eat, and fill their water bags.

A very tentative time scale for the journey is set out below. I've estimated these times from the distances involved and from the Israelites' need to rest and regroup:

Rameses to Gulf of Aqaba	8 days
Cross Gulf of Aqaba and camp	2 days
From Gulf of Aqaba to Marah	3 days
Camp at Marah	2 days
Marah to Elim and camp	3 days
Elim to Red Sea (Wadi Tiryam) and camp	2 days
Total	20 days

At Wadi Tiryam, as we've seen in the previous chapter, they left the trade route running along the coast of the Red Sea and traveled inland to the Desert of Sin, I suggest using the trade route that went first along the Wadi Tiryam and then along the Wadi Sadr, climbing up and down along the natural passes through the layers of the Shifa Mountains to the high plateau of the Hisma Desert, which I identify with the Desert of Sin. This would have been a slow and quite difficult journey. The explorer Richard Burton did a similar journey in 1878 from Muwaylah, just south of Wadi Tiryam, to where the Wadi Sadr enters the Hisma, and from his account in *The Land of Midian* this took him six days in February, although his journey included halts for explorations. It is not unreasonable to suppose that this journey through mountain passes could have taken the Israelites, with their children and elderly, nine or ten days, particularly in April–May when it is much hotter than in February. Thus a very tentative estimate of the journey time of the Israelites from Rameses to the Desert of Sin is about thirty days, consistent with the lunar month (twenty-nine or thirty days) recorded in the Bible for this journey.

Origin of Sin

The name Sin has, of course, nothing to do with the English word *sin*. I am reminded of the story of the British general Napier who captured Sind in Pakistan in 1843. He reported his success back to the prime minister in a single Latin word *Peccari*, meaning "I have sinned." So what does Sin with a capital *S* mean? Biblical scholars are divided on this. Some say that the meaning is unknown, whereas others agree with Lucas, who writes in *The Route of the Exodus,* "The name 'Sin' for the wilderness [desert] is almost certainly derived from the Babylonian Moon-god, Sin."

What are the facts? Most ancient civilizations were polytheistic, and throughout the Middle East the moon was regarded as one of their many deities. In a number of cities, for example Harran in ancient Mesopotamia (modern east Syria to north Iraq), Ur in Babylonia (modern south Iraq), Tayma in Midian (see map 4.2, pg. 52, for these sites), and at various places in south Arabia, it is known that the moon was the principal god who was worshiped above all others. For example, James Montgomery, who was professor of Hebrew and Aramaic at the University of Pennsylvania, states in his book *Arabia and the Bible,* "There stands out [in south Arabia] a definite astral triad of highest deities: Moon, Sun and Morning (or Evening) Star [Venus]. The Moon has the pre-eminence, even as he had in the elder Babylonian religion, before settled agricultural society had shifted the center of gravity to the Sun."

It may seem strange to us today that the moon was the principal god in many Middle Eastern places. Surely if we were going to choose a chief god from one of the heavenly bodies we would choose the sun, which is easily the brightest body in the sky. Ancient civilizations in the Middle East didn't all see it that way. To these people, surrounded by deserts, the sun was a harsh, cruel, and scorching light, whereas moonlight was gentle, welcome, and enabled travelers to find their way by night. In addition, most Middle Eastern nations had a lunar calendar, not a solar calendar like ours, so the moon was absolutely central in regulating both their lives and their religious festivals. It was the new light from the new moon that determined the start of each new month.

The ancient Israelites would have known all about moon worship. The Old Testament patriarch Abraham (who probably lived some time in the period 2000–1750 B.C.) spent part of his life living in Harran (also spelled Haran) in Mesopotamia, twenty miles southeast of Edessa in Turkey (Genesis 11:31). Ancient texts reveal that Harran was a major center for the worship of the Moon-god, Sin, from before 2000 B.C., and it contained a large temple dedicated to Sin. Before living in Harran, Abraham lived in Ur of the Chaldees (Genesis 11:31), which was another major center for Moon-god worship. Ur of the Chaldees is modern Tell el-Muqayyer on the River Euphrates in southern Iraq (map 4.2, pg. 52). The massive ruins of a ziggurat (stepped temple), built around 2150–2050 B.C., still dominate the site, and we know from inscriptions that this temple was dedicated to the Moon-god.

I've said above that the Moon-god was the major god at Tayma in Midian. How do we know this, and how old is the settlement at Tayma? Perhaps the most important archaeological book ever written about Midian is *Ancient Records from North Arabia* by Winnett and Reed. They state, "The presence at Tayma of the great well called al-Haddaj makes it highly probable that human occupation of the oasis dates back to a very remote period." The Assyrian king Tiglath-pileser III

(747–727 B.C.) claims in an inscription to have received tribute from Tayma. The first book in the Bible states that Tema was the son of Ishmael (the son of Abraham), who ruled a settlement named after him at Tema (Genesis 25:15–16). Isaiah 21:13–14 explicitly states that Tema is in Arabia, and we can have little doubt that the biblical Tema is modern Tayma (notice again the preservation of the consonants). The archaeologists Parr, Harding, and Dayton in 1968 found Midianite pottery at Tayma, which strongly suggests the settlement there dates back to at least the thirteenth to twelfth centuries B.C.

In about 552 B.C. a most remarkable event happened at Tayma, which is well documented in ancient literature. Nabonidus, the king of Babylonia from 555 to 539 B.C., traveled five hundred miles to Tayma and spent ten of the sixteen years of his reign there. (Incidentally, Nabonidus is the father of the Belshazzar mentioned in the fifth chapter of the biblical book of Daniel). Historians were baffled as to why a Babylonian king should make this very long journey to the foreign land of Midian, and live there for ten years, until an inscription was found in 1956 at Harran in modern Turkey, where Abraham once lived. It seems from this inscription that Nabonidus was particularly devoted to the Moon-god Sin, installing his daughter as priestess at the Temple of Sin in Ur. His mother was particularly devoted to the Temple of Sin in Harran. Nabonidus planned to rebuild the great temple of Sin at Harran, but he was opposed by the priests of another Babylonian god, called Marduk. The Moon-god Sin had been the principal god at Harran from before 2000 B.C., but gradually Marduk had taken over. The situation became so serious that Nabonidus left Babylonia, putting his son Belshazzar in charge, and he traveled to Tayma in Midian, where he lived for ten years.

I was intrigued by this story of Nabonidus. It seems clear from Babylonian inscriptions that King Nabonidus left Babylonia because he found himself in conflict with the priests of Marduk over his total devotion to the Moon-god Sin. But why did he choose to settle in Tayma in Midian, five hundred miles away? I asked William Facey this question. He replied, "Winnett and Reed's *Ancient Records from North Arabia* firmly links Tayma with a moon cult, and moreover with a moon cult that pre-dates Nabonidus's arrival there. Indeed, his journey would only make sense if there was already an important moon cult established there. Tayma's moon cult may reach back to the Bronze Age and beyond." So it seems probable that Tayma in Midian was a major center for Moon-god worship from well before the time of Nabonidus.

A number of carvings on stone have been found at Tayma depicting the crescent moon and a bull's head with crescent-shaped horns, both symbols of the Moon-god. Perhaps the most fascinating of these is the Tayma Cube (photograph 18.2, pg. 301), discovered near the ancient city wall of Tayma in 1980 during an excavation by the Saudi Arabian Department of Antiquities. The length of a side of the cube is fifteen inches, and the cube dates from the sixth century B.C. On one face of the cube are the crescent moon and a bull's head with crescent horns, both known to represent the Moon-god. On another face (photograph 18.3, pg. 301) is another bull with crescent horns. The disc between the bull's horns (photographs 18.2 and 18.3) is usually interpreted as a sun disc, but given the bull's association with moon worship in ancient Arabia, the disc probably represents the full moon.

The evidence of Moon-god worship from Tayma, together with archaeological discoveries from temples in south Arabia dedicated to the Moon-god, strongly suggests that the Moon-god may have been the main god throughout Arabia.

When Moses fled Egypt after killing the slave master, he came to live in Midian, where the Moon-god was worshiped, and so Moses would have been familiar with worship of the Moon-god. In particular, Moses lived with the family of Jethro and married Jethro's daughter. The Bible describes Jethro as "the priest of Midian," and I suggest, for reasons I will give in the next chapter, that Jethro was probably the priest of the Moon-god.

It may therefore seem obvious that the Desert of Sin in the Exodus refers to the Moon-god, Sin, but there is a difficulty with this interpretation that we need to consider. The difficulty is that the Moon-god had a different name in different languages, and it is clear from ancient texts that sometimes each tribe, and even each city, called the Moon-god by a different name. Let me give some examples. The name of the Moon-god was Sin in Babylonian, and it was Nanna in Sumerian (the language of southern Babylonia). In Ugarit in Syria he was Yarih. In southern Arabia (modern Yemen) archaeologists have

18.2. The Tayma Cube. The crescent moon is in the top right corner. In the center is a full-frontal bull's head with crescent horns.

18.3. Another face of the Tayma Cube. The bull occupies almost half of the face and the bull's head is turned full-frontal to show the crescent horns, symbol of the Moon-god.

discovered spectacular temples dedicated to the Moon-god, decorated with crescent moons and bulls with crescent-shaped horns. However, different southern Arabian tribes, who occupied different territories, called the Moon-god by different names.

What name or names did the Midianites in northwest Arabia use for the Moon-god? Winnett and Reed, in *Ancient Records from North Arabia,* record that the names discovered so far on ancient inscriptions include Wadd and possibly Salm, but the records are very incomplete because little archaeology has been carried out in northwest Arabia. In addition, the name used for the Moon-god in a given place may have changed over time—if one tribe conquered another.

So although we can say with reasonable certainty that the local Midianite tribespeople living around the Hisma Desert at the time of the Exodus would have worshiped the Moon-god, we don't know what name they would have used for this god. But could the author of the book of Exodus have used the name Sin to refer to the Moon-god? I specifically asked Professor Millard this question. He replied, "There's an excellent scholarly book on these matters called the *Dictionary of Deities and Demons in the Bible.* I suggest you try to find this at Cambridge. It's the second edition you want, published in 1999. The first edition contained a number of mistakes which have now been corrected."

So off I went to Cambridge University Library to find this splendidly titled book, edited by van der Toorn and others. This is what it says under "Sin": "Sin is the name of the Babylonian Moon-god. . . . It is striking that the name appears twice as *San-* in a Hebrew context, in Sanherib and Sanballat." The name Sanherib, also called Sennacherib, occurs twenty times in the Old Testament, and it means "[The god] Sin has replaced the brothers." Sanballat occurs ten times in the Old Testament and means "[The god] Sin gives life." So there is evidence that the name Sin was used, at least indirectly, by the Israelites.

Although the names of the Moon-god differed from place to place, we know from various archaeological discoveries that its symbols remained the same throughout the Middle East. For example, a cylinder seal from Babylonia depicts the Moon-god Sin holding a crescent on a pole and standing on the backs of two young bulls with horns like crescents. As we have seen, the same symbols for the Moon-god have been found in Tayma (see photographs 18.2 and 18.3, pg. 301) and in southern Arabia.

Hence the symbols of the Moon-god, Sin, were a crescent, representing the crescent shape of the new moon, and a bull, particularly a young bull, probably because of its crescent-shaped horns. In fact, even today we sometimes call the crescent shape of a new moon the horns of the moon. In ancient Egypt, the moon was often called the bull of heaven.

I've previously identified the Desert of Sin with the high sandy plain called the Hisma. Was there a reason for associating the Moon-god with the Hisma? The Hisma was a clearly defined desert separating the red granite Shifa mountain range from the black basalt volcanic lava flows of the Harrah (see map 4.1, pg. 46).

Wallin calls the Hisma the "yellow plain": it was the same color as the moon. The color combinations would have been dramatic. Think of approaching the Hisma from the Red Sea coast, as the Israelites did. You would have climbed up through the red Shifa Mountains and then seen the yellow sand of the Hisma Desert against a backdrop of the black lava fields, like seeing a yellow moon set in a black night sky. Was this the reason the Hisma was called the Desert of Sin?

Musil, in *The Northern Hegaz,* describes the Hisma as follows: "Above the dense haze there rose like islets countless horns, cones and truncated cones, pyramids, obelisks, and other quaint shapes, fashioned by the action of rain, frost and wind, which had gnawed at the layers of rock and carried away the softer ingredients." So the Hisma is a desert containing a variety of fantastic rock formations, but the first type that Musil mentions are rocks shaped like *horns.* Now imagine the superstitious Moon-worshiping Midianites walking in the Hisma among these rocks shaped like horns, the symbol of the Moon-god. Isn't it likely that they would call the Hisma the Desert of the Moon-god?

I tentatively suggest they did this, using their local name for the Moon-god, and the Hebrews called it the Desert of Sin. I will provide some intriguing new evidence for this in the next chapter.

Decoding Dophkah

Where did the Israelites go after the Desert of Sin? Numbers 33:12 tells us precisely: "They left the Desert of Sin and camped at Dophkah." So where was Dophkah? The first thing to note is that Dophkah was not in the Desert of Sin, since the Israelites left the Desert of Sin to camp at Dophkah. Hence, if our identification of the Desert of Sin with the Hisma is correct, Dophkah was not in the Hisma. It therefore must have been either across the Hisma in the black volcanic lava fields, called the Harrah, extending for mile after mile, or it must have been back across the Shifa mountain range.

Biblical scholars have no idea where Dophkah was. So little is known about Dophkah that it does not even rate a mention in the *New Bible Dictionary* or in the *Illustrated Encyclopaedia of Bible Places.* Do we have any clues about Dophkah? The word *Dophkah* is related in Hebrew to a word meaning "knock" or "strike." Some scholars therefore believe that Dophkah may refer to mining or metalworking. So are there any settlements that had mining or metalworking operations near to where the Israelites entered the Hisma? The answer is yes. About forty miles (as the crow flies) southeast of this point are the mines of two major settlements, Shaghab and Shuwak (which Musil calls Sarab and Swek, respectively). Burton writes that a Muslim pilgrim route passed through these places. Hence I tentatively suggest that the earlier ancient trade route from the Wadi Tiryam passed through Shaghab and Shuwak (see map 4.1, pg. 46).

These settlements really were substantial. Burton, in *The Land of Midian,* writes, "Shuwak proper is nearly a mile and a half long, and could hardly have lodged less than twenty thousand souls." So there must have been plenty of drinking water here, enough for the twenty thousand (I believe) Israelites to drink and fill their water bags. Now for the really interesting part. Burton writes, "The arrangements touching fuel and water in this great metal-working establishment are on a large scale. The biggest of the *Afran* (furnaces) lies to the northwest . . . originally some five or six feet high. They are built of firebrick and of the Hisma stone. . . ."

So there was a site for both mining and metalworking operations at Shuwak. For the Israelites to have reached Shuwak they would have traveled southeast along the Hisma and then left the Hisma, traveling southwest along one of the five substantial wadis that cross the Shifa mountain range and lead down to Shuwak. Their motivation for going to Shuwak would have been the plentiful water supply there, from the various wadis that flow into this region. Here they would have found refreshment and rest and been able to fill up their water bags for the next stage of their journey. I tentatively suggest they called this place Dophkah because of its mining and metalworking operations.

How old were the ruins of the smelting furnaces Burton observed at Shuwak? Burton does not estimate this, and I can find no archaeological record of it. However, as we have seen, the smelting sites found at Timna in the Arabah, which were used by the Midianites, were dated by Beno Rothenberg back to the thirteenth century B.C. (see *Midian, Moab and Edom*). Thus we know that the Midianites were smelting metal at that time. It is therefore possible that the ancient smelting site at Shuwak, which I tentatively identify with Dophkah, may have been operating in the thirteenth century B.C., which is precisely at the same time as the Exodus. However, a detailed archaeological survey is needed to date the antiquity of Shuwak. All we can say at present is that Shuwak is between the Hisma (Desert of Sin) and my location of Mount Sinai. It has a plentiful supply of water, and it probably was on a trade route. Hence I believe it likely that the Israelites camped at Shuwak on their way to Mount Sinai, and I tentatively identify Dophkah with Shuwak.

Water from the Rock

After Dophkah the Israelites camped at Alush and Rephidim, the last campsites before reaching Mount Sinai. *Alush* is not obviously related to a Hebrew word, and *Rephidim* may be related to the Hebrew for camps or resting places. Without further information it is difficult to locate them with any certainty. Alush could possibly be a wadi called al-Hallas, in which Musil states there is a spring, but it is best not to speculate further.

However, near Rephidim an amazing event happened: Moses obtained water from a rock. Here is the description in the book of Exodus:

They camped at Rephidim, but there was no water for the people to drink. So they quarrelled with Moses and said, "Give us water to drink.". . . Then Moses cried out to the Lord, "What am I to do with these people? They are almost ready to stone me." The Lord answered Moses, "Walk on ahead of the people. Take with you some of the elders of Israel and take in your hand the staff with which you struck the Nile, and go. I will stand there before you by the rock at Horeb. Strike the rock, and water will come out of it for the people to drink." So Moses did this in the sight of the elders of Israel. And he called the place Massah and Meribah because the Israelites quarrelled and because they tempted the Lord. (Exodus 17:1–7)

I've suggested that there are natural explanations for all the major miracles in the Exodus account (and also argued that they are still miracles). But can there possibly be a natural explanation for Moses' getting water out of a rock? "Like getting blood out of a stone," is a popular expression for something that is virtually impossible. Getting copious quantities of water out of a rock seems even less possible.

Well, in fact it isn't, and here is an eyewitness account of its happening, reported by Major C. S. Jarvis, the British governor of Sinai, in his book *Yesterday and Today in Sinai,* published in 1936:

The striking of the rock at Rephidim by Moses and the gushing forth of water sounds like a veritable miracle, but the writer [Major Jarvis] has actually seen it happen. Some of the Sinai Camel Corps had halted in a wadi and were digging in the loose gravel accumulated at one of the rocky sides to obtain water that was slowing trickling through the limestone rock. The men were working slowly, and the Bash Shawish, the Colour-Sergeant, said, "Give it to me," and seizing a shovel from one of the men he began to dig with great vigour. . . . One of his lusty blows hit the rock, when the polished hard face that forms on weathered limestone cracked and fell away, exposing the soft porous rock beneath, and out of the porous rock came a great gush of clear water. It is regrettable that these Sudanese Camel Corps hailed their N.C.O. [Non Commissioned Officer] with shouts of "What ho, the Prophet Moses!"

So what is happening here? The answer is that some rocks are porous whereas others are not. Porous rocks include sandstone and limestone. These rocks can absorb huge quantities of water from rain. In a desert, rocks undergo a particular type of weathering because of sandstorms, in which sand, dust, and organic matter from decayed plants and animals are swept against the rocks at high speed by the wind. Over time this can result in a hard impervious crust forming on the surface of the rock, rather like a layer of cement. If this crust is broken by a sharp blow, then water can flow out of a porous rock. This effect is well known to hydrogeologists.

It seems clear that this is the natural explanation of the event witnessed by Major Jarvis. The account in the book of Exodus is so similar, and it fits so closely with what is known from geology, that I believe we can say, beyond reasonable doubt, that this is the natural explanation of the "water from the rock."

However, one point about the story puzzled me. Exodus 17:6 says, "I [God] will stand before you by *the rock at Horeb* [my italics]." Houtman's commentary on Exodus says that the sense of this text is, "the well-known rock at Horeb." Clearly Mount Horeb (Sinai) itself isn't meant, or else the text would have called the rock at Horeb "Mount Horeb." So the implication of the text is that at Sinai there is a well-known rock in addition to Mount Sinai. Further, the story implies that a lot of water came out of the rock, enough to quench the thirst of many Israelites. So the rock must have been a very large porous rock, capable of holding lots of water, and it also must have been of considerable height so that the water gushed out under pressure to make an impressive display, worthy of recording in the book of Exodus. So what was this well-known rock at Horeb? We will find out in the next chapter.

The Hebrew word translated "strike" in "strike the rock" is translated "smite" in the KJV. The same Hebrew word is used in Exodus 21:18: "If men quarrel and one hits [strikes] the other with a stone . . ." A heavy blow is implied, not a light tap, consistent with the need to break the cementlike surface crust on the rock. So, once again, the details of the story fit like a glove what we now know from science about obtaining water from a rock.

Can we use our scientific understanding of what happened at the miracle of the water from the rock to pinpoint where this event occurred? Unfortunately the answer is no because, as I've said before, several different types of rock are porous and can store large quantities of water, including sandstone and limestone. Both of these rocks are common in Midian (see, for example, the geological map in *Arabia Deserta* by Doughty). Moses called the place where the water from the rock miracle occurred Massah (Hebrew for "testing") and Meribah (Hebrew for "quarreling"), but because these are specific Hebrew names not related to the local geography, they are of no help in locating where this event occurred. All we know is that the event occurred "at Horeb," that is, at or close to Mount Sinai, which we will discover in the next chapter.

The Amalekite Attack

Shortly after the water from the rock incident, "The Amalekites came and attacked the Israelites at Rephidim" (Exodus 17:8). The Amalekites were an ancient nomadic people, and the Old Testament book of Samuel records that the first king of Israel, King Saul (c.1045–1010 B.C.), "attacked the Amalekites all the way from Havilah to Shur" (1 Samuel 15:7). As we have seen in an earlier chapter, Havilah was probably a region in south Arabia, and Shur was a region at the head of the Gulf of Aqaba, so this text is saying that the Amalekites could be found in most of Arabia and that Saul attacked them there. Other Old Testament passages suggest they also roamed in Edom and the Negev. Being nomadic, they might be located in one place at one time and in a different place at another time.

Here is another puzzle. It is clear from the description of the all-day battle given in Exodus 17:8–13 that the Israelites had great difficulty in winning: first the Amalekites were on top, then the Israelites, then the Amalekites, and so on, until the Israelites finally won. Since there were about five thousand Israelite men over the age of twenty, if my interpretation of the figures in Numbers is correct, there must have been a substantial number of Amalekites for them to have decided not only to initiate the attack but also to keep the battle going all day. My guess is that there must have been thousands of Amalekites who attacked the Israelites near Mount Sinai. What were all these nomads doing at Mount Sinai at this time? I will suggest the answer in the next chapter.

In this book we have followed the story of Moses from his birth to the start of the Exodus from Rameses. We have then identified in detail the Exodus route taken to the Desert of Sin, locating many ancient sites never identified before. I've also tentatively identified Dophkah. After Dophkah came Alush, Rephidim, and Mount Sinai. I have not found it possible to identify Alush and Rephidim from the evidence we have. The million-dollar question now is, Can we identify Mount Sinai after three thousand years? Can we do this conclusively, or are there several possibilities? Is it really possible, in our generation, to find beyond reasonable doubt the true Mount Sinai? Come with me into the final chapter of this book, where all will be revealed.

NINETEEN

THE SPECTACULAR SITE
OF MOUNT SINAI

*In the third month after the Israelites left Egypt—on the very day—
they came to the Desert of Sinai. . . . Mount Sinai was covered with
smoke, because the Lord descended on it in fire. The smoke billowed up
from it like smoke from a furnace, the whole mountain trembled violently, and the sound of the trumpet grew louder and louder. Then
Moses spoke and the voice of God answered him.*

Exodus 19:1, 18, 19

Bruce Feiler, in his beautifully crafted book *Walking the Bible,*
writes, "God could have given the Israelites the Ten Commandments wherever he wanted. He chose Mount Sinai. The
place, we can conclude, must be vital to the event." And so it was.
Read again the quotation above from the book of Exodus. This was
no ordinary mountain. It was covered with smoke. Flames of fire
leaped up from its summit. The mountain blazed like a gigantic furnace. It throbbed and trembled. This terrifying, awe-inspiring, visual
pyrotechnic display was accompanied by the sound of a trumpet blast
growing louder and louder in a great crescendo, as if heralding the arrival of a mighty king. Then Moses spoke, and God answered.

For over 1,600 years, ever since Mount Sinai was identified with
the nonvolcanic Jebel Musa in the Sinai Peninsula, in A.D. 400, people
have believed that the biblical description of Mount Sinai as a mountain blazing with fire is poetic language. And, of course, there is poetic
language in many places in the Bible, but it is usually clear when it is
being used. However, as we saw in chapter 6, the Old Testament description of Mount Sinai fits perfectly an eyewitness description of an
erupting volcano, even down to details like the loud trumpet sound

produced by gases escaping through cracks in the rocks. So I believe that the biblical description of Mount Sinai is literally true. This was no ordinary mountain; it was a very special mountain—a volcano. And not an extinct volcano either, but a volcano that erupted at precisely the time of the Exodus, so that in this majestic setting Moses heard the voice of God and the Ten Commandments were given. Once again we have a magnificent miracle of timing. If the Exodus story is true, doesn't it make sense that Mount Sinai was a very special mountain?

However, for 1,600 years nearly everyone has reduced Mount Sinai from being an awe-inspiring mountain of fire to an everyday, ordinary mountain. For 1,600 years scholars, pilgrims, and tourists have visited the traditional site, Jebel Musa, the Mountain of Moses, in the south of the Sinai Peninsula, believing this to be the real Mount Sinai. However, increasingly biblical scholars have become unhappy with this site and have suggested other sites, but not normally volcanic ones. If you are interested in knowing about these, then Professor Har-el summarizes the arguments for and against no fewer than thirteen proposed sites for Mount Sinai in his book *The Sinai Journeys, The Route of the Exodus.*

Recently the Americans Ron Wyatt, David Fasold, Larry Williams, and Bob Cornuke have gained considerable publicity with their claim that the true Mount Sinai is in Saudi Arabia at a mountain called Jabal al-Lawz, and several popular books have been written about this, for example that by Howard Blum, *The Gold of Exodus: The Discovery of the True Mount Sinai.* However, Jabal al-Lawz is not a volcano, and thus it doesn't satisfy the biblical description of Mount Sinai.

It is my belief that we can identify the true Mount Sinai uniquely. There is one, and only one, mountain in the whole world that satisfies completely the detailed biblical description of Mount Sinai. In this chapter we are going to find it. I think this final chapter is the most important one in the book, because if it is correct, many history books, encyclopedias, dictionaries, maps, schoolbooks, biblical commentaries, and travel books will all have to be rewritten because they all wrongly put Mount Sinai on the Sinai Peninsula.

So how do we find the real Mount Sinai? I'm going to use the same methods that I've used throughout this book for unlocking the secrets of the Exodus. First, we look for the key clues in the biblical account, and then we use the understanding of nature provided by modern science, in this case the study of volcanoes, to help us locate the true Mount Sinai.

Volcanoes and Lava Fields

As we saw in chapter 6, Mount Sinai was an active volcano. The Old Testament description of Mount Sinai contains no fewer than seven characteristic features of an erupting volcano. This rules out all the mountains in the Sinai Peninsula as being Mount Sinai, as there are no historically active volcanoes in the Sinai Peninsula. Since Moses led the Israelites out of Egypt, across the Sinai Peninsula, and into Arabia, Mount Sinai must therefore be in Arabia. But where?

In my reading of the books of intrepid explorers of Arabia, and in looking at maps, I kept coming across the words *harra, harrah,* and *harrat* in connection with lava fields. What do these words mean? *Harrah* (also spelled *harra*) is a general word that means a lava field. *Harrat* also means a lava field, but it is used for a specific named lava field, for example the Harrat 'Uwayrid. *Harra, harrah,* and *harrat* all come from an Arabic word meaning "burned land." So what is a lava field? I would love to go to Saudi Arabia to see these lava fields (and the true Mount Sinai!) with my own eyes, but, unfortunately, visits to Saudi Arabia in order to explore sites where Moses and the Israelites might have been are forbidden. So in April 2002 I contented myself with visiting the lava fields of Mount Etna in Sicily, as I mentioned earlier. Mount Etna consists of four main craters on top of, and surrounded by, mile after mile of black volcanic lava. When lava comes out of a volcano it is red molten rock, but when it solidifies it is jet black. Lava fields are not easy to walk over because the many sharp, loose pieces of lava slide about and turn over when you walk on them. It is easy to twist an ankle walking on lava. In addition, our guide told us that in the summer sun, the lava heats up and becomes like hot black coals, which burn your feet as you walk on them.

Having visited Mount Etna, I was puzzled. How could twenty thousand Israelites have survived for eleven months, as stated in the Bible (see Exodus 19:1 and Numbers 10:11) in the barren lava fields around an active volcano? It seemed impossible. However, I was somewhat consoled by the fact that so far in my Exodus route I didn't have the Israelites walking over lava.

How many volcanoes are there in Arabia? The answer is hundreds. Doughty, in *Arabia Deserta,* describes his visit to a very large lava field called Harrat Aueyrid (usually spelled 'Uwayrid): "We encamped amidst innumerable volcanelli hillian [crater hills of small volcanoes], the greater of those about us might be 500 feet in height, above the mountain plain: there seemed to be some such crater hills in about every square mile." So this lava field is covered with small crater hills along with some larger volcanoes, since Doughty continues, "Over the open lava fields is seen the great volcanic cone Anaz, with a long train of volcanic bergs and craters."

Reading all this, I began to understand why no one has convincingly identified the true Mount Sinai. The few people who have appreciated that Mount Sinai was a volcano then have hundreds to choose from! Also, there are volcanoes throughout Arabia, from Midian in the north down to modern-day Yemen in the south. It seems an impossible task to identify the true Mount Sinai out of all the possibilities. Can it be done? My only hope was to look for key clues in the biblical account.

The Clue of the Eleven Days

The Old Testament book of Deuteronomy gives an absolutely key clue if only we can understand its meaning. It states, "It takes eleven days to go from Horeb to Kadesh Barnea by the Mount Seir road" (Deuteronomy 1:2). As we saw in earlier chapters, Mount Horeb is another name for Mount Sinai. The reference to eleven days is intriguing. As we've seen, the Bible, and other ancient literature, doesn't always intend certain numbers to be taken literally; for example, the number three often literally means three, but it can also mean several. Somewhat similarly, today the number one thousand sometimes literally means one thousand, but it sometimes means "many," as in, "I've told you a thousand times." However, I've never come across the number eleven being used when it is not intended literally. "Eleven days" has a ring of precision to me. So I think we can deduce that "eleven days" means precisely that.

Where was Kadesh Barnea? The vast majority of scholars identify Kadesh Barnea with the region around a small spring called 'Ain Qudeis (Alan Millard tells me that the Hebrew *Kadesh* is better transcribed as *Qadesh,* and the Arabic equivalent is *Qudeis:* they are all from the same consonantal root) about fifty miles southwest of Beersheba (see map 12.3, pg. 181).

The region includes 'Ain Qudeirat, five miles from 'Ain Qudeis, another spring containing much more water (incidentally, *'Ain* means "spring"). I'm going to take Kadesh Barnea to be the broad region around 'Ain Qudeis, including 'Ain Qudeirat, because I've looked at the evidence and I believe it is reasonably strong.

Where was the Mount Seir road? Musil, in *The Northern Hegaz,* locates Mount Seir as a ridge of mountains about forty miles northeast of the head of the Gulf of Aqaba (see map 12.3, pg. 181).

The description "from Horeb to Kadesh Barnea by the Mount Seir road" implies that there was a well-known road, called the Mount Seir road, going from Kadesh Barnea (or close to it) to Horeb (or close to it). I write "or close to it" because if I say "I traveled from Cambridge to London by the M11 highway," this doesn't mean that the M11 highway actually passes through Cambridge (it doesn't), but it passes close to Cambridge. I'm going to come back to what is meant by "the Mount Seir road" later in this chapter.

Finally, what is meant by "It takes eleven days"? I don't think it means that it actually took Moses and the Israelites eleven days to make this journey. In fact, I don't think it means that they made this journey at all. It is simply the way that distances between places were estimated in ancient times, before there were maps. So I suggest it means that Horeb (Sinai) was an eleven-day journey from Kadesh Barnea in the sense that a traveler, or a trader, would have taken eleven days to make this journey, stopping at the known campsites, each one day's journey apart, along the way. So by counting up the stopping places along the route, which was the well-known (at the time) Mount Seir road, the writer and the original readers would have known that Mount Sinai was eleven days' journey from Kadesh Barnea. So what was "a day's journey" in ancient Arabia? This is such an important question for locating Mount Sinai that I will summarize what we found out in earlier chapters.

In the ancient world, if you were not traveling along a trade route with known stopping places, then a day's journey was frequently taken to be 24 miles, the equivalent of walking at three miles per hour for eight hours. Eleven days' journey would then correspond to a distance of 264 miles. However, on a trade route, a day's journey was determined by where the designated stopping places were, which were usually chosen because of the availability of water. A stopping place would be guarded by local tribesmen, who provided food, water, safety, and a bed for the night (or for the day if you walked by night).

Musil, in *The Northern Hegaz,* states that on the pilgrim route from Egypt to Mecca, in Arabia, which followed the earlier trade route, daily marches were typically 28 to 31 miles each. Houtman, in his biblical commentary *Exodus,* states, "Pilgrims covered about 50 km (31 miles) per day." Eleven days would then correspond to a distance of 344 miles. For the pilgrim route from Damascus, in Syria, to Mecca, in Arabia, Musil writes, "A day's march on the Pilgrim Route always amounts to about sixty kilometres (37.5 miles)." This would make an eleven-day journey a distance of 412 miles. Why was a day's march longer on one route than on another? Because the stopping places depended upon the availability of water.

Although these pilgrim marches used camels, as mentioned earlier, the front camel was led on foot, and not every pilgrim had a camel, so many pilgrims walked. The pilgrim marches were therefore at walking pace, and they marched for long hours to travel from one stopping place to the next. As we've seen, in Moses' time, donkeys would have been used instead of camels, but the stopping places on the trade routes were probably identical to those on the later pilgrim routes because these places were determined by the availability of water.

Since we don't yet know where Mount Sinai is, we don't know which trade route, if any, it might have been near to. So how far was Mount Sinai from Kadesh Barnea? Looking at the numbers in the paragraph above, and remembering that the distance as the crow flies is always less than the actual journey distance, the absolute maximum distance as the crow flies from Mount Sinai to Kadesh Barnea is 412 miles. This means that if I take a map and draw on it a circle of radius 412 miles, centered on 'Ain Qudeis, then Mount Sinai must be somewhere within this circle.

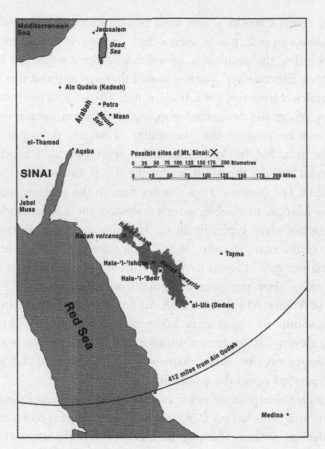

19.1. Map with an arc of a circle drawn on it, radius 412 miles, centered on Kadesh. Mount Sinai must be a historically active volcano lying within this circle. The three possibilities are marked with crosses.

I've drawn part of this circle on the map above. We can immediately see that the clue of Mount Sinai's being eleven days' journey from Kadesh Barnea is useful because we can rule out all volcanoes outside of this circle. For example, all the volcanoes in south Arabia (modern Yemen) are much too far away. Similarly, volcanoes around Mecca and Medina lie outside the circle and are therefore too far away (Mecca is off the map to the south). We now have only a limited number of volcanoes to consider as possible sites for Mount Sinai: those within the circle.

Historically Active Volcanoes

Is it possible to say which of the volcanoes within the circle could have been Mount Sinai? I'm now going to use another key clue from the Bible: Mount Sinai was erupting at the time of the Exodus, about 3,300 years ago. This is an important clue because according to Doughty and other explorers, most of the volcanoes in Arabia are extinct. So is it possible to find out which volcanoes in Arabia are extinct and which have been active in the last 3,300 years? If we can do this we can eliminate all the extinct volcanoes from our search for Mount Sinai and further narrow the field of possible volcanoes.

Back in 1996 I already realized that the biblical description of Mount Sinai matched closely that of an erupting volcano, so I jumped at the opportunity to go to a conference on the Greek volcanic island of Santorini. While I was there I met a geology student, Helena Tasker, who not only told me about a Smithsonian Institution book called *Volcanoes of the World,* but also kindly mailed me her copy of this book when she returned to England.

Volcanoes of the World is written by leading volcanologists, and it is a comprehensive collection of data from all volcanoes in the world known to have been active in the last ten thousand years. There are 1,511 such volcanoes listed. The latest edition, published in 1994, lists eighteen volcanoes in Arabia that have been active in the last ten thousand years. It calls them "historically active volcanoes." If I'm correctly interpreting the Bible as describing Mount Sinai as an active volcano, then Mount Sinai must have been one of these eighteen volcanoes. From the latitude and longitude given for each volcano in *Volcanoes of the World,* we can identify each one on a map. Only three of these lie within the circle drawn on the map. That is, only three are within a radius of 412 miles of Kadesh Barnea. All the other volcanoes active in the last ten thousand years are too far away. So Mount Sinai must be one of these three volcanoes: we have really narrowed down the field. Some people think that scientists don't have emotions. Well, this one does! And I have to tell you that by now I am really excited. Out of all the volcanoes in the whole world there are only three possible candidates that could be Mount Sinai. Can we narrow the field still further, to two or even just one volcano?

Volcanoes of the World lists the first of these three volcanoes as being in a large lava field called Harrat Rahah, but it doesn't give the volcano a name. The other two are in a more southerly lava field called Harrat 'Uwayrid and their names are Hala-'l-'Ishqua and Hala-'l-Bedr. (*Hala* is Arabic for "volcanic hill," so Hala-'l-Bedr means "volcanic Mount Bedr.") I've marked the locations of these volcanoes on map 19.1, pg. 316.

Is it possible to identify one of these volcanoes with Mount Sinai and reject the other two? Let's look next at the type of volcano. Volcanoes come in a huge range of types, from craters gently emitting steam to those engaging in terrifying explosive eruptions. *Volcanoes of the World* classifies all the volcanoes it lists according to a volcanic explosivity index (VEI). A VEI value of 0 is for a gentle, nonexplosive eruption in which the height of the column cloud is less than 300 feet. Eruptions that from their descriptions were definitely explosive but that we know nothing else about are assigned a VEI value of 2. This describes a moderate volcanic eruption with a cloud column up to three miles high above the crater.

Volcanoes of the World lists no information at all about the unnamed volcano in the Harrat Rahah and does not give it a VEI value; this column is left blank. How frustrating—I needed to know more about this volcano since it could be Mount Sinai! Fortunately, the introduction to *Volcanoes of the World* states that a major source of its data was the twenty-two-volume *Catalog of Active Volcanoes of the World*. I tracked this down to the library of the Department of Earth Sciences at Cambridge University. The very helpful librarian said that this catalog had not been looked at for years and that it was stored in a corridor outside the library in a locked cupboard high up off the floor. I thought she was exaggerating, but she wasn't! First, we had to find a long ladder, and then she had to find a key to the cupboard. I climbed up ten steps of the ladder, reached the cupboard, unlocked it, and there was the twenty-two-volume *Catalog of Active Volcanoes of the World*. Perched precariously on top of the ladder, I blew the dust off the books and pulled out the volumes one by one until I found the volume I wanted: volume 16, *Arabia and the Indian Ocean,* by M. Neumann van Padang.

Neumann van Padang's volume does indeed describe the unnamed volcano in the Harrat Rahah. It says that it lies at the western end of the lava field and that it is a small volcanic cone, called a tuff cone, sitting on lava flows. I believe we can rule out such an unimpressive small hill as being Mount Sinai: it simply does not fit the description in the book of Exodus.

Arabic texts report a volcanic eruption in A.D. 640 in the volcanic Harrah region north of Medina, but they do not identify the volcano involved. A search by volcanologists revealed two volcanoes with relatively "fresh" lava flows, either or both of which could have been responsible for the A.D. 640 eruption: these volcanoes were Bedr and 'Ishqua. Data about Hala-'l-'Ishqua and Hala-'l-Bedr are presented in slightly different forms in the 1981 and 1994 editions of *Volcanoes of the World*. Hala-'l-'Ishqua is given a volcanic explosivity index of 0, which means that its eruption was "nonexplosive" and "gentle," with a cloud height of up to only 300 feet. Such a low pillar of cloud certainly would not have been visible from many miles away, as recorded in the book of Exodus, and we can therefore rule out this volcano as being Mount Sinai.

The third, and final, historically active volcano in Arabia within eleven days' journey of Kadesh Barnea is Hala-'l-Bedr. *Volcanoes of the World* gives this a VEI value of 2, which means that it was an explosive volcano, with a cloud column height of up to three miles above its crater. In addition, *Volcanoes of the World* states, "Eruptions that were definitely explosive, but carry no other descriptive information in their record, have been assigned a default VEI of 2." In other words, Mount Bedr has been judged to have had a *minimum* VEI of 2, but it could have been significantly greater than this, so that the cloud column height could have been much greater than three miles.

So we have one, and only one, possible candidate for Mount Sinai, if this was an explosively erupting volcano as described in the Bible. Out of the 1,511 historically active volcanoes listed in *Volcanoes of the World*, only three are within eleven days' journey from Kadesh Barnea, and only one of these emitted a high pillar of cloud and fire: Mount Bedr.

Is Mount Sinai Really Mount Bedr?

To see if Mount Sinai really is Mount Bedr, I'm going to look at the description of Mount Sinai given in the Old Testament and see if it fits, in detail, what we know about Mount Bedr. The only eye-witness description of Mount Bedr I can find is given by Musil, in *The Northern Hegaz*. Fortunately, this is a superb and detailed description.

What does Mount Bedr look like? Musil writes, "The volcano of al-Bedr presented a fine view, rising as it does above the grey table mountain of Tadra, which stands in the midst of the fertile, pale green basin of al-Gaw [also spelled al-Jaw]." Where is Mount Bedr? The *Catalog of Active Volcanoes of the World* gives the precise geographical position of Mount Bedr as latitude 27°15' north and longitude 37°12' east, and thus we can locate Bedr on a map. Using a good map, for example the U.S. Geological Survey map I–205B (1959) or the Arabian Peninsula map published by HMSO London, map 2–GSGS (1980), we can see that Mount Bedr is a solitary, isolated volcano (on the HMSO map Hala-'l-Bedr is called Hallat al-Badr). All the other volcanoes in Midian rise up from huge lava fields, either Harrat Rahah or Harrat 'Uwayrid. But Bedr is different. It is situated *between* these two lava fields, and it sits on a high, flat, gray, sandstone table mountain called Tadra, which is 5,000 feet (almost one mile) above sea level. Bedr is a black basalt volcanic cone that rises up about 500 feet above the Tadra table mountain. The table mountain itself has a large diameter of about six miles.

What a magnificent site! Picture a huge, flat, table mountain six miles across. The most famous table mountain in the world (up until now!) is Table Mountain in Cape Town, South Africa. It is 3,500 feet above sea level and less than two miles long. The table mountain on which Bedr stands is over three times as long. What a staggering spectacle! And then standing on top of this huge gray table is the black volcanic cone of Bedr, rising to a height of about 500 feet above the top of the table mountain. When we want to emphasize the importance of an object we often put it on a pedestal: for example, the Statue of Liberty stands on a tall column. So it is with Bedr: the isolated volcanic cone is displayed atop the massive natural plinth of one of the largest table mountains in the world.

So we have a truly magnificent candidate for Mount Sinai. But does what we know about Mount Bedr fit the biblical description? I'm going to explore below the clues the Bible provides about

Mount Sinai, and we will see how Mount Bedr fulfills not just one clue, but all the clues, in a most remarkable way. We'll start with some small clues.

The Public Square

Exodus chapters 25 and 26 describe the Israelites constructing a complex tent called the Tabernacle close to Mount Sinai. The Tabernacle was a large enclosure 150 feet long and 75 feet wide that contained the sacred Ark of the Covenant. The second chapter of the book of Numbers describes how the Israelites (I believe twenty thousand people) formed four camps around the Tabernacle, north, south, east, and west of it. The huge flat table mountain called Tadra, with Mount Bedr (Sinai) at one end of it, would have been an ideal "public square" for the Tabernacle surrounded by twenty thousand Israelites.

The Rock at Horeb

As we saw in the previous chapter, the rock at Horeb (Sinai) that Moses struck must have been porous, large, and well known. Now if Mount Sinai is at its traditional site of Jebel Musa in the Sinai Peninsula, then there are so many rocks there that the statement "the rock at Horeb" is totally meaningless. However, if Mount Horeb (Sinai) is Mount Bedr, then I believe the meaning of "the rock at Horeb" is totally clear: it is the magnificent table mountain on which Mount Horeb (Sinai) sits. In addition, this sandstone mountain would hold large quantities of rainwater.

The Isolated Mountain

We can deduce that Mount Sinai was an isolated mountain, and not part of a mountain chain, because Exodus 19:12 states, "Put limits for the people around the mountain and tell them, 'Be careful that you do not go up the mountain or touch it.'" The picture painted in this passage from Exodus is not of a mountain peak in a range of mountains, but of an isolated mountain rising up from a surrounding plain and with a well-defined circumference around its base. The solitary volcanic cone of Mount Bedr is consistent with this description of putting limits around the mountain.

The Mountain Stream

There was a stream of water flowing down the mountain. Deuteronomy 9:21 records, "I crushed it [the golden calf] and ground it to powder as fine as dust and threw the dust into a stream that flowed down the mountain." Musil, in *The Northern Hegaz,* writes, "Upon the eastern slope of the grey table mountain of Tadra is situated the black volcano Hala'-l-Bedr. On the western slope there used to flow a spring now said to have been clogged up by the collapse of a rock."

Water and Vegetation Around Mount Sinai

We now come to a big issue. Could twenty thousand Israelites have survived around Mount Bedr for eleven months? Pause for a moment and think of the water and food requirements of twenty thousand people, not just for a day or a week or even a month, but for eleven whole months. If you go back to the start of this book, you will see that one of the major doubts I had about the traditional Mount Sinai, Jebel Musa in the Sinai Peninsula, was that it is surrounded by barren desert. I couldn't see how twenty thousand Israelites with their flocks could possibly have survived there for about one year. Do the surroundings of Mount Bedr contain any more water and vegetation than the land around the traditional Mount Sinai?

We've already seen that Musil says Mount Bedr is on a table mountain that stands in the fertile green basin of al-Gaw, but what exactly is this fertile green basin? Just listen to Musil's description of his own approach to Mount Bedr:

> The valley broadens out into a basin enclosed on all sides by low, but steep, slopes, and known as al-Gaw (the watering place) because it contains many rain-water wells. The plain is covered with a fairly deep layer of clay in which various plants thrive luxuriantly, and it therefore forms the best winter encampment of the Beli. The guide proudly pointed out to us the abundant

withered pasturage through which we were passing, and asked whether throughout our journey from Tebuk we had seen so many and such various plants. The annuals were yellowish, while the shrubs were a brilliant green.

What a beautiful and fertile place for the Israelites to have lived in for eleven months! Incidentally, who are the Beli referred to above? They are an Arabian tribe, and Hogarth, in the second edition (1917) of *Hejaz before World War I,* writes, "The Billi [his spelling of Beli] in Hejaz number, probably, at least forty thousand souls." So when Musil wrote *The Northern Hegaz* in 1926, there would have been at least forty thousand Beli. If forty thousand Beli tribespeople, with their flocks and herds, can survive around Mount Bedr, then twenty thousand Israelites certainly could have done so. To my mind, one of the most difficult questions about the Exodus is now solved. There must have been extremely few places where twenty thousand Israelites could have survived for eleven months, and around Mount Bedr was one of them.

The Israelites not only survived, but they flourished there. For example, there was enough water for twenty thousand Israelites not only to drink but also to wash their clothes: "After Moses had gone down the mountain [Sinai] to the people, he consecrated them, and they washed their clothes" (Exodus 19:14). If water is really scarce, you don't waste it by washing your clothes. However, it is clear from Musil that water is plentiful around Mount Bedr. I can assure you from my visit to the traditional Mount Sinai that for twenty thousand Israelites to have washed their clothes there would have been impossible.

The Caves of the Servants of Moses

Musil, in *The Northern Hegaz,* makes a fascinating remark about a volcano called Mount Asi, which is only sixteen miles southeast of Mount Bedr. He writes, "To the southeast [of Mount Bedr] we perceived the volcano of al-Asi, in which are the Morajer Abid Musa, 'the caves of the servants of Moses.' Our guide explained that the servants of Moses sojourned in them when their master was abiding with

Allah." How amazing! So there is an ancient Arabian tradition that Moses was in this part of Arabia.

As far as I am aware, there are only two places in the whole of Arabia named Musa, the Arabic for Moses, and both of these are in Midian. The first is the well of Musa, which is in ancient Madian, modern al-Bad'. As we have seen, the tradition that Moses lived for some years with the family of Jethro at ancient Madian is a strong tradition, and it is consistent with the biblical account. The second is the "caves of the servants of Musa," on Mount Asi, sixteen miles from Mount Bedr, where Moses lived for about a year, if my identification of Mount Bedr with Mount Sinai is correct.

We must be careful not to put too much weight on traditions; nevertheless, if Moses spent some time living in Madian and around Mount Bedr, surely we would expect there to be traditions about this, and this is precisely what we find.

The Altar of Twelve Stones

When Moses was at Mount Sinai he built an altar of twelve stones on which animals were sacrificed to God. Here is how the book of Exodus describes the building of the altar: "He [Moses] got up early the next morning and built an altar at the foot of the mountain and set up twelve stone pillars representing the twelve tribes of Israel." Now listen to this passage from *The Northern Hegaz* describing a holy site under the northern slopes of the mountain: "Another sacred spot is situated by the well of al-Hzer. It is called al-Manhal, and upon it are twelve stones known as al-Madbah [the place of slaughter], where the Beli [the local tribesmen] still offer up sacrifices when they are encamped close by."

The parallel between this account of the Beli tribesmen in 1910, when Musil visited Bedr, and the ancient Israelites three thousand years earlier is striking. Both regarded Bedr as a sacred mountain. Both made sacrifices on an altar of twelve stones erected at the foot of Mount Bedr. This may of course be a coincidence. On the other hand, the twelve-stone altar of the Beli at the foot of Mount Bedr may preserve the memory of the twelve-stone altar of the Israelites, perhaps at the very same spot, and perhaps using the very same stones.

How do we tell if events are curious coincidences or if they are more meaningful? Strange coincidences happen surprisingly frequently. For example, the English painter William Hyde came to live in Westminster in London and found that the person living in the next room of the same house was Dr. Jekyll. Thomas Jefferson, the chief author of the American Declaration of Independence, died on its fiftieth anniversary, on July 4, 1826, as did his old rival, John Adams. Mark Twain was born in November 1835, when Halley's comet blazed in the night sky, and he died in April 1910, when Halley's comet returned. All these events are, I think, pure coincidence. In life we have to be really careful not to take coincidences too seriously.

On the other hand, it can be equally foolish to dismiss repeated coincidences as chance events. Recently, in my house in Cambridge I noticed on the kitchen ceiling a small damp patch that rapidly dried. It occurred several hours after I had taken a shower in the bathroom above, and since it didn't happen immediately afterward, I put it down to coincidence. However, when it happened a second and then a third time, I knew it was no coincidence. Somehow water must have been leaking through from the bathroom to the kitchen, and indeed it was. To have continued believing this was a coincidence would have been an expensive mistake: our kitchen ceiling could have come down. So it is with the events of the Exodus: if "coincidences" happen often, then they are probably not coincidences. So apart from the altar, are there any more striking parallels between the behavior of the ancient Israelites at Mount Sinai and the modern Beli at Mount Bedr?

Do Not Touch Mount Sinai

Mount Sinai was so holy to the Israelites that Moses didn't allow either humans or animals to touch it. Here is what the book of Exodus records God as saying to Moses:

Put limits for the people around the mountain [Sinai] and tell them, "Be careful that you do not go up the mountain or touch the foot of it. Whoever touches the mountain shall surely be put to death. He shall surely be stoned or shot with arrows; not a hand is to be laid on him. Whether man or animal, he shall not be permitted to live." (Exodus 19:12–13)

What a stern injunction! Neither humans nor animals were even to touch Mount Sinai. If they did they had to be stoned to death. No other mountain in the whole Bible is given this respect, not even Mount Zion in Jerusalem.

Now listen to the words of Musil in *The Northern Hegaz:* "The Bedouin have been afraid to ascend this volcano [Mount Bedr] and they drive away their animals, not allowing them to graze upon the slopes or upon the grey ridge of Tadra [the table mountain on which Bedr stands]." So Mount Bedr [Sinai] was sacred to both the Israelites three thousand years ago and the Beli a hundred years ago, and neither people nor animals were permitted to approach it.

Musil's explanation of the Belis' fear of Mount Bedr is their memory of its erupting many years ago. However, as we've seen, there are other volcanoes in Midian that have been active in historical times, but Musil doesn't record the local tribesmen forbidding people and animals from touching these volcanoes, only Mount Bedr. It is therefore reasonable to ask whether the modern, very curious prohibition of people and animals touching Mount Bedr is a tradition that goes back to Moses. Whether or not this is the case, the identical respect shown for Mount Bedr and for Mount Sinai by the Beli and the Israelites, respectively, is striking and is consistent with Bedr's being Sinai.

Why Did Musil Not Believe Bedr Was Sinai?

As we've just seen, the description of Mount Bedr by Musil in *The Northern Hegaz* matches almost word for word the biblical description of Mount Sinai. Mount Sinai is depicted as an erupting volcano; Bedr is an active volcano. The mountain must stand in isolation so that "bounds" could be set around it, and Bedr is entirely isolated from the surrounding hills. There is the flat tabletop Tadra, on which Bedr stands, providing a "public square" for the Israelites to camp around the Tabernacle. There is the adjacent, plentiful water supply, plus the stream down the mountain, just as described in the Bible. There is the tradition that the servants of Moses lived in caves in the vicinity. Both people and animals were forbidden to touch the mountain. The locality we are seeking must provide water and vegetation for twenty thousand Israelites for eleven months; the fertile plain around Mount Bedr provides the best pasturage and watering place for many miles around. Moses obtained plentiful water from "the rock at Horeb"; the huge porous sandstone table mountain called Tadra is an ideal rock for this event. Moses built an altar of twelve stones at the foot of the mountain; here, at the foot of Mount Bedr, the Bedouin still sacrifice on an altar of twelve stones. It is difficult to conceive of any mountain in the world satisfying the biblical description of Mount Sinai more completely than Mount Bedr.

Surely the well-educated Musil must have realized the striking similarity between Mount Bedr and the biblical Mount Sinai, yet he never once mentions this in *The Northern Hegaz*. Why not? This really puzzled me, so I looked into it, and what I discovered is fascinating. When Musil returned from his perilous journey to Midian in 1910, he was in fact convinced that the volcanic Mount Bedr *was* Mount Sinai, and he stated this in a preliminary report on his visit, published in 1911. However, he rapidly discovered that the location of Mount Sinai was an extremely controversial topic. For example, a distinguished British scholar, Dr. Charles Beke, had previously claimed that Mount Sinai was an unnamed volcano in Arabia, and for this "heresy" his opponents had forced him to return a gold medal awarded to him by the Royal Geographical Society. Beke later retracted his theory that Mount Sinai was a volcano because he couldn't justify it, and he located Sinai instead at the nonvolcanic Mount Ithm (also known as Bagir), close to the head of the Gulf of Aqaba.

Musil, very reasonably, was asked to justify his belief that Mount Sinai was Mount Bedr by constructing a plausible route of the Exodus from Egypt to Mount Bedr. He spent the next fifteen years of his life trying to do this, and he failed. So he retracted his view that Sinai was Bedr and then published details of his travels in *The Northern Hegaz* in 1926, sixteen years after his visit there. As I've said above, nowhere in his book does he mention even the possibility that Mount Sinai might be Mount Bedr; instead, he goes for a more northerly nonvolcanic site, but one that is still in Midian. Musil rather vaguely writes, "Sinai must have been an isolated peak . . . presumably near the seib [small watercourse or valley] of al-Hrob. . . . [It] must be located in the land of Midian to the south-east of the modern settlement of al-Aqaba." Musil seems to be influenced by the similarity of the Arabic Hrob with Horeb, which I suspect *is* a coincidence! The Frenchman Jean Koenig and Canon W. J. Phythian-Adams, from Britain, following the initial lead of Musil, have both argued in a series of papers (see bibliography) that Bedr is Sinai, but their work has never been taken seriously because they haven't had a convincing Exodus route to Mount Bedr.

I've tried in this book to reconstruct in detail the Exodus route to Mount Bedr. I believe this fits the biblical account like a glove, and it is the first time this route has been produced. I've sketched this route on the following map (19.2). I've also shown, from *Volcanoes of the World* and other sources, that if Mount Sinai was an active volcano as described in the book of Exodus, then there is one, and only one, possible mountain that could be Mount Sinai, and that is Mount Bedr. No one has used these arguments before. I therefore suggest that we now have both a convincing route of the Exodus and a convincing site for Mount Sinai. But the story isn't yet finished!

Mount Bedr: Mountain of the Moon God

Does the name Bedr have a meaning? I looked this up in a standard Arabic dictionary, and the answer is intriguing: *bedr* means "full moon." Why was this mountain given this name? I've seen a number of volcanic craters in Iceland, Italy, and elsewhere. Usually they are irregularly shaped, but just occasionally they look like a perfect round circle, just like the circle of the full moon. Satellite photographs of Mount Bedr reveal that its crater is indeed a perfect circle, and the ancient Midianites would have seen this by climbing up the mountain (before such contact was forbidden) to the top of the crater. So once again, place-names have a meaning. Mount Bedr is the mountain of the full moon.

Does the name Sinai have a meaning? As we've seen, the Desert of Sinai and Mount Sinai are close geographically to the Desert of Sin, and I was puzzled by the similarity of the words *Sin* and *Sinai*. So are these words related? As the French scholar Jean Koenig has pointed out, Sinai may mean "from Sin" or, equivalently, "belonging to Sin"

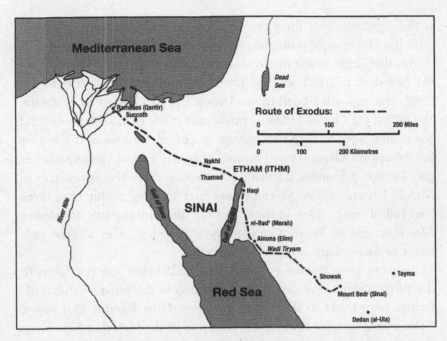

19.2. The route of the Exodus to the true Mount Sinai (Mount Bedr).

or "of Sin." The name Mount Sinai then means the mountain of the Moon-god Sin, and the Desert of Sinai is the desert containing this mountain. Robert Gordon, the Regius Professor of Hebrew at Cambridge University, has also told me that the ending *ai* could be an ancient Hebrew feminine ending, so Sinai could have been an ancient female form of Sin, suggesting that Mount Sinai was possibly the mountain of the Moon-goddess.

So the name Mount Bedr means the mountain of the full moon, and the name Mount Sinai may mean the mountain of the Moon-god or -goddess. What a remarkable connection! Let me spell out just how intriguing the connection is. As we've seen in chapter 6, in the ancient world volcanoes were sacred mountains, so Bedr the volcano would have been a holy mountain. But to which god? The "full moon crater" of Bedr, I think, makes this crystal clear. Bedr would have been sacred to the Moon-god or his consort. So the Midianites would have called it the mountain of the Moon-god, and I suggest the Hebrews then took over this name and called it Mount Sinai, meaning the mountain of the Moon-god (or goddess)—and I suggest that this is the significance of the name Sinai, whether the name originated with the Hebrews or someone else.

Another angle on the moon connection suggested itself to me when the first draft of this book had just been finished. It was August 15, 2002, and my wife's birthday, so I took her to London to celebrate. We visited the Queen of Sheba exhibition at the British Museum, and Sarah then went to an ATM, leaving me briefly to look at the nearby bookshops on Great Russell Street. This was a great mistake on her part because I found a fascinating bookshop there that specializes in Middle Eastern books. Several hours later I emerged clutching three bags full of books. One of these had the unpromising title *Babylonian Menologies and the Semitic Calendars* by S. Langdon, who was the professor of Assyriology at Oxford University.

Langdon gives textual evidence that in Babylon, on the fifteenth day of the month, the day of the full moon in the lunar calendar, offerings were made to the Moon-god, Sin. Now Exodus 16:1 states, "The whole Israelite community . . . came to the Desert of Sin . . . on the fifteenth day of the second month." So the book of Exodus explicitly states that the Israelites arrived at the Desert of Sin on the precise day of the month, full-moon time, that was sacred to Sin.

Similarly, Exodus 19:1 spells out the same thing for the arrival of the Israelites at Sinai one month later: "In the third month after the Israelites left Egypt—on the very day—they came to the Desert of Sinai." What does "on the very day" mean? Well, as we saw in chapter 11, the Israelites left Egypt on the fifteenth day of the first month, at full-moon time. So they arrived at the Desert of Sinai on the fifteenth day (full-moon time again in the lunar calendar) of the third month. Another special day for the worship of the Moon-god.

However, the fifteenth day of the *third month* was regarded as a *very* special day for the Moon-god. Langdon states that both in the early Assyrian calendar and in the early south Arabian calendar, the third month, corresponding to May–June in our solar calendar, was sacred to the Moon-god. Mark Cohen, in his scholarly book *The Cultic Calendars of the Ancient Near East,* gives textual evidence that in Assyria the third month was known as the month of Sin.

It is not unreasonable to suppose that the third month would have been sacred to the Moon-god in the Midianite lunar calendar as well, since the Midianites were traders who would have known about the religious festivals of their neighbors. So the fifteenth day of the third month may have been the most important day in the year for worship of the Moon-god in Midian. It was "on this very day" that the book of Exodus emphasizes the Israelites arrived at Sinai and took it over. How remarkable! Now that we know the real Mount Sinai was Mount Bedr, notice how this helps us to understand better key details in the book of Exodus such as the significance of arriving at Sin and Sinai on the fifteenth day of the month.

I should probably make it plain that I'm definitely not suggesting that the Israelites' worship of their God grew out of moon worship. What I am saying is that Mount Bedr was already a holy mountain, dedicated to the Moon-god, before the Israelites arrived. The Israelites then "took over" this pagan mountain and made it the mountain of *their* God: the mountain where Moses received the Ten Commandments. I'm reminded of why Christians celebrate Christmas on December 25: they "took over" a pagan Roman festival that occurred on this day, called "Sol Invictus," the festival of the Invincible Sun, and they renamed it Christmas, to celebrate the birth of Christ, the Invincible Son.

Why does the Bible use Mount Horeb as an alternative name to Mount Sinai? I can think of two possible reasons. The first arises from my suggestion that the Israelites took over Mount Bedr as the mountain of their God. I believe they named it Sinai because it was originally the mountain of the Moon-god. However, I suggest that some Israelites didn't like to use the name Sinai for their holy mountain because of its Moon-god connotations. So they invented another name for this mountain, Horeb. *Horeb* is Hebrew for "desolate," and a black basalt volcanic mountain is indeed a desolate place. So the Bible sometimes uses the name Sinai for this mountain and sometimes Horeb, but both names refer to the same mountain. An alternative possibility is that Mount Sinai refers specifically to the volcanic Mount Bedr while Mount Horeb refers more broadly both to the table mountain called Tadra in Arabic and to Mount Bedr, which rises from Mount Tadra.

I believe we can also understand why so many Amalekites attacked the Israelites near Mount Sinai. I suggest they had assembled around Mount Sinai before the fifteenth day of the third month in order to worship their Moon-god on this special day. When they heard that the Israelites were coming they staged a preemptive strike. But they lost, leaving the Israelites free to occupy the Desert of Sinai and the very fertile land in the al-Gaw basin adjacent to Mount Sinai.

Jethro: The Priest of Midian

What type of priest was Jethro? I've already suggested that since the Moon-god was probably the principal god in Midian, Jethro was probably a priest of the Moon-god. So when Moses "led the flock [of Jethro] to the far side of the desert and came to Horeb, the mountain of God" (Exodus 3:1), Moses was almost certainly traveling to a sacred mountain that was well known to Jethro. As the priest of the Moon-god, Jethro probably would have visited this holy Mountain of the Full Moon many times previously and made sacrifices there. He would also have known about the fine pastureland nearby in the basin of al-Gaw. So our identification of Mount Sinai (Horeb) with the Mountain of the Full Moon (Bedr) helps us to understand better the story of Moses and Jethro's sheep in Exodus 3.

It may be interesting to note that Jethro later visited Moses and the Israelites when they were at Mount Sinai. Jethro said to Moses there, "Now I know that the Lord is greater than all other gods" (Exodus 28:11). So Jethro, the priest of Midian, finally realized that the God of Israel, whom he calls "the Lord," is greater than all other gods, including of course the Moon-god and the other gods he and the Midianites worshiped.

The Incident of the Golden Calf

Our knowledge that Mount Sinai is Mount Bedr helps us to understand better the curious incident of the golden calf recorded in the book of Exodus (see figure 1.2, pg. 8). The background is that Moses had climbed up Mount Sinai, the summit of which was covered in volcanic smoke, and he had not been seen for forty days and forty nights. Exodus 32:1 records the Israelites' going to Aaron and saying, "As for this fellow Moses who brought us up out of Egypt, we don't know what has happened to him." But we can guess what they thought. Moses had gone up to the top of the fiery mountain of the Moon-god and had disappeared. The Israelites must have thought Moses had been slain at the top of this terrifying mountain and that the Moon-god had triumphed over Moses. So the Israelites, forgetting all the good things their God had done for them, quickly changed sides and made an idol to worship that represented the Moon-god. And what animal represented the Moon-god, carved on his temples from Babylon to southern Arabia, including carvings found in Tayma in Midian (see photographs 18.2 and 18.3, pg. 301)? As we've seen, it was a young bull, otherwise called a calf. The Israelites then sacrificed to this golden calf, until Moses appeared and broke the idol into pieces. The Israelites remained susceptible to Moon-god worship for many years. For example, 1 Kings 12 records with disapproval that a king of Israel called Jeroboam made two golden calves. This was in about 920 B.C., some 350 years after the Exodus. And when did Jeroboam make sacrifices to these golden calves? The Old Testament tells us it was on "the fifteenth day" of the month (1 Kings 12:32–33), precisely at full-moon time in the lunar calendar. This suggests to me that Jeroboam was probably sacrificing to the Moon-god. A later king of Israel, Josiah, who reigned for thirty-one years (c.640–609 B.C.), did away with the worship of the sun, moon, and stars in Israel (2 Kings 23:4–5).

I believe the new understanding we've gained in this book about the Exodus really illuminates incidents like the building of the golden calf. There are a number of other Exodus events I could comment on, but this book is already long!

Now that we know where Mount Sinai really is, I would like to finish this chapter by revisiting the eleven days' journey from Kadesh Barnea to Mount Sinai. In particular, was this distance precisely eleven days or not?

The Clue of the Eleven Days' Journey Revisited

I want to reexamine Deuteronomy 1:2, "It takes eleven days to go from Horeb to Kadesh Barnea by the Mount Seir road," because I want to show that this distance is precisely eleven days' journey if Horeb [Sinai] is Bedr. However, if you find detailed routes tedious, then please fast-forward to the epilogue following this chapter.

Where was Mount Seir? Bible dictionaries and commentaries are rather vague on this, usually saying that Mount Seir may be on the east or the west of the Arabah. However, Musil has made a detailed study from both biblical and Arabic sources, and he concludes that Mount Seir was a mountain range now called as-Sera, which rises close to modern Petra, on the east of the Arabah in Edom/Seir, and then extends southeast (see map 19.1, pg. 316).

The British explorer Philby says that Mount Seir is the modern Mount Shara range, and from his map it is clear that this is the same as Musil's Sera range (note the similarity of the consonants in *Seir, Sera,* and *Shara*). The Arabic expert St. John Armitage also tells me that ash-Shara is ancient Mount Seir.

Why don't any of the Bible dictionaries I've consulted mention this location of Mount Seir? Again I suspect it is because of the mind-set of many biblical scholars that Mount Sinai is in the Sinai Peninsula, on the *west* of the Arabah. If Kadesh Barnea is on the *west* of the Arabah, as it is, then it doesn't make sense to go from Kadesh Barnea to the traditional Mount Sinai in the Sinai Peninsula, which is on the *west* of the Arabah, via Mount Seir, which is on the *east* of the Arabah. It is rather like saying that I traveled from Seattle to San Francisco (both on the west coast) via the road to New York (on the east coast); it makes no sense. So the fact that Mount Seir is located to the east of the Arabah is yet another reason for saying that Mount Sinai cannot be in the Sinai Peninsula.

So we've identified Mount Seir: it is a mountain range, or a peak in this range, that starts at the fabulous rose red city of Petra in ancient Seir/Edom, modern Jordan, and then runs southeast, past ancient Maan (see map 19.1, pg. 316).

What was the Mount Seir road? For the writer of Deuteronomy 1:2 to specify the Mount Seir road in this way, it must have been a major route, probably a trade route, well known to the original readers.

There were only a limited number of trade routes in the Middle East three thousand years ago. One of these was an inland route that ran roughly south to north through Arabia, passing through Dedan (modern al-Ula) and Tabuk in Midian (see map 4.2, pg. 52).

This ancient trade route, described in detail in Musil's *The Northern Hegaz,* later became the Muslim pilgrim route from Damascus in

Syria to Mecca and Medina. Much later a major railway line, called the Hejaz Line, was built from Damascus to Medina under the engineering supervision of a German for the Turks, and this line follows closely the ancient pilgrimage route. Later still, Lawrence of Arabia blew up this line with explosives.

This ancient trade route is only thirty-four miles away from Mount Bedr as the crow flies. However, to get to this trade route the Harrat 'Uwayrid has to be crossed (see map 4.1, pg. 46), but there is a nearby route. T. E. Lawrence (Lawrence of Arabia) describes this in *The Seven Pillars of Wisdom*. He set off from al-Wajh on the coast of the Red Sea, traveled up to Abu Raqah, close to Mount Bedr (see map 4.1, pg. 46), and then crossed the Harrat 'Uwayrid to get to the trade route. Musil also traveled from Mount Bedr across to this trade route.

Three thousand years ago this trade route passed through the oasis of Maan, close to Petra, which was at the crossroads of some of the key trading routes in the Middle East. We know this route existed in the thirteenth century B.C. from archaeological surveys of Peter Parr and others (see bibliography). Apart from this route from Maan to southern Arabia, there was a route north to Damascus, routes east to the Persian Gulf and Babylonia, and routes west to ports on the Mediterranean and northern Egypt. Some of these routes are shown in map 4.2, pg. 52.

Maan and Petra are both on the Mount Seir range. In fact, you go around this range to travel from Maan to Petra. So when Deuteronomy refers to going from Horeb (Mount Sinai) by the Mount Seir road, I believe it means going north from Mount Sinai (Bedr) up toward Mount Seir along the ancient inland trade route through Arabia that is accessible from Mount Bedr. So this part of the route is solved.

What about traveling on to Kadesh Barnea, on the west of the Arabah, from the east of the Arabah? The difficulty here was crossing the walls of mountains on both sides of the Arabah, which were impenetrable except at a few natural passes. However, a trade route running northwest from Maan/Petra/Mount Seir to Gaza and el Arish on the Mediterranean coast went through natural passes. Kadesh Barnea was less than twenty miles from this trade route (see map 4.2, pg. 52). So when Deuteronomy refers to going "from Horeb to Kadesh

Barnea by the Mount Seir road," I believe the meaning of this to the original readers was clear, and we've just reconstructed this route.

What about the journey's taking eleven days? As we've seen, this refers to the number of known stopping points, a day's journey apart, on the trade routes. I must emphasize that it does *not* mean that the Israelites made this journey in eleven days. I've spent a lot of time studying the route, from Musil and elsewhere, and will summarize the known stopping points on the journey from Bedr to Maan (Mount Seir). The nearest stopping point to Bedr on the inland Arabian trade route was at a place called Mu'azzam, about thirty-seven miles away. We know it is possible to travel from Bedr to Mu'azzam because Musil did this route himself. From Mu'azzam to Maan is on the trade route all the way. The known stopping points, and the distances between them, are as follows:

Bedr to Mu'azzam (37 miles) to Akhdar (35 miles) to Tabuk (39 miles) to Hazm (25 miles) to Hajj (31 miles) to Sorer (25 miles) to Akabat (31 miles) to Maan (Mount Seir, 37 miles).

If we assume that from Mount Bedr to Mu'azzam was reckoned as a day's journey, then, counting up the days from the list above, from Mount Bedr to Mount Seir was eight days' journey. From Maan to Kadesh Barnea you go along the ancient spice route from Mount Seir toward Gaza, leaving this route at a place called Mazad Neqavot to get to Kadesh Barnea. The route is:

Maan (Mount Seir) to Petra (24 miles) to Mazad Neqavot (34 miles) to Kadesh Barnea (34 miles).

So from Mount Seir (Maan) to Kadesh Barnea was three days' journey. Thus the total journey time from Mount Sinai (Bedr) to Kadesh Barnea by the Mount Seir road was eleven days (eight plus three), precisely as stated in the book of Deuteronomy, not a day more or less.

As far as I'm aware, all the evidence in the Bible on the location and nature of Mount Sinai fits its identification with Mount Bedr in Arabia, and I know of no evidence against.

EPILOGUE

We have followed Moses and the Israelites on an epic journey from Egypt to Mount Sinai, where the Ten Commandments were given and a nation was born—surely one of the most significant journeys in history. We've used a combination of modern science and ancient texts to throw light upon the miracles recorded in the biblical account of the Exodus, and we've shown that many, if not all, of these miracles have natural explanations. However, I've emphasized that they are still miracles: miracles of *timing*. Some of the miracles have very specific explanations, for example the crossing of the Red Sea, which enables the exact geographical location to be specified. These key marker sites greatly help in the reconstruction of the Exodus route, and a new route is proposed in this book.

I've suggested a large number of novel interpretations of the events of the Exodus, but probably most important, I've shown that Mount Sinai is not in the Sinai Peninsula but in Arabia. In particular, Mount Sinai is Mount Bedr, a volcano active in historical times in Arabia. We've also seen that the greatest miracle in the Old Testament, the crossing of the Red Sea and the subsequent drowning of Pharaoh's army, occurred at the head of the Gulf of Aqaba, and modern science

enables us to understand in detail how these momentous events occurred.

If my theory is correct—and I believe the evidence is strong—history books, maps, footnotes in Bibles, biblical commentaries, and
travel guides to the Middle East will all have to be rewritten. The
many Web sites about the Exodus will have to be updated.

Is there further evidence we can seek to confirm my proposal that
Mount Sinai was the volcanic Mount Bedr? I think there is. The main
test would be a scientific investigation to determine whether or not
Mount Bedr erupted at the time of the Exodus, between 1300 and
1250 B.C. I predict that it did. If so, it would be strong evidence supporting both the date of the Exodus and also the view that Mount
Sinai was Mount Bedr. In addition, if Mount Sinai was Mount Bedr,
the mountain of the Moon-god, as I have tentatively suggested, I
would expect to find archaeological evidence of Midianite sacrifices to
the Moon-god at Mount Bedr.

Dating the eruption(s) of Mount Bedr will require considerable scientific care. As we saw earlier, Mount Bedr may well have been the
volcano north of Medina that erupted in A.D. 640, described by Arabic writers. In addition, the Old Testament records that the prophet
Elijah visited "Horeb, the mountain of God" in the ninth century B.C.
When Elijah stood on the mountain there was an earthquake and fire
(1 Kings 19:12), which strongly suggests that Mount Sinai was erupting at the time. Hence Mount Sinai (Mount Bedr) may have erupted
several times since the Exodus and there may be layers of lava on top
of one another, corresponding to volcanic eruptions at different times.
Careful scientific work will be required to date each eruption.

So dating an eruption of Mount Bedr to the period 1300–1250
B.C. and looking for evidence of sacrifices to the Moon-god are, I
suggest, the two main topics that a scientific expedition to Mount
Bedr should concentrate on. Can we expect to find archaeological evidence for the Israelites themselves being at Mount Bedr? The problem here is that the Israelites lived in tents, which leave little or no
archaeological remains. Also they were at Mount Sinai for only eleven
months, and this was over three thousand years ago. For these reasons,
I think we shouldn't expect to find any evidence from archaeology
that the Israelites were at Mount Bedr, but if we did then clearly it

would be a remarkable bonus. (Imagine finding fragments of the original stone tablets on which the Ten Commandments were written, which Moses broke to pieces in his anger over the golden calf idol; Exodus 32:19.)

At the start of this book I asked a number of important questions. Let's see if we can now answer them. First, is the Old Testament account of the Exodus from Egypt a coherent and consistent account (many scholars believe it isn't)? My answer to this is a resounding yes.

Second, is the Exodus account in the Bible factually accurate? When I started my research on this book in 1995, I really wondered just how accurate the biblical text was. I was well aware that most scholars believe it is riddled with errors and inconsistencies. I've subjected the biblical text to a real grilling in this book, and I can only stand back in amazement at its accuracy and consistency, down to points of tiny detail.

Third, can we understand the miracles? The answer again is yes. I've used modern science to explain every miracle in the Exodus story. Conversely, tiny details of the miracles, like the water's stopping at Adam at the crossing of the Jordan, or like the lightning and the sound of a trumpet at the erupting Mount Sinai, fit precisely what we know about these events from modern science.

Fourth, has the Exodus text been misinterpreted? The insights provided by modern science suggest that the Exodus text has often been misinterpreted by scholars. The real meaning of the text, suggested in this book, is frequently more dramatic than the traditional interpretation. The Exodus story revealed in this book is truly astonishing, amazing, and inspirational.

Fifth, can we reconstruct the Exodus route and find the true Mount Sinai after three thousand years? Again, another yes. I suggest that the real Mount Sinai is the volcanic Mount Bedr, standing on top of one of the largest table mountains in the world.

Finally, I asked in the first chapter, Is there any evidence of a "guiding hand" in the events of the Exodus? What I've found is that the Exodus story describes a series of natural events like earthquakes, volcanoes, hail, and strong winds occurring time after time at precisely the right moment for the deliverance of Moses and the Israelites. Any one of these events occurring at the right time could be ascribed to lucky chance. When a whole sequence of events happens at just the right moment, then it is either incredibly lucky chance or else there is a God who works in, with, and through natural events to guide the affairs and the destinies of individuals and of nations. Which belief is correct: Chance or God? I'm not going to answer that question for you; you must answer it yourself.

We have come to the end of an extraordinary journey. I would like you, the readers, to think of yourselves as members of a jury, assessing and weighing the evidence. What do you, the members of the jury, think of the evidence I've presented? Please think long and hard, because if the arguments I've given are correct, then this book has rewritten our understanding of a major event in world history: the Exodus from Egypt.

BIBLIOGRAPHY

Browsing in bookshops has been one of the pleasures of writing this book. I have read and consulted a huge amount of literature covering a wide range of topics while researching the Exodus story. In this bibliography I want to give a selection of the books and articles that I have found most useful so that readers can carry out further study if they are interested.

First, a few words on the books to which I have referred constantly in my research. All the biblical quotations in this book, unless otherwise stated, come from the New International Version (NIV) of the Bible. This is one of the best modern English translations: it is easy to read and aims to be accurate. I have also consulted a number of other translations, including the King James Version (KJV), the Revised Standard Version (RSV), the New Revised Standard Version (NRSV), and the New American Standard Bible (NASB). I have used Bible dictionaries extensively. The one I like the best for its clarity is the *New Bible Dictionary* (Leicester, England; Downers Grove, IL: InterVarsity Press, 1996), which was always by my side. The *Lion Handbook to the Bible* is a readable guide to the Bible that assumes no background knowledge.

There are many biblical commentaries on the book of Exodus. The one I have used the most is *Commentary on Exodus*, by James Philip

Hyatt (London: Oliphants, 1971). My paperback edition has been opened so many times it has now fallen apart! This verse-by-verse commentary is very readable and well balanced. A more advanced commentary that I frequently consulted is in three volumes: *Exodus,* by Cornelis Houtman (Kampen, Netherlands: Kak, 1993–). Readers will notice that I sometimes disagree with these commentaries and with some articles in the *New Bible Dictionary;* nevertheless, they are excellent books.

It is difficult to appreciate what a desert in the Middle East is really like unless you have traveled there yourself. Bruce Feiler's *Walking the Bible* (New York: Perennial, 2002) describes his ten-thousand-mile journey retracing the steps of the main biblical characters in the first five books of the Bible. This beautifully written book really evokes the spirit and the atmosphere of Middle Eastern lands. If you have never been to Egypt and the Sinai Peninsula, then reading Feiler's book is the next best thing.

Part 1

The most useful book I found for setting the scene of the Exodus story was James Hoffmeier's *Israel in Egypt* (New York: Oxford University Press, 1997), which contains a wealth of useful and up-to-date information. Helpful background reading was provided by *The Oxford History of the Biblical World,* edited by Michael Coogan (New York: Oxford University Press, 1998), and *The Cambridge Ancient History* (London: Cambridge University Press, 1970), particularly Volume 2, part 2, *The Middle East and the Aegean Region c.1380–1000 B.C.*

Concerning the chronology of the pharaohs of ancient Egypt, I was interested to read the radically new dating of the pharaohs given recently by David Rohl in *A Test of Time* (London: Century, 1995), although I am not persuaded by him because of the mass of interlocking evidence supporting the conventional chronology. This conventional Egyptian chronology is set out in *Cambridge Ancient History* and in Kenneth Kitchen's *Pharaoh Triumphant* (Warminster, England: Aris & Phillips, 1983), which concentrates particularly on Ramesses II, who I believe was the pharaoh at the time of the Exodus. A very useful book that gives information on ancient Israel, including the length of a generation in ancient times, is *A History of Israel,* by John Bright (London: SCM Press, 1959). An excellent book on both the geography of Bible lands and on how place-names have changed over time is *The Land of the Bible,* by Yohanan Aharoni (Philadelphia: Westminster Press, 1979).

Part 2

To understand as much as possible about the land of Midian, I immersed myself in the books of intrepid explorers who literally risked their lives about one hundred years ago to travel there. Some of these books have been recently reprinted, and the others are available secondhand or in libraries. Some are very rare and cost hundreds of dollars in good condition, but if, like me, you are a reader rather than a collector, then damaged copies are available much more cheaply. The two-volume *The Land of Midian,* published in 1879 by Richard Burton (London: C. Kegan Paul), is a delight to read, as is his *The Gold-Mines of Midian* (Cambridge: Oleander Press, 1979). Georg Wallin's *Travels in Arabia* (Cambridge: Oleander Press, 1979), contains much useful information. *Arabia Deserta,* by Charles Doughty (London: Bloomsbury, 1989), is a more difficult read but repays the effort. Easily the most useful book on Midian is *The Northern Hegaz,* by Alois Musil (New York: AMS Press, 1978), but I would recommend reading a less detailed book on Midian first, like those of Richard Burton, or H. St. John Philby's *The Land of Midian* (London: Benn, 1957), a relatively recent book by a Midian explorer. Each of these books on Midian provides different nuggets of information and helps build a complete picture of the land.

Archaeological studies of Midian are very limited compared to the huge amount of work performed in Israel, Egypt, and the Sinai Peninsula. The best introduction to these is *Ancient Records from North Arabia,* by F. V. Winnett and W. L. Reed (Toronto: University of Toronto Press, 1970). *Midian, Moab, and Edom,* edited by John Sawyer and David Clines (Shieffield, England: JSOT Press, 1983), contains several informative articles, particularly one by Beno Rothenberg and Jonathon Glass on Midianite pottery. William Facey's *Riyadh: The Old City* (London: IMMEL, 1992) also has some relevant chapters. There are a number of useful archaeology articles in *Atlal: The Journal of Saudi Arabian Archaeology,* particularly by Peter Parr. The small handbook by David Hogarth, *Hejaz Before World War I* (New York: Oleander, 1978), also contains some helpful information, particularly on Midianite tribes. Lawrence of Arabia's classic book *The Seven Pillars of Wisdom* (Garden City, NY: Doubleday, Doran, 1935), is a tremendous adventure story largely set in Arabia.

One of the first books to consider the route of the Exodus to a mountain in Midian is Alfred Lucas's *The Route of the Exodus of the Israelites from Egypt* (London: Edward Arnold, 1938). This is an excellent book, although Lucas places Mount Sinai at Mount Ithm (also called Bagir) in Midian. Like Lucas, Major Claude Jarvis lived in Egypt for many years, and his *Yesterday and To-day in Sinai* (Edinburgh: W. Blackwood, 1943) is a delightful and informative description of the Sinai Peninsula.

On various occasions when writing this book I needed to know what a Hebrew word really meant, and I needed a specialist dictionary. The *Dictionary of Classical Hebrew,* edited by David Clines (Sheffield: Sheffield Academic Press, 1993–1998), is a mine of authoritative information. Another dictionary that I found very useful for detailed information on people and places in the Near East is *Dictionary of the Ancient Near East,* edited by Piotr Bienkowski and Alan Millard (Philadelphia: University of Pennsylvania Press, 2000).

A huge number of general books about volcanoes have been published. An excellent small book is *Volcanoes: Fire from the Earth* by Maurice Krafft (New York: H. N. Abrams, 1993), who was tragically killed by an erupting volcano. This book contains many useful historical descriptions of volcanoes. Another excellent book is *Mountains of Fire* by Robert and Barbara Decker (Cambridge: Cambridge University Press, 1991).

Part 3

The classic papers by Greta Hort, which described the plagues of Egypt in terms of natural mechanisms, were published in the journal *Zeitschrift für Alttestamentliche Wissenschaft,* volumes 69 and 70 (1957–1958). John Marr and Curtis Malloy have updated the work of

Hort and published their research in a paper, "An Epidemiologic Analysis of the Ten Plagues of Egypt," in the May 1996 issue of *Caduceus*. Nahum Sarna has discussed the explanation of the plagues in terms of natural mechanisms in his wide-ranging book *Exploring Exodus* (New York: Schocken Books, 1986).

Part 4

A landmark book on ancient Egypt is *Egypt of the Pharaohs* by Sir Alan Gardiner (Oxford: Clarendon, 1961). He also wrote a classic paper on what the Bible calls the "way of the Philistines," "The Ancient Military Route Between Egypt and Palestine." This was published in the *Journal of Egyptian Archaeology,* volume 6 (1920).

Information on how far away pillars of volcanic fire can be seen is given in the very useful historical review of earthquakes, which also includes some volcanoes, *The Seismicity of Egypt, Arabia, and the Red Sea,* by N. N. Ambraseys, C. P. Melville, and R. D. Adams (Cambridge: Cambridge University Press, 1994).

A fascinating account of traveling in the Middle East, with graphic descriptions of storms on the Gulf of Aqaba and so forth, is given in John Lloyd Stephens's *Incidents of Travel in Egypt, Arabia Petraea, and the Holy Land* (1838; reprint, Norman: University of Oklahoma Press, 1970). Details of what it is really like to travel through the Sinai Peninsula, and the availability of water, are given in Edward Robinson's *Biblical Researches in Palestine* (1838; reprint, New York: Arno Press, 1977) and E. H. Palmer's *The Desert of the Exodus* (1871; reprint, New York: Arno Press, 1977), as well as in several of the books mentioned earlier, particularly those by Jarvis and Lucas. The extent to which places like the Gulf of Suez and the Bitter Lakes may have been different in Old Testament times relative to today is discussed by J. Simons in *The Geographical and Topographical Texts of the Old Testament* (Leiden: E. J. Brill, 1959). Colin Willock's Time-Life book *Africa's Rift Valley* (Amsterdam: Time-Life Books, 1974) gives some striking photographs of the Great Rift Valley.

Ian Wilson's *Exodus: The True Story Behind the Biblical Account* (San Francisco: Harper & Row, 1985) repeats the claim made by Hans Goedicke and others that the crossing of the Red Sea was due to a tsunami that resulted from the eruption of the volcano Santorini. Doron Nof and Nathan Paldor proposed a different mechanism, wind setdown, for the crossing of the Red Sea, which they took to be at the Gulf of Suez. Their detailed mathematical analysis, which I've applied to the Gulf of Aqaba, was published in 1992 in the *Bulletin of the American Meteorological Society*.

Part 5

Many different mountains have been proposed for Mount Sinai. Menasche Har-el summarizes the arguments for and against thirteen different sites in *The Sinai Journeys: The Route of the Exodus* (Los Angeles: Ridgefield, 1983). One of these sites, Jabal al-Lawz in Midian, has recently received considerable publicity and is the subject of a popular book, *The Gold of Exodus: The Discovery of the True Mount Sinai,* by Howard Blum (New York: Simon & Schuster, 1998). Much earlier, Charles Beke had proposed that Mount Sinai was in Midian, at Mount Ithm (Bagir) (the site chosen later by Lucas), and he gave his reasoning in a fascinating book, *Sinai in Arabia*, which also includes details of the heated arguments he had with many prominent people who believed that Mount Sinai was at Jebel Musa.

However, as I have shown, the arguments that Mount Sinai was a volcano are strong, which rules out Jabal al-Lawz and Mount Ithm. An indispensable book for finding out about historically active volcanoes is the Smithsonian Institution's *Volcanoes of the World,* edited by T. Simkin and others (Tucson: Geoscience Press, 1994). Alois Musil originally suggested that one of these historically active volcanoes, Mount Bedr, was Mount Sinai, but he later retracted this because he could not construct a suitable Exodus route to Mount Bedr. Canon W. T. Phythian-Adams revived Musil's original idea in two delightfully written articles published in 1930 in the *Palestine Exploration Quarterly.* Jean Koenig also argued that Mount Sinai was Bedr in his book *Le Site de Al-Jaw dans L'Ancien Pays de Madian*, published in 1973, and also in some journal papers referred to in this book. However, like Musil, neither Phythian-Adams nor Koenig could give a convincing Exodus route to Mount Bedr and so their work has largely been forgotten.

The possible connection of Mount Sinai and Mount Bedr with the

Moon-god Sin is intriguing. James Pritchard's *Ancient Near Eastern Texts* (Princeton: Princeton University Press, 1992) shows the large number of references to Sin in ancient Near Eastern literature. S. Langdon's *Babylonian Menologies and the Semitic Calendars* (London: Oxford University Press, 1935) gives useful information on the worship of Sin. A more recent book, by Mark Cohen, *The Cultic Calendars of the Ancient Near East* (Bethesda, MD: CDL Press, 1993), updates Langdon's book and is very informative.

The Web is a very useful source of information, but also of misinformation! I plan to have a Web site dedicated to this book. If you look up the words *Colin Humphreys Exodus* in a search engine, then I am sure you will find it. I plan to put up information not only about this book but also about the developing story of the acceptance of the Exodus route proposed in this book, the natural explanations of the miracles, and the latest information on Mount Sinai's being Mount Bedr in Arabia. E-mail enquiries to me at that site will be welcome.

ACKNOWLEDGMENTS

Three people helped me enormously in the writing of this book. Robert Gordon, professor of Hebrew at Cambridge University, read every chapter and pointed out with expertise and dry humor many places where my arguments were weak or dubious. Thank you, Robert, for all the time you spent on this in your very busy schedule. My wife, Sarah, made a huge contribution. She is responsible for a number of the ideas in this book; for example, to her it was intuitively obvious that the Israelites would cross the Red Sea at the head of the Gulf of Aqaba. She has also accompanied me on our annual holidays to the Middle East each year since 1995, which have turned out to be "working holidays," and she has found many relevant books in second-hand bookshops and on the Web. She has even mowed the grass so that I could spend more time writing! My daughter Kate also read every chapter, corrected my spelling and punctuation, and suggested many improvements. Many, many thanks to Robert, Sarah, and Kate.

I also extend my great thanks to the following people:

William Facey, director of the London Centre for Arab Studies, read the entire book and has been particularly helpful over the chapters on Arabia, supplying much information that is impossible to find in books. Alan Millard, of Liverpool University, commented in detail on four chapters and saved me from making a number of mistakes on, for example, the archaeology of Arabia.

Tony Kelly, of Cambridge University, read a number of chapters and made very useful comments, particularly about the relationship between religious beliefs and modern science.

My daughter Liz located a number of very useful Web sites and made good suggestions for figures. Conny Schönjahn spent many hours translating some really difficult German texts into English, written by scholars such as Martin Noth. Geerjapersad Ramloll, the father of one of my research students, Sandra, spent a lot of time translating a long French article by Jean Koenig into English.

I would like to thank John Spence, of Arizona State University, for his encouragement and for sending me a number of useful books. Many thanks to Matthew Taylor and Kate Spence for drawing the maps and for help with figures. Also special thanks to Clifford McAleese for drawing the figures illustrating the effect of wind setdown in the Gulf of Aqaba.

John Ray, head of Egyptology at Cambridge University, made a number of very helpful comments about ancient Egypt. Nick Butterfield, Department of Earth Sciences, Cambridge University, read my chapters on the plagues of Egypt and made many extremely helpful points. Ian Muir, of the same department, commented on the burning bush chapter. Peter Parr was very helpful on the archaeology of Arabia, and St. John Armitage enlightened me about life in Arabia from his firsthand knowledge.

Graeme Waddington, of Oxford University, was an ever-helpful source of knowledge about astronomy and ancient calendars. Amos Nur, of Stanford University, kindly sent me information about earthquakes on the Jericho fault. Herbert Huppert and Mark Hallworth, of Cambridge University, supplied some of the magnificent images of erupting volcanoes used in this book. Robert Hodge provided several very useful books about Arabia, and Kate Garrett and Janet Herdman helped with typing.

On many occasions I have spent lunchtimes in some splendid libraries. I would like to thank the staff of the following libraries for all their help: Oriental Studies Library, Cambridge; Tyndale House Library,

Cambridge; Department of Earth Sciences Library, Cambridge; University Library, Cambridge; British and Foreign Bible Society Library, within the University Library, Cambridge; St. Anthony's College Library, Oxford; Selwyn College Library, Cambridge.

Finally, many thanks to my agent, Al Zuckerman, and his assistant, Fay Greenfield, for all their help and encouragement, and to my publishers, Harper San Francisco and their staff, particularly John Loudon, Terri Leonard, Kris Ashley, and Priscilla Stuckey for all their support, encouragement, and helpful suggestions for improving this book.

Really finally, a special thanks to Margaret Beeston for typing the manuscript of this book during evenings and weekends with great patience as I kept updating the chapters.

INDEX

Page numbers of maps, illustrations, or photographs appear in italics.